Wilfried Raussert

Off the Grid

Art Practices and Public Space

Wilfried Raussert

Off the Grid

Art Practices and Public Space

uuut Wissenschaftlicher Verlag Trier

Copublished by
UNO University of New Orleans Press

Off the Grid:
Art Practices and Public Space /
Wilfried Raussert. –
(Inter-American Studies | Estudios Interamericanos; 35)
Trier: WVT Wissenschaftlicher Verlag Trier, 2021
      ISBN 978-3-86821-835-0
New Orleans, LA: University of New Orleans Press, 2021
      ISBN 978-1-60801-213-8

SPONSORED BY THE

Federal Ministry
of Education
and Research

The project, on which this book is based, has been funded by the German Federal Ministry of Education and Research (Bundesministerium für Bildung und Forschung, BMBF). The responsibility for the content of this publication lies with the author.

Cover Image: Public Reading (copyright Wilfried Raussert)

Cover Design: Brigitta Disseldorf

Library of Congress Cataloging-in-Publication Data
Names: Raussert, Wilfried, author.
Title: Off the grid : art practices and public space / Wilfried Raussert.
Description: Trier : Wissenschaftlicher Verlag Trier ; New Orleans, LA :
   copublished by University of New Orleans Press, [2021] | Series:
   Inter-American studies = Estudios interamericanos ; volume 35 | Includes
   bibliographical references.
Identifiers: LCCN 2020044535 | ISBN 9781608012138 (paperback)
Subjects: LCSH: Social practice (Art)--America. | Art and
   society--America--History--20th century. | Art and
   society--America--History--20th century.
Classification: LCC N7433.915 .R38 2021 | DDC 701/.03--dc23
LC record available at https://lccn.loc.gov/2020044535

Publisher: WVT Wissenschaftlicher Verlag Trier, Postfach 4005, D-54230 Trier,
Bergstraße 27, D-54295 Trier, Tel. 0049 651 41503, Fax 41504, www.wvttrier.de, wvt@wvttrier.de

Copublisher: University of New Orleans Press, 2000 Lakeshore Drive, Earl K. Long Library,
Room 221, New Orleans, LA 70148, United States, 504-280-7457, unopress.org

This book is dedicated to all artists
making public space a site of belonging.

Contents

Introduction

Public Space, Art Practice, and the Social

Contested public space

Protest and revolution tend to begin in the street. On October 28th, 2016 *The Guardian* announced the following news:

> Law enforcement officials arrested 141 people in North Dakota after police surrounded protesters, deploying pepper spray and armored vehicles in order to clear hundreds of Native American activists and supporters from land owned by an oil pipeline company. (*The Guardian* 2016, n. pag.)

This was the most violent day in the three-month long standoff between police and hundreds of members of more than ninety Native American tribes, who were attempting to block the construction of the Dakota Access pipeline. Operated by Texas-based Energy Transfer Partners and intended to transport fracked crude from the Bakken oil field in North Dakota to a refinery near Chicago, the $3.7 billion pipeline was seen by tribes as a threat to their water supplies and numerous sacred sites. As the demonstrations of the Standing Rock tribe and supporting groups of Native American activists show, the rethinking of public space remains central to public conceptions of the common good in the twenty-first century. Many Native American community movements defend sacred and community space in opposition to extractivist capitalist intrusion from hegemonic national and multinational companies. As with other contemporary grassroots movements, art practices in the Dakota movement – such as chant, performance, poster art, and on-the-spot sculpture – were primary vehicles for expressing dissidence and resistance. Not simply creative responses to moments of crisis, these practices serve as community-building forces, promoting sociability through helping people reimagine the social. Practices like these that engage with and in public space highlight art's central role for social creativity. In the first place they produce and receive a high degree of visibility. They also intensify the potential for dialogue between art and a larger public. The artist becomes a creator and activist. Walter Benjamin famously labeled the author a "producer" and equipped him with an "organizing function" (1986, 221–223). Benjamin's creative agent has become an inspirational image for socially and politically minded artists who create imaginaries of the social embedded in dissident, democratic, utopian, and egalitarian thinking. Such linkage in art between the creative and the social has roots in the utopian ideals that were part of the colonial foundations of South and North America.

The Dakota events are just one instance of a new wave of social protest across the global. The Occupy movement, the Arab Spring movement, the Dreamer's movement, the Resist movement, the student movement in Chile, the "Ni Una Más" [Not One More (Woman)] in Latin America, and the Black Lives Matter movement have been among the most mediatized examples of current sociocultural practices of (re)claiming, (re)interpreting, (re)constructing public space. At the same time, we are witnessing privatizations of public space in the sales of land to private companies, and in the sales of streets, squares, and plazas to private developers. In cities like Quito, Toronto, and New York people are increasingly vulnerable to displacement by gentrification. In the wake of these developments, street art projects, communal gardening, and housing projects in urban centers that promote a grassroots approach to the use of public space. Public space outs itself as the very testing ground for rethinking history and heritage, reflecting on and installing power relations, performing culture wars, and staging new communal visions.

While grassroots movements led by artist-activists frequently struggle to regain public space for communal get-togethers, recreation, and alternative forms of urban mobility, an increasing technological surveillance of public squares by governmental agents facilitates the hegemonic control of everyday life in contemporary cities. Massacres and terrorist attacks rationalized as part of a culture war have added a new violent dimension to the struggle over the use of public space. This struggle shows that public space remains open, liberating, ambiguous, and conflicted at the same time. Furthermore, it is fragile. As Jorge de la Barre and Blagoveste Momchedjikova maintain, "Space (public, private, physical, virtual, augmented) has never been so highly monitored and controlled; paradoxically it has never been so vulnerable" (2016, 9).

New ways of thinking public space

Strongly influenced by Henri Lefebvre's reconceptualization of space, poststructuralist theories in geography have brought forth new ways of thinking the relation between place, everyday culture, and people. Time-space compression in the digital age (David Harvey 1989) shows that the boundaries between time and space, public and private, real and virtual, horizontal and vertical are being blurred by contemporaneity. While community building and social change have always been intertwined with space, action-oriented theory has enabled new ways of asserting alternative identities, ways of life, and cultural and social interaction (Chiara Tornaghi and Sabine Knierbein 2014). As a result, we have deepened our understanding of cultural, economic, and political change in relation to space. Publicness, public life (Arendt 1989; Sennett 1990), public opinion, public sphere (Habermas 1989), – they all have been revisited, their meanings challenged and multiplied. From debates about the privatization of public space (Sorkin 1992; Low and Smith 2005; Minton 2012) to the re-creation of new collective spaces (Watson 2006; Franck and Stevens 2007; Hou 2010), space has been conceived anew, in relational and plural ways. Such redefinitions focus on the power inequalities underlying distribution of and access to space. For instance, in the spirit of action-oriented theory, bell hooks contemplates the relationality of black identities in a spatial dimension. The socio-spatial marginality associated with gender and race becomes a position that opens up "the possibility of radical perspectives from which to see and imagine alternatives and new worlds" (hooks 1990, 149).

Conceptions of space are changing, as are the people taking their life concerns to the streets. Storming public streets for protest, strike, and resistance has historically been associated with working-class masses. However, youth and citizens' revolts in recent years in Santiago de Chile, New York, Mexico City, Cairo, London, Madrid, Tel Aviv, and Tunis have consisted largely of young, middle-class, well-educated people, including artists and intellectuals. The reclamation of public space that can be observed in these protest actions – which are frequently labelled "social media revolutions" – raises the question as to how public space is being reimagined, how it is designed physically or digitally in each case, and what new actor-constellations are involved (Leonardi 2017, 47–48).

Without a doubt, public space remains a real material presence. It exists tangibly, beyond the spaces of cultural consumption and advertisement. Via material and electronic billboards, an international commercial culture has laid itself across public space in many cities around the world. Public space is the area where American and now global mass culture most visibly advertises itself, creating the desire, if not demand, for its consumption (Kroes 2008, 70–72). With the arrival of new media and the digital realm as a new global player in the reconceptualization of public space, one may wonder to what extent the public space has been abstracted into a metaphor that represents interrelationship for people who are striving to communicate in public beyond the solitary mind, the private home, and the closed institutional space.[1] If so, new questions emerge, such as: "Which aspect of communication attracts particular attention?" "What new communal ties are imagined?" and "What role does the artist play in the reconceptualization of public space?" When public space is increasingly viewed metaphorically, the role of the artist in public-space politics can only grow in importance. Beyond the need to rethink public space as metaphor and as material space, more

---

1   http://www.goethe.de/ges/prj/rue/pgm/enindex.htm.

questions evolve. Whose public space is it? How far does the public space reach? What are the relations between material and virtual public space? How global can the site-specific place be? These and many more questions related to public spaces and their importance for free speech, borderless space, communitarian networks, and identity politics have been addressed by artists, intellectuals, and writers in the twentieth and twenty-first centuries.

The role of artistic practice for urban spaces

It is increasingly common today for architects and city planners to design public spaces (or illusions thereof) that blend, rather than contrast, with their hyper-consumerist surroundings. This trend marks a new step in the history of place making in the Americas. In this latest conception of public space, the ideal city no longer shapes the real city. Instead, the malls, entertainment complexes, and art museums represent important interventions in public space by creating an ideal city based on consumption (Orvell and Meikle 2009a, 9–10). As a consequence of these developments the common symbols of public space are more and more excerpts from the nexus of aesthetic display and commercial culture. Artistic participation in this context means a direct involvement in the market circuits of cultural production and consumption. Hyper-consumerism in present-day metropolises is part of an expanding festival culture that embraces culture and art as commodity and entertainment. George Yúdice asserts that "the role of culture has expanded in an unprecedented way into the political and economic" (2003, 9). Culture then no longer functions as a realm of legitimation, but, rather, must itself be legitimized by its political and economic utility. By cherishing festival and spectacle culture, contemporary urban politics also promote a re-aestheticization of public space. Without doubt, this re-aestheticization creates new opportunities for artists to help remodel city space. Nevertheless, it has also been criticized, particularly by leftist and neo-Marxist intellectuals who see true political participation in public space threatened by the spectacularization of urban spaces

(Debord 1995). As they argue, modern spectacle and festival grounds provide communal meeting places but are, at the same time, monitored public sites for mass entertainment (Costa, Guerra, and Soares Neves 2017, 8–9).

City space becomes an expression of a culture-oriented use of space in late capitalism, when the production of festive public space encourages urban desire and facilitates controlled consumption. Artistic practice then is potentially condemned to be only part of what Sharon Zukin dubs "pacification by cappuccino" (Zukin 1995, 28) or what Herbert Marcuse calls "repressive tolerance" (112). Yúdice (2003) points toward the radical changes that these urban developments imply for our understanding of culture. Culture is not only multiplied, it is strongly embedded in intersections of politics and economics. There is general critical consensus that the culture of spectacle commodifies all forms of social, cultural, and political life. Yet, critics like Goldstein and Gotham arrive at a more complex vision of spectacle culture. Amid the clear commodity interests, they locate a potential for rebellion, resistance, and subversion in contemporary urban spectacles. Goldstein claims that "spectacles, like other public events, are systems for not only the performance but also the creation or transformation of social order" (2004, 16). Referencing New Orleans's Mardi Gras, Gotham maintains that public spectacles have the potential to create "a radical critique" particularly with respect to "class and race inequalities" (2005, 235).

With a nod to Gotham, I argue that commodified public spaces still allow artists opportunities for genuine ideological critique. Artists are adept at embracing new versions of counterculture's "anti-authoritarian humanism" (Goffman 2004, 31). Hence, art, commissioned or trespassing, intervenes in urban development as part of consumer culture. Art also continues to thrive as an expression of grassroots urban politics and as an agent for turning communal and public spaces into fora for *convivencia*, environmentalist community, dialog, participation, and resistance. Art practice continues to break with urban convention, social norms, and spatial configurations, and it does so even more effectively in the high visibility provided by open accessible public spaces.

Avant-gardism(s), art practice, the social

For rethinking art practices in relation to public space and the public sphere, it seems worthwhile to address the conception of art as a social and aesthetic spearhead, a notion closely intertwined with debates about avant-gardism in its political and aesthetic dimensions. The French term l'avant-garde originally held a specific military significance (Huyssen 1987, 101–120); it referred to distinguished front-line soldiers that led troop movements. After the general politicization of life as a result of the French Revolution, new semantic fields opened up for the word, whereupon avant-gardism came to be seen as a cultural component of modern society and its optimism. Yet, at the same time, "countercultures are transgressive, avant-garde movements" (Goffman 2004, 33). The transfer of the topos avant-garde from the military into the social sector added to the term's spatial significance a theologically-oriented sense of time. Historical developments are thought of as time-forward, linear processes. Accordingly, the vanguard, representing a lateral spearhead, embodies the part of society that drives new developments.

In the social conception of the Saint-Simonians, the scientifically, politically, and aesthetically defined avant-garde earned an elite position through their leadership role. The scattering of avant-garde impulses to different areas of society also illustrates that the aesthetic and political discourses in France in the early twentieth century were separated. Trying to equate the beginning of an artistic avant-garde movement with the French Revolution is historically unjustifiable from today's perspective. Nevertheless, the term already appears in the 1820s in connection with art, society, and politics. Saint Simons' scholar Olinde Rodriguez connected the term avant-garde with art in his dialog *L'artiste, le savant et l'industriel.*

Saint Simon himself had the idea that art is progressive in that it forms the way for a new social order. At the same time, there is a role assignment: artists must be philosophical revolutionaries. In Saint-Simon's conception, artists, scientists, and industry leaders work together to design and realize a new form of government. In the competition among the groups, the artists take over the leading role, which is described as avant-garde. Art is thus equated with a social avant-garde; its primary purpose is to promote the new social design by spreading relevant new ideas. This social positioning of art shows that the concept of the avant-garde did not originally include a pioneering role in the development of art. In the mid-nineteenth century, the phrase was used mainly in a political sense and gained particular currency in socialist utopian circles. In the writings of Fourier (1829) and Laverdants (1845), the idea of art as an avant-garde social development through to ideational society is sustained.

The transformation of "avant-garde" from a term of social discourse into one of aesthetics takes place only gradually. As stated by Francis Haskell, political and social metaphors are generally not used before the second half of the nineteenth century in art criticism (1990, 124–127). In criticism of Rimbaud's poetry, impressionist painters like Manet used the term in reference to art and literature. At the same time, a blurring of discourses commonly occurred whereby artistic radicalism was automatically equated with its counterpart (133). As the terminus of art-history and art criticism, the term avant-garde was established not until the early twentieth century and mainly signaled a spearheading of artistic development.

Consequent historiography of the topos avant-garde distinguishes three phases of usage of the term. In the nineteenth century, art acts as a social avant-garde and has no autonomous status in the utopian visions of Saint-Simon and Rodriguez. Early modernism in the twentieth-century second phase is characterized by the emergence of an artistic avant-garde, which looks for innovative form and content and finds the most radical manifestation in the Dadaist and Surrealist risings in the early decades of the twentieth century. These artists rebelled not only against traditional practices in art and literature but intended to release art from its pristine isolation and return it to life practice (Bürger 1974). Geographic and cultural shifts from Europe to the Americas contributed to the launching of a third phase, which has been characterized by a decentralizing within art. The avant-garde has turned into a heterogeneous phenomenon (Crane 1987, 14–15; Hadjinicolaou 1978, 56).[2] In addition to the individualistic aspects of the contemporary avant-garde, Christopher Butler (1980) emphasizes the avant-garde's pluralistic nature and eclectic practices. In contrast to the historical avant-garde (Bürger 1974), which clearly defined itself as a counter-culture, today's avant-garde art appears diverse. Within this scattering/diversity, avant-gardism appears in the contemporary debate as a sanctioned form of aesthetic thinking and an artistic practice that is striving for renewal across society as well as individually and aesthetically (Russell 1981, 3–5). From today's perspective, it appears wise to use the term "avant-garde" to identify "the critical and canonical tradition of classification" while applying the term 'vanguard' "to locate the cultural and political radicalism of art practice in context" (Filewod 2011b, 144). This distinction is important because ideas take on new meaning as they move from context to context. What occurs as innovation in one context may be considered a reiteration of tradition in another. For example, the seemingly progressive agenda of moving art into public spaces in one context may become neocolonial practice in a different context. As Harding emphasizes with reference to radical art practice, "innovation is always tied to the experimental, which, in turn is tied to potential success and potential failure" (2011, 19). In relation to art practices in public space, the outcomes depend on the power relation between the actual space inhabited and the transformative power of art practice.

Artists with the impulse for social change and renewal have come from different backgrounds and followed different routes. Grassroots social movements develop radical artistic practices, as do vanguard groups emerging from well-established artistic circles.

---

2   Köhne emphasizes that the boundaries between the avant-garde, mass
     culture, and popular culture are blurred (2000, 49).

At times, their projects and ideas merge, at other times collide. Not only are artistic approaches to public space manifold; so too are metaphorical constructions of public space. Frequently, the artistically driven metaphors of public space reach back to culturally defined meanings of individual and communal space. With respect to the Americas, it is significant that public space in many Amerindian communities has been considered communal property. For other Amerindian communities based upon nomadic life styles space has been regarded as temporary and in transit. European associations of property with identity have led to land distribution and distinctions between private and public, agricultural and industrial uses. The resulting processes of institutionalization and commodification have helped produce a divide between art and life in many parts of the western world. Amerindian cultures have tended to favor a holistic approach to cultural life, however. Their traditions also mark different approaches to the artistic conceptualization of public space. For instance, public tribal rituals remain a stronghold in Amerindian cultures.

Because art practices can cross boundaries, crisscross time and space, and "collage" worlds anew, they can anticipate social change, quickly respond to social crisis, and expose the fluidity and ambiguity of public space faster than official city planning can envision new sites and spaces for creative and critical expression. While the power of art practices should not be romanticized, it is safe to say that art continues to play a pivotal role in defining and designing public space, thus intervening in debates about the public sphere. Art's importance looms large behind Richard Sennett's reflection that cosmopolitanism is a one key test of a city's condition. A lack of difference and diversity diminishes the quality of urban public space (Sennett 1977). Or, as Simon Parker puts it, "Without religious, ethnic, or cultural difference, the city lacks the ecological diversity to recombine in new and surprising ways" (2004, 156). Art practices tend to give voice precisely to that: difference and diversity.

While art flourishes within those new commodified urban spaces as merchandise, it can nonetheless challenge the surveillance and control of spectacularized urban spaces. This rings true because imagination and art ultimately cannot be controlled. Hence, even within the context of commissioned art projects, be they commissioned by city planners, government officials, or entrepreneurs, there is always the possibility of uncontrolled action and expression. And art regularly defends its claims by providing individual and public space for play, improvisation, experimentation and creation. Its high degree of performativity in particular underscores art's expressive potential to influence place and space making.

Public art: what is it?

In order to dig deeper into the relationship between art practices and public space, it is helpful to come up with a tentative definition of what public art can be. At its most basic level, public art is just that: art in public spaces. Beyond that, it can be many other things. It can solidify the social status quo or call for resistance. It may take the form of historic statues of monarchs or soldiers on horseback in squares or parks. Alternatively, it can be events, performances, and installations that raise public consciousness and express social critique of contemporary issues, such as those pertaining to human rights or the environment. With the emergence of the new media age public art has become even more diversified. It can take a wide range of forms, sizes, and scales. It can be permanent or play with transitory presence. Public art includes murals, graffiti, human sculpture, memorials, integrated architectural or landscape architectural work, community art, digital new media, light and sound projections on and from public buildings, and street performances and festivals.

Public art is particularly essential for social creativity because it is often site-specific, in the sense that it is created in response to the place and community in which it resides. In its more conventional or historic shape it often interprets the history of the place and its people, and in its more critical fashion it addresses social, political, and environmental issues. The work may be created individually or in groups, and more recently, in collaboration with the community, reflecting the ideas and values of those whom it addresses. Being public, the art is ideally free, open, and accessible to everyone. Public art creates a heightened awareness in the viewer of the site, the people, and the broader social and cultural environment around them.

Public art occupies a central role in connecting different public sites, spaces, and spheres. In the twenty-first century especially, we have witnessed a reconfiguration of art practices in the public. Participation culture lets artists and spectators diffuse the site-specific installation or performance, thanks to smartphones and streaming platforms. Such diffusion through the new media mobilizes site-specific art and sends it anywhere in the world, creating new virtual public spaces and communities. It is also increasingly common for media installations to be designed from the very beginning to have a nomadic reach. Whatever its form, public art instills and reflects meaning – and creates a sense of place, where people live, work, struggle, and visit.

What concerns us most here is the role of art in public spaces in the Americas, its interAmerican flows, networks, and social meaning. Art in the streets has a long history in the Americas. South and North America, with alternating loci of enunciation, have been key global players when it comes to expanding the horizons of political and public-space defining art practices, as can been seen in muralism, happenings, graffiti, and hip hop cultures. From Brazil to the Caribbean to the U.S., individual and collaborative public art practices have highlighted art's function as a seismograph of crisis and laboratory for social and political change. Art practices outside of schools, institutions, museums, and galleries have provided the backstage and frontstage for rethinking and reconstructing public space in experimental, provocative, and innovative ways. This holds true for elitist radical art and grassroots art alike. Particularly through technologized and amplified performance arts and digital diffusion, public art has gained new momentum to create interAmerican and global communities for rethinking the social and the environment. High speed virtual distribution has replaced the train wagon to give public art unprecedented power to spread its visions, aesthetics, and critique. As much as concert halls, galleries, and museums still separate art from life, art practices in public spaces show art to be part of the social, shaping, changing, and solidifying it.

InterAmerican approach

Beyond the idea of "a hemispheric America" and certainly ever since the collapse of Spanish imperial claims in 1898, concrete cultural, political, and economic dynamics, tensions, and processes within the Americas have increasingly created interAmerican networks that manifest mutual entanglements between locations, regions, and nations beyond a North-South divide (Raussert 2017, 3). The development of such international interconnectedness is reflected in the aesthetic and political aspirations of public art today. Exploring the ways in which "America/América" as a geopolitical, cultural and social manifestation should be seen instead as "entangled Americas" beyond closed national spaces is one of the goals in studying the relationship between art practice and public space.

If pan-Americanism was the trial run for a specifically U.S. vision of global governance, it is equally true that liberal ideals have firm roots in the Latin American struggles for independence. This may explain that the history of positive responses to U.S. proposals for more intense hemispheric cooperation. Intellectuals like Oswald de Andrade from Brazil, Gabriela Mistral from Chile, Carlos Pellicer from Mexico, Pedro Henríquez Ureña from the Dominican Republic, and José Enrique Rodó from Uruquay rhetorically expressed an "American ideal." These thinkers felt that the U.S.'s hegemonic aspirations undermined that ideal, they nevertheless shared a larger understanding of America/América's mission in the world. While many U.S. Americans might erroneously have mistaken values like freedom, individuality, and self-governance as uniquely part of their national fabric, they were also Latin American aspirations as the region sought to escape from being an Old World that moved from war to war, crisis to crisis – particularly in the aftermath of World War II. Americanisms have underlain a defense and promotion of "universal values" from different local and national positionings throughout the Americas (Smith 2017, 6–7).

From the late nineteenth century to the mid-twentieth century, pan-Americanism repeatedly acted as a "horizon of expectation" (Koselleck 2000) within which hopes and anxieties collided as intellectuals and artists from the various Americas created their visions for future models of community and coexistence. The conflicts and contradictions inherent to the emergence of pan-Americanism find explication in Hannah Arendt's political definition of community building, written in *The Human Condition* (1989). She contended that political communities take shape through the contention of different groups and individuals attempting to recreate the world around one "sovereign mastery" (9). Power and positioning play a pivotal role in whose vision is to gain mastery. Arendt's understanding of political community is conflict-based, and art and cultural work assume an important role within this community-building process. In Arendt's vision, they create "as if" worlds and provide exploratory space for ideas, challenges, and visions (9). In the Americas, art practice that reclaims public space is highly present, giving Arendt's visions particular urgency, as well as relevance to processes of social critique and change.

Art practice, like other social practices in the Americas, is strongly embedded in a space-community continuum that is constantly renegotiated and marked by colonial and neocolonial history and related local, regional, and hemispheric power struggles. An example of this point can be seen in the utopian social aspirations that have historically underlain Latin and North American societies. On the other hand, the collectivization of the "*convivencia*" claims among Latin American groups and the "community" politics in North America have historically helped redefine social coexistence (Berkovitch 1978; Slotkin 2000; Quijano 2014) in the American hemispheres. A focus on interAmerican connectedness opens venues to see the politics, cultural productions, and thought systems among, for instance, indigenous cultures and African Caribbean, African American and Latin African American cultures, and diaspora cultures within the Americas as providing optional discourses to comprehend the constellation of the Americas as hemispherically-related beyond and also outside of the Old World-New World axis. In that sense, an interAmerican lens not only provides new insights into the Americas as being defined regionally or nationally, transatlantic and transpacific studies of the Americas, but additionally, helps us tackle one of the weak spots of area studies, namely its lack of theory building. Area should first of all be envisioned in the plural version, related to a mobile "progressive sense of place" (Massey 2001, 156.) that is intrinsically connected to synchronic as well as uneven temporalities. Thus, synchronicity, simultaneity, and the investigation of vertical as well as horizontal relations with respect to knowledge and power systems shape the general theoretical framework. The critical analysis directs itself at issues of process, relation, and interaction to come to terms with areas as spaces of political, economic and cultural entanglement (Raussert 2014).

This book departs from unterritorialized definitions of art, the social, and public space – terms that should not be reduced to state, nation, or society. Its chapters draw on contemporary space research (Lefèbvre 1991; Löw 2016; Massey 2001; Soja 1989; Canclini 1990) to investigate which imaginative, conceptual, and practical daily-life spatializations and uses of public space have emerged in artistic representations and performances. Spatial units keep changing over time, and such evolution can help us consider the interconnectivity between localities, regions, and nations within the Americas in a diachronic as well as synchronic way. The conceptualization of space as porous, fluid, mobile, framed, controlled, and channeled dialectically permits us to study the transversal flows that have shaped cultural, economic, and political processes within the Americas without losing awareness of the hierarchies and power structures involved. Linking spatial mobility with time, one begins to discover new links and connections, as well as gaps and borderlines that characterize the complex, multidirectional, and multirelational diffusion of cultures in the Americas.

Three periods of crisis and change

Looking at three historically distinct conjunctures of artistic practice, this book claims public space for renegotiating art and community, art and politics, and art and economy. Such an approach is selective and risks falling prey to potentially closed narratives of history by evading developments that occurred outside the selected time frames. Its advantage, however, lies in its potential for highlighting certain epochs, identifying major ruptures, and emphasizing relationality in historical and cultural manifestations and developments. With that in mind, this book investigates the changing relations between art practice and public space, between art and community, and between art and resistance in the selected periods. It argues that rereading art history through the lens of art practice in public space enables new insights into the close relationship between art and community-building in the Americas and brings to light flows of art practices within interAmerican cultural and social entanglements.

The three periods of historical crisis and change that the book addresses are treated as eras of renewed critical intellectual debate about the nation, of new visions of culture, community, and public space in the U.S. and Latin America. These eras are further defined as heydays of artistic innovation and provocation, ranging from grassroots to avant-garde practices, and of art practices that reclaimed public spaces. All three periods chosen are marked by cultural, social, and political movements that privileged the street and other public spaces as effective sites for political communication.

In a nutshell, the period of the 1920–1930s witnessed a fierce challenge to modernism and modernity. Both concepts encountered numerous challenges in the Americas. Indigenous and black movements in particular challenged orthodox conceptions of community, culture, and public space through art practices aimed at aesthetic and political renewal. Indigenous movements, immigrant groups, and Afro-descendant groups struggled for visibility and inclusion throughout the Americas. As he traveled throughout the Americas, Marcus Garvey advocated culturally- and politically-minded art practices in public spaces as a way to promote his Pan-African vision. In the U.S. in particular, African American artists and intellectuals challenged Anglo-Saxon nativist agendas of society and culture. For Alain Locke, art represented the link between cultures, races, and ethnic groups. He believed it would be the driving force of a new conceptualization of "America" and American society, and it needed the visibility of public space. He explicitly combined his notion of art with the avant-garde in his introduction to the anthology *The New Negro* (1970 [1925]). He designated Harlem as an African American center in multicultural New York and argued that the music, literature, and art of the Harlem Renaissance was an expression of African American renewal, signifying the willingness to establish a new social consciousness.[3] Locke defined this consciousness as "the consciousness of acting as the advance-guard of African Peoples in their contact with Twentieth Century civilization" (14). As Locke's definition suggests, in the teeth of racial discrimination, many authors and artists of the Harlem Renaissance saw themselves as not only a piece of American society, but also as a spearhead of modern American literature and a multiethnic cultural consciousness spanning various cultures in the Americas. This view accorded with other currents of U.S. thought, specifically with William James's pluralistic view of society, John Dewey's critique on dualistic thought structures, and Franz Boa's renegotiation of traditional conceptions of race and culture (cf. Hutchinson 1995, 30–31). Recognizing that their convictions were in line with modernist thought, Harlem Renaissance writers and artists nurtured the hope that art could transform society. African American intellectuals like

---

3   Ann Douglas stresses that the financial sponsorship of the Afro-American art and culture contributed to an optimistic tenor (cf. 1995, 90).

Alain Locke and W.E.B. DuBois sought a dialog within pragmatism to promote change toward a truly multicultural societal form.[4]

Similar to the Harlem Renaissance and its artistic and cultural critique of a white-centered modernism in the North, Latin American *modernismo,* frequently reduced by others to an aestheticist and anti-political stance, also brought forth harsh critiques of the social status quo and the colonial injustices against indigenous peoples in Latin America. The early twentieth century witnessed the rise of a movement dedicated to representing indigenous cultures and promoting their struggle against colonial oppression. Intellectuals and writers like the Peruvian José María Arguedas and the Mexican Rosario Castellanos inserted a strong political discourse into *modernismo*. In "Our América," the Cuban poet Martí challenged colonial structures and their injustices against indigenous cultures in the Americas. Visual artists in post-revolutionary Mexico like Diego Rivera dedicated themselves to a new national vision that embraced a "Mexicanized" and "indigenized" modernity. This championing of indigenous and black cultures of the Americas paved the way for Pan-American visions that attempted to overcome the larger North-South divide in the American hemisphere. Rivera's penchant for utopian visions left him captivated simultaneously by the dream of a rich mass-producing capitalism in the making, and by socialism's claim of the attainability of a new revolutionary society (Rochfort 1998, 123). A decade later, Aimé Césaire's *Négritude* movement, which was inspired by African thinkers, shook colonial rule in the French Caribbean.

The second period is the turbulent 1960s and 1970s, in which art practices fueled by anti-colonial, anti-war and, civil rights movements redefined public spaces in terms of new forms of community-building, political protest against authoritarian and totalitarian structures, and critique of technocratic global village utopias (Roszak 1995). The 1960s and 1970s marked an intense challenge to social

---

4   In relation to pragmatism and the Harlem Renaissance, cf. Hutchinson
      (1995, 42–52).

and political hierarchies around the globe. The Cuban Missile Crisis marked the apex of the Cold War. The anti-Vietnam protest movement expanded to a global scale. Anti-colonial movements in Africa and Asia, indigenous movements throughout the Americas, anti-totalitarian protests in Latin American countries, and the civil rights and Black Nationalist movements in the U.S. – which influenced other black cultural and political movements in Latin America and Brazil – helped create what is commonly regarded as the most turbulent and counter-cultural period in the history of the twentieth century. In the U.S., Native Americans, Hispanics, and Asian Americans followed the example of African American protests against racial discrimination and politics. The demands and rights of minorities were met with increasing attention and understanding in the broader population. Intercultural and interethnic conflicts and tensions within the U.S. and anticolonial tendencies, as observed in Latin America, Asia, and Africa, brought forth a worldwide public sensitivity toward forms of ethnic discrimination and societal disadvantage. This fact explains why the civil rights movement in the USA and its radical Black Nationalist formations inspired protests against existing state and social orders throughout the Americas and around the globe.

Artistic practice, while frequently shaped by the prospering of playful postmodernist artistic expression, gained new prominence as a way to create new social and cultural visions. Since the late 1960s, regimes of public space in most cities have developed around the need for more democratic, inclusive, and tolerant forms of interaction. Political demonstrations, performances, and festivals have made public spaces more dynamic, more attractive, and more open to different social groups. Public spaces have also attracted people who once were limited to narrow areas of the city such as drug users, dealers in illegal goods, and the homeless (Orvell and Meikle 2009b). Beginning in the 1970s in the U.S., and, a few decades later, in Latin American cities, support for the preservation of landmark buildings, gentrification processes, movements of artists and professionals into old districts, and capital investment in new festival cultures and shopping malls as theme parks radically changed urban appearance and life. The new developments brought forth a revalorization of street markets, the installation of public art and building of art museums, and a new appreciation of historic urban identities in conjunction with public art practices (Orvell and Meikle 2009b). The 1960s and early 1970s marked a pivotal period in the history of public space, as (counter) community-building art helped create new possibilities for what the space could be and how it could be used.

The third period is the post-Cold War, post-Berlin Wall, and neoliberal world of globalization in which art practices flourish as integral parts of commodified and disneyfied metropolitan spaces of consumption. Yet, at the same time, they occupy public spaces in the form of radical street art and performance practices that challenge surveillance, control, and censorship in public space. With the end of the Cold War and the spread of neoliberal and neocapitalist agendas in politics, economy, and cultural policy, new schisms emerged making even more visible divides between a prospering global North and a global South frequently exploited and marginalized in new waves of globalization. The social divide between rich and poor has kept growing, and local and communal resistance to the threat of global homogenization has brought forth numerous grassroots movements, human rights organizations, ecological movements, and regional independence movements around the globe. Huntington's claim of a new culture war, especially between the Christian and Muslim world, has found sad fulfillment in neocolonial practices and global terrorist threats.

A new variety of youth and citizens' revolts have characterized the early period of the twenty-first century. From Cairo, London, Madrid, Moscow, and New York to Tel Aviv and Tunis, primarily young, well-educated people have taken to the streets. The reclamation of public space that can be observed in these protests – which are frequently called social media revolutions – raises the question of how views of the function of public space have altered, and how that space is designed physically or digitally in each case.

In response to the new crisis, art practice has entered a new, intensified phase of (re)claiming public space. At the intersection of artistic expression, political commentary, and commercial advertisement, graffiti, spray paint, posters, and murals infuse contemporary urban life with a new visual semiotics. The city's public spaces are increasingly shaped by a symbolic appropriation of grassroots movements, activists, and artists (Youkhana and Förster 2015, 7). It is safe to say that in the urban centers in the Americas, as in other parts of the world, street art and graffiti function as a medium for communication, resistance, and commercialization. By the 1990s, re-aestheticization of public space depended on a huge and still expanding symbolic economy: on the one hand, on Planet Hollywood, Imax movie theaters, and Disney stores – all of which can be found today in Los Angeles and many other cities around the globe – and on the other hand, in new elitist contemporary art museum cultures representing such brand names as "Frank Gehry." In the United States, this model of re-aestheticizing public space has gone to a consumerist extreme by promoting retail space – coffee bars, restaurants, shops – as public space. Likewise, street, parks, and recreation areas are designed as if they were spaces of consumption (Orvell and Meikle 2009b). Art practices in public space today shape and are shaped by political dissent and consumerist marketing strategies, walking a tightrope between grassroots activism and participation in consumer culture. As they respond to current social, political, and economic crises, they also mold changing urban imaginaries of individual expression, communal vision, and dissent.

Art practice, public space, and the social

Public space in its real and virtual facets manifests itself as a conflicted, productive, and interactive zone. Bourdieu sees in the social space a first and last reality that produces differences and hierarchies, and also shapes social actors' imaginaries of the social (Bourdieu 2006, 365–367). Artists and activists create, respond to, and rethink the social in relation to public space. The great importance

that social narratives currently hold is strongly supported by two social developments that are closely linked: today's rapid emergence
of grassroots and other social movements in the Americas confronting neoliberal globalization – from Occupy Wallstreet to contemporary popular movements that since the early 2000s have supported
leftist Latin American governments. These movements have attempted to critically challenge the social status quo of systems of
domination. Protest movements against Donald Trump's presiden-
tial election and his presidency in the United States and the Black
Lives Matter movement, as well as indigenous movements in Latin
America and Canada protesting exclusion and marching for recognition of rights and redistribution of land keep challenging the power
of new right-wing politics. These complex dynamics demonstrate
the social's high sociopolitical volatility staggering between utopia
and dystopia (Kaltmeier and Raussert 2019, 8–10). These cultural,
social, and political developments ask for further analysis both from
synchronic and diachronic perspectives. The following chapters ex-
amine the interface of art practice, public space, and community vision in different historical periods.

By analyzing manifestations, developments, and entanglements
of public art practices, this book looks at public art's contribution to
making, changing, and simulating the social. As Baudrillard puts it,
"the social is not a clear and unequivocal process" (2007, 65). The
approach taken here entertains a relational grasp of the social while
looking at artistic practices in public space. Contrary to the tendencies in social and politic sciences to reify and fix the social order,
this book aims to point out the fluidity (Bauman 2000) and contin-
gency of the social and the ways it is negotiated by art practices that
reoccupy and redefine public space. As Castoriadis (1997) believes,
social orders and social imaginations can emerge from the social.
However, they are always subject to processes of transformation.
The central concern of the chapters is art's power for social creativity. In this respect, the question about which self-reflective processes
break up conventional social formations and give rise, through performance in public spaces, to new forms and imaginations of the so-

cial is of special interest to scholars of twentieth and twenty-first century radical art. This book addresses the creativity and performativity of the social in public space as central categories. In keeping with current debates among the cultural, historical, and social sciences, the book identifies artistic practices from avant-garde, radical, and grassroots artists and collectives as a heuristic field that stands particularly for a creative and self-reflective (new) performance of the social.

The book pursues the relational approach to the triad of artistic actor, public space, and the social (to the extent that alterity becomes a central category of the social). Social philosopher Bernhard Waldenfels asserts that the individual can be considered a *homo respondens* (2015, 5) who re-thinks the social in response to the presence and activity of others. Hence, there is no better place than a public site to stimulate a rethinking and restaging of the social via art practice. In artistic creations and performances of the social, interdependence and interaction with others must always be included and performed. This being in touch with the other is essential for art practices that represent and perform the social in public space – practices that aim to provide connectivity, coalition, resistance, and hegemony.

Works cited

Arendt, Hannah. 1989. *The Human Condition.* Chicago: University of Chicago Press. Print.

Baudrillard, Jean. 2007 [1978]. *In the Shadow of the Silent Majorities, or The End of the Social.* Los Angeles: Semiotext(e)/Foreign Agents. Print.

Bauman, Zygmunt. 2000. *Liquid Modernity.* Cambridge: Polity Press. Print.

Benjamin, Walter. 1986. "The Author as Producer." In *Reflections: Essays, Aphorisms, and Autobiographical Writings*, ed. Peter Demetz, 220–238. New York: Schocken. Print.

Berkovitch, Sacvan. 1978. *The American Jeremiad.* Madison: University of Wisconsin Press, Madison. Print.

Bourdieu, Pierre. 2006. "Sozialer Raum, symbolischer Raum." In *Raumtheorie: Grundlagentexte aus Philosophie und Kulturwissenschaften*, ed. Jörg Dünne and Stephan Günzel, 354–374. Frankfurt a. M.: Suhrkamp. Print.

Bürger, Peter. 1974. *Theorie der Avantgarde.* Frankfurt a. M.: Suhrkamp. Print.

Butler, Christopher. 1980. *After the Wake: An Essay on Contemporary Avant-garde.* Oxford: Clarendon Press. Print.

Canclini, Néstor García. 1990. *Culturas híbridas: Estrategias para entrary salir de la modernidad.* México: Grijalbo. Print.

Castoriadis, Cornelius. 1997. *The Imaginary Institution of Society.* Cambridge: MIT Press. Print.

Costa, Pedro, Paula Guerra, and Pedro Soares Neves. 2017. *Urban Interventions, Street Art, and Public Space.* Lissabon: Urban Creativeorg. Print.

Crane, Diane. 1987. *The Transformations of the Avant-Garde: The New York Art World 1940–1985.* Chicago: University of Chicago Press. Print.

De la Barre, Jorge, and Blagoveste Momchedjikova. 2016. "Between Spectacle and Resistance: Some Thoughts on Public Space Today." In *Street Notes* 25: 1–12. Print.

Debord, Guy. 1995. *The Society of the Spectacle.* New York: Zone Books. Print.

Douglas, Ann. 1995. *Terrible Honesty: Mongrel Manhattan in the 1920s.* New York: Farrar, Strauss and Giroux. Print.

Filewod, Alan. 2011a. "Maoist Performativities: Milton Acorn and the Canadian Liberation Movement." In *Avant-Garde Performance and Material Exchange: Vectors of the Radical*, ed. Mike Sell, 122–139. New York: Palgrave Macmillan. Print.

Filewod, Alan. 2011b. "Introduction (Section III: Divergences)." In *Avant-Garde Performance and Material Exchange: Vectors of the Radical*, ed. Mike Sell, 143–148. New York: Palgrave Macmillan. Print.

Fourier, Charles. 1829. *Le nouveau monde industriel et sociétaire.* Paris. Print.

Franck, Karen A., and Quentin Stevens, eds. 2007. *Loose Space: Possibility and Diversity in Urban Life.* London/New York: Routledge. Print.

Goffman, Ken. 2004. *Counterculture through the Ages. From Abraham to Acid House.* New York: Villard Books. Print.

Goldstein, Daniel. 2004. *The Spectacular City: Violence and Performance in Urban Bolivia.* Durham: Duke University Press. Print.

Gotham, Kevin Fox. 2005. "Theorizing Urban Spectacles: Festivals, Tourism and the Transformation of Urban Space." *City* 9.2: 225–246. Print.

Habermas, Jürgen. 1989. *The Structural Transformation of the Public Sphere: An Inquiry into a Category of Bourgeois Society.* Cambridge: The MIT Press. Print.

Hadjinicolaou, Nicos. 1978. "Sur l'ideologie de l'avantgardisme." In *Histoire et Critique des Arts* 6.2: 50–73. Print.

Harding, James A. 2011. "Introduction to Intersections." In *Avant-Garde Performance and Material Exchange: Vectors of the Radical,* ed. Mike Sell, 17–22. New York: Palgrave Macmillan. Print.

Harvey, David. 1989. *The Condition of Postmodernity: An Enquiry into the Origins of Cultural Change.* London: Sage Publishers. Print.

Haskell, Francis. 1990. "Die Kunst und die Sprache der Politik." In *Wandel der Kunst in Stil und Geschmack: Ausgewählte Schriften,* ed. Francis Haskell, 122–138. Köln: DuMont. Print.

hooks, bell. 1990. *Yearning: Race, Gender, and Cultural Politics.* Boston: South End Press. Print.

Hou, Jeffrey. 2010. *Insurgent Public Space: Guerilla Urbanism and the Remaking of Contemporary Cities.* London/New York: Routledge. Print.

Hutchinson, George. 1995. *The Harlem Renaissance in Black and White.* Cambridge: The Belknap Press of Harvard University Press. Print.

Huyssen, Andreas. 1987. *After the Great Divide: Modernism, Five Faces of Modernity: Modernism, Avant-Garde, Decadence, Kitsch, Postmodernism*. Durham: Duke University Press. Print.

Kaltmeier, Olaf, and Wilfried Raussert. "Introduction." 2019. *Sonic Politics. Music and Social Movements*, ed. Olaf Kaltmeier and Wilfried Raussert, 1–14. London/New York: Routledge. Print.

Köhne, Karen. 2000. *La vie est d'hommage: Autobiographie und Fiktion, Tradition und Avantgarde im Erzählwerk Jack Kerouacs*. Würzburg: Königshausen & Neumann. Print.

Koselleck, Reinhart. 2000. *Zeitgeschichten: Studien zur Historik*. Frankfurt a. M.: Suhrkamp. Print.

Kroes, Rob. 2008. "Imaginary Americas in Europe's Public Space." In *Transcultural Visions of Identities in Images and Texts. Transatlantic American Studies*, ed. Wilfried Raussert and Reinhard Isensee, 69–94. Heidelberg: Winter. Print.

Laverdant, Gabriel-Désiré. 1845. *De la mission de l'art et du rôle des artistes: Salon de 1845*. Paris. Print.

Lefèbvre, Henri. 1991. *The Production of Space*. Hoboken: Wiley-Blackwell. Print.

Leonardi, Paul. 2017. "The Social Media Revolution: Sharing and Learning in the Age of Leaky Knowledge." *ScienceDirect* 27.1: 47–59.

Locke, Alain. 1970 [1925]. "The New Negro." *The New Negro*, ed. Alain Locke, 3–16. New York: Atheneum. Print.

Löw, Martina. 2016. *The Sociology of Space. Materiality, Social Structures, and Action*. New York: Palgrave. Print.

Low, Setha, and Neil Smith, ed. 2005. *The Politics of Public Space*. London/New York: Routledge. Print.

Marcuse, Herbert. 1969. "Repressive Tolerance." In *Critique of Pure Tolerance*, ed. R. Barrington Moore and Herbert Marcuse, 95–137. Boston: Beacon Press.

Massey, Doreen. 2001. "A Global Sense of Place." *Space, Place and Gender*, ed. Doreen Massey, 146–156. Minneapolis: University of Minnesota Press. Print.

Minton, Anna. 2012. *Ground Control: Fear and Happiness in the Twenty-First Century City*. New York: Penguin Books. Print.

Murphy, Richard. 1999. *Theorizing the Avant-Garde: Modernism, Expressionism, and the Problems of Postmodernity*. Cambridge: Cambridge University Press. Print.

Nancy, Jean-Luc. 1991. *The Inoperative Community*. Minneapolis: University of Minnesota Press. Print.

Orvell, Miles, and Jeffrey L. Meikle. 2009a. "Introduction." In *Public Space and the Ideology of Place in American Culture*, ed. Miles Orvell and Jeffrey L. Meikle, 9–17. Amsterdam: Rodopi. Print.

———, eds. 2009b. *Public Space and the Ideology of Place in American Culture*. Amsterdam: Rodopi.

Parker, Simon. 2004. *Urban Theory and the Urban Experience. Encountering the City*. London/New York: Routledge. Print.

Quijano, Aníbal. 2014. *Colonialidad del poder, eurocentrismo y América Latina*. Lima: Clacso. Print.

Raussert, Wilfried. "Introduction." 2017. In *The Routledge Companion to Inter-American Studies*, ed. Wilfried Raussert, 1–12. London/New York: Routledge. Print.

———. 2014. "Mobilizing 'America/América': Toward Entangled Americas and a Blueprint for Inter-American 'Area Studies.'" *Forum for Inter-American Research* 7.3: 59–97. www.inter americana.de.

———. 2003. *Avantgarden in den USA 1940–70: Zwischen Mainstream und Erneuerung*. New York/Frankfurt a. M.: Campus. Print.

Rochfort, Desmond. 1998. *Mexican Muralists: Orozco, Rivera, Siquieros*. San Francisco: Chronicle Books. Print.

Roszak, Theodore. 1995 [1968]. *The Making of Counterculture. Reflections on the Technocratic Society and Its Youthful Opposition*. Berkeley: University of California Press. Print.

Russell, Charles, ed. 1981. *The Avant-Garde Today: An International Anthology*. Urbana: University of Illinois Press. Print.

Sennett, Richard. 1977. *The Fall of Public Man*. New York: Knopf. Print.

———. 1990. *The Conscience of the Eye: The Design and Social Life of Cities*. New York/London: W.W. Norton & Company. Print.

Slotkin, Richard. 2000. *Regeneration Through Violence: The Mythology of the American Frontier, 1600–1860*. Oklahoma City: University of Oklahoma Press. Print.

Smith, Richard Cándida. 2017. *Improvised Continent. Pan-Americanism and Cultural Exchange*. Philadelphia: University of Pennsylvania Press. Print.

Soja, Edward. 1989. *Postmodern Geographies: The Reassertion of Space in Critical Social Theory*. New York: Verso. Print.

Sorkin, Michael. 1992. *Variations on a Theme Park: The New American City and the End of Public Space*. Paris: Farrar, Straus and Giroux. Print.

The Guardian. 2016. "North Dakota Pipeline: 141 Arrests as Protesters Pushed Back From Site." https://www.theguardian.com/us-news/2016/oct/27/north-dakota-access-pipeline-protest-arrests-pepper-spray.

Tornaghi, Chiara, and Sabine Knierbein, eds. 2014. *Public Spaces and Relational Perspectives: New Challenges for Architectural Planning*. New York/London: Routledge. Print.

Waldenfels, Bernhard. 2015. *Sozialität und Alterität*. Frankfurt a. M.: Suhrkamp. Print.

Watson, Sophia. 2006. *City Publics*. London/New York: Routledge. Print.

Youkhana, Eva, and Larissa Förster, 2015. "Introduction." In *Grafficitity: Visual Practices and Contestations in Urban Space*, ed. Eva Youkhana and Larissa Förster, 7-17. Köln: Morphomata. Print.

Yúdice, George. 2003. *The Expediency of Culture: Uses of Culture in the Global Era*. Durham: Duke University Press. Print.

Zukin, Sharon. 1995. *The Cultures of Cities*. Malden: Blackwell Publishers. Print.

Chapter I

Parading and Performing in the Streets:
Cultural and Artistic Practices in Garveyism
and the Harlem Renaissance

Mexico City and New York became central sites for art practices to revisit and redefine public space in the early decades of the twentieth century. They also turned into important contact zones for artists, intellectuals, and movements. At the same time, they functioned as centers of art practice with a strong interAmerican outreach that introduced new forms of modernist art and expression, redefining modernity in its social and artistic dimensions. To understand how art interpreted and fashioned public space aesthetically, socially, and politically, one must look at artistic and cultural practices conducted by black cultural workers, intellectuals, and artists who came from the Caribbean, Latin America, and different areas of the United States to engage in rich collaborations and exchange in Harlem, the mecca of black culture in New York in the 1920s. Equally important is it to revisit the literary and chiefly visual avant-gardes in Mexico City that not only shaped post-revolutionary Mexican society and cultural expression, but became a magnet for interAmerican cultural exchange, particularly in the context of Mexican muralist painting, which forcefully claimed public sites and had a transcultural, at times Pan-American outreach. Both examples show that art practice in public space was central for reinventing the social along the lines of new communal and national imaginaries in the Americas.

Historical context and the emergence of "The New Negro"

At the turn of the twentieth century, a call for a gathering of intellectuals in London in order to explore the situation of peoples of African ancestry living in Africa, North and Latin America, and the Caribbean captured the attention of black activists, artists, and intellectuals. Along with a hope of overcoming allegations of "Negro inferiority" in scientific circles, a Pan-African movement emerged to confront global issues of colonial discrimination against peoples of African descent. Participating thinkers from different peoples of African ancestry shared the belief that historical experience, cultural values, social anxieties, and strong hopes united many black cultures around the globe. London's Pan-African conference echoed the impact of the "American Negro Exhibit" that had taken place a few months prior at the *Rue des Nations* in Paris. This exhibit combined books, photography, and visual, industrial, and fine art products to celebrate black cultural and industrial production of the post-slavery period of the U.S., and to document black presence in the public sphere of the Western world. The common tenor among black intellectuals celebrated the evidence of black equality and productivity "once the veil of slavery had been lifted" (Powell 2002, 24). Pan-African ideas gained momentum and encountered a new exotic fascination with the black continent and its diasporic offspring in the so-called "African craze." This opened venues for black cultural and artistic practices to enter public space. During the 1920s, the channels through which blues and jazz reached the public multiplied rapidly. The phonograph, the radio, and talking pictures took the market by storm and helped spread various forms of black music from the Americas (Raussert 2000, 29; cf. Ogren 1989a). A somewhat ambiguous embrace and clichéd representation of African cultural expression pushed artistic expression in music, cabaret, visual arts, and literature to new horizons. Thus, in U.S. America began a reinvention of modernity, nourished by the desire for a truly "American" aesthetic and vernacular.

Various social factors influenced and shaped Harlem's unique role in the development of African American art, music, and literature in the 1920s. After a short period of postwar decline, the American economy soared because of the tremendous profits earned from World War I. African Americans in the Northern cities also profited from this economic boom. In years of general prosperity, African American artists found a way in the cultural business industry.

Wealthy patrons sponsored black artists, inviting the latter to regular salon gatherings of artists and patrons. Harlem was an economically prospering area of New York City and a place where optimism developed in the black community. James De Jongh points out that Harlem provided the matrix for the growth of new ideas and new concepts of race: "new kinds of Negroes, with new ways of thinking could flourish" (1990, 9). The early decades of the twentieth century marked a period of tremendous social and geographical change within the black communities. The large migration from the South to the North between 1914 and 1918 and the emergence of World War I had great significance for black people in the United States (Drake and Cayton 1945, 55–64).

The outbreak of World War I launched a reversal of European migration. At the beginning of the war, immigration had actually reached a standstill. Many a foreign-born citizen returned to his home country in Europe to join the troops in combat. While U.S. American industry experienced increasing production during the war years, it had to confront a lack of labor force, too. Many recruiting agents travelled South to attract black people to the urban centers up North. Cotton farming had repeatedly been set back through flood, famine, and the boll weevil epidemic (Raussert 2000, 19). Due to harsh social and economic conditions – not to mention the local racial problems – many African Americans moved to the big cities up North.

While industrial centers up North faced a steadily increasing wave of black migrants from the South, Harlem witnessed the arrival of many black artists and intellectuals of varied national descent. They arrived from the Caribbean, Latin America, and Africa. Despite their individual differences in politics and ethics, most of the black intellectuals at the time pursued the goal of establishing an alternative aesthetic to the modernist forms of Euro-American art. This aesthetic was "tied to a sense of myth, geography, history, and culture that was truly indigenous to the countries, rather than merely reflective of European trends, whether conservative or avant-garde" (Rampersad 1989, 67). As the international makeup of the artistic and literary Harlem scene suggests, multiple approaches to aesthetics, politics, and history gained access to the cultural discourse. At a time when ritual lynchings in the South and race riots against African Americans in the North were still popular, Harlem was taken to be an enclave of change. Whereas colonial policy continued worldwide suppression of black people, Harlem profited from the African craze accompanying the modernist period and a tremendous intellectual and artistic exchange between various black cultural traditions. Arguably the strongest interAmerican connection during the early decades of the twentieth century developed between writers and intellectuals from Jamaica and their black counterparts from Harlem. This link is especially significant because it enhanced an artistic re-appropriation of public space by black literary, musical, and artistic agents. Performance arts like jazz, public poetry readings, street performances, parades, and cabaret shows fed the literary and artistic imagination (Ogren 1989b) and developed along an interAmerican exchange between actors and sites in Harlem and Kingston, Jamaica. These artistic practices highlighted the significance of the connection between performance and public space for rethinking modernist aesthetics and politics from Afro-descendent perspectives.

As a frequent traveler between Jamaica and the U.S., Marcus Garvey embraced ideas of Pan-Africanism, ideas inflected by his additional knowledge of Jamaican and Southern U.S. cultural traditions. Garvey is the intellectual figure among black radical thinkers who most stressed the importance of public space and visibility in public space for the advancement of black people. Performance in public space was crucial to his politics and aesthetics of change. In parades, public theatre performances, and variety shows, Garvey demonstrated his performative style of excess and his knack for "exploiting the subversive potential of multiple sites of cultural production" (Ford-Smith 2004, 20).

Garvey's Universal Negro Improvement Association (UNIA) was arguably the most influential anticolonial organization in Jamaica in the first decades of the twentieth century. His legacy included his mastery of heterogeneous performance languages. He integrated spectacular parades, elocution competitions, variety concerts, pageants, ceremonial rites, choirs, dance, plays, public debates, and speeches in his programs to mobilize, educate, inform, and transform his followers. As Ford-Smith points out, "UNIA performances were as crucial to the making of Jamaican identity as they were to anticolonial resistance" (19; cf. Hill 18–19). Garvey employed performances to create an imagined anticolonial nation (McClintock 1995). Through performance in public space, he could reach a huge audience, including those who had not had the resources to acquire literacy. Performance skills to Garvey and his followers opened doors to knowledge unauthorized by dominant systems of knowledge. He used performances in streets and public sites to envision communities of resistance by unleashing memory and alternative ways of knowing encoded in body, movement, dress, and voice (cf. Hamilton 1987; Gaines 1996). With thousands of people participating in his parades and many thousands more witnessing them, Garvey established public space as a black domain for spectacle and cultural and political affirmation.

Garvey's spectacular UNIA parades came out of a tradition of parade culture that had developed in Harlem in the early twentieth century. James Weldon Johnson describes Harlem's parade culture in *Black Manhattan*:

> Harlem is also a parade ground. During the warmer months of the year no Sunday passes without several parades. There are brass bands, marchers in resplendent regalia, and high dignitaries with gorgeous insignia riding in automobiles. Almost any excuse for parading is sufficient – the funeral of a member of the lodge, the laying of a corner stone, the annual sermon to the order, or just a general desire to turn out …. [G]enerally these parades are lively and add greatly to the movement, colour and gaiety of Harlem. (1930, 168)

Parades brought music, religion, performance, and protest into the streets. Arguably, the first massive African American public protest took place on July 28, 1917 in New York City. Among the demonstrators were many children who participated in the Silent Protest Parade against the East St. Louis Riots. According to press releases, between 8,000 and 10,000 African Americans marched against lynching and anti-black violence. The march was precipitated by the East St. Louis Riots of May and July of that year, which were an outbreak of labor-, class-, and race-related violence.[1]

But it was another parade that announced the beginning of a new era for African Americans in the aftermath of World War I: the return of the 369th Regiment in 1919. That parade literally marched through Harlem, starting at 61st Street, proceeding up 5th Avenue, across 110th Street, and up Lenox Avenue. When the UNIA parade for the 1922 convention transgressed into the area occupied by whites, according to a report in the *New York World*, banners appeared reading, "White man rules America, black man shall rule Africa," "We want a black civilization," and "God and Negro Shall Triumph" (Robertson 2011, n. pag.). Many thousands of blacks, from the West Indies and the American South, were migrating to New York between 1910 and 1920, particularly during the labor shortages of the war, and Marcus Garvey's and the UNIA's message of black unity, pride, and economic self-sufficiency took root and flourished among a disaffected people.[2]

For the African American community, which had repeatedly faced segregation, exclusion, violence, and lynching in public spaces, an occupation of public sites meant an act of cultural and political empowerment. Responding also to housing situations in Harlem, a large part of African American communal life took to the streets, stoops, and sidewalks.

---

1   http://newyorknatives.com/black-new-yorkers-rose-up-on-this-day-in-nycs-history/.

2   http://www.nydailynews.com/new-york/marcus-garvey-powerful-man-harlem-article-1.796006.

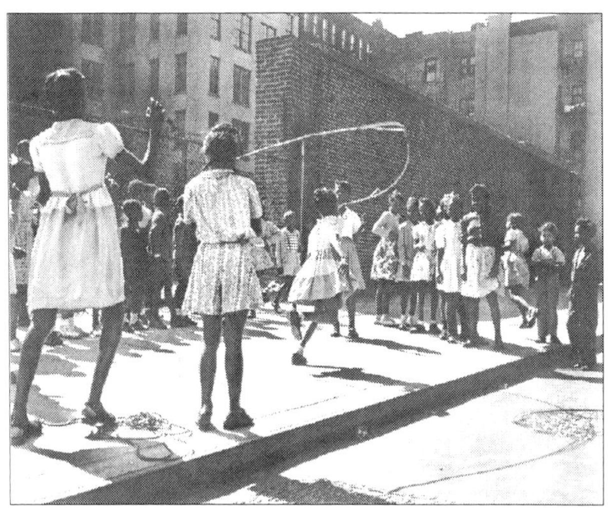

Figure 1: Children playing on sidewalk, 1940s (© Schomburg Center).[3]

Hence, singing in groups, preaching in public, delivering soap-box political speeches, and enjoying verbal games like "playing the dozens" formed a crucial part of social life and community-building during the spring and summer months in Harlem. Partly an escape from the confines of crowded apartment houses, these gatherings in public an environment for sharing ideas, developing community, and practicing art in public (cf. Compton 2017, 60). With the arrival of migrants from the Caribbean, Latin America, and Africa, further creolization of black cultural and political life in streets, marketplaces, and shopping zones took shape.

The spaces in Harlem that served to educate and strengthen were "the play street, the speaker's corner, the parade route." They "provided a precarious safety and doubled as the crucible in which resistance movements were fomented" (Reid 2018, 7). In a way these public sites turned into "homeplaces," which were often shaped by women and fostered the growth of community from home to the

---

3   Source: Sid Grossman, photographs and Prints Division, Schomburg Center for Research in Black Culture. The New York Public Library, Astor, Lenox and Tilden Foundations.

larger Harlem public (hooks 1991, 72). As Reid reminds us, Harlem was rich in small public spaces "to empower community enrichment through performance and expression of culture" (2018, 7). The development of Harlem as an urban enclave for the black population brought about a production and re-shaping of space: external social and economic conditions, cultural and political strategies of power, and social confinement by way of exclusion led to the emergence of these homeplaces, even if they were only of a tenuous nature. These homeplaces led to an intense epoch of social organization and cultural production in Harlem. Amidst the abundance of artistry in music clubs, theaters (e.g., the National Black Theater, the Harlem Suitcase Theater, and the American Negro Theater), and poetry readings in literary salons, the venues for social and cultural performance ranged "from sidewalk to ballroom to backroom rent party" (44–45). It was Harlem's sidewalk and community art practices in particular that built a sense of black pride and community. Harlem's development illustrated that grassroots creative expression in public space could make a significant difference in the living conditions of disenfranchised communities. Grassroots rituals and public art practices situated in community spaces during the Harlem Renaissance fostered a dialogic and communal development of cultural expression that tremendously shaped the social life in Harlem.

For a population facing constant oppression, public sites in the enclave of Harlem provided venues for free artistic expression and individual as well as communal empowerment. A striking performance of self was represented by the "soapbox or street corner" speaking practice (Reid 2018, 56). This expression of oral culture included poetry, history lessons, exchanges about culture, and promotion of new concepts of blackness, all of which took place in parks, streets, and on sidewalks accessible to all who took the time to listen. Black agency took its fullest force in the act of public assembly and parades. As concerns the latter, the preparation of the pageantry was just as important as the practice of parading itself. Both were acts of self-empowerment that created a spirit of group solidarity to give voice to what had labelled the "New Negro" consciousness. The pageantry provided a space for reinventing the self through costuming and puffery. While it was playful, it contained the power to subvert and resist to colonial practices of domination. No simple mimicry and mockery, it included a deep sense of self-reflexivity about self-positioning, social conditioning, and historical change. Reid sums it up nicely:

> In Harlem, urbanity was evidenced by parades, which utilized space as a forum for peacocking and pageantry and provided a release for artistry; play streets as safe containers for creative play; community art spaces as sites to educate and nourish the body to prepare for political action; and speakers' corners as public spheres spaces serving as incubators for nascent resistance movements which ultimately advanced civil rights. (2018, 66)

This rich tapestry of performing self, culture, and politics is inconceivable without the tremendous exchange that took place between different black cultures in Harlem. In practice, Garveyism was a series of early performances of black power. As in most Caribbean anticolonial settings, in Jamaica performances played a key role in carving narratives of identity and community. Garvey's spectacular parades could draw on long established Caribbean tradition and represented an exemplary educational tool to teach black history to the masses. While the parades recreated narratives of black colonial history, they also provided a venue for contemporary protest and militancy. Garvey's plays such as "Slavery from Hut to Mansion," frequently performed in theaters as well as open public sites, carried out cultural memory work that unraveled the pain and grief of enslavement. At the same time, they served as effective provocations to social and political action.

Most powerful, though, were Garvey's UNIA parades for the propagation of black nationalism both in Jamaica and Harlem (Ford-Smith 2004, 20). The parades in Jamaica and Harlem enacted a Pan-African vision of communal bonding.

Participants could be identified by their African liberation colors and, at ceremonials, by their elegant military uniforms. Participants carried banners and flags with symbolic images borrowed from Egyptian history. They also integrated swords, weaponry, and other regalia into "a complete *mise en scène*" (Ford-Smith 2004, 24). In sum, large numbers of black people occupied public space, conveying the UNIA's message of black pride and nationalism through the parades. In addition, these practices were extended, for UNIA members, through intense exercises in controlled public-speaking and effective rhetoric. Rituals and regal displays, too, were deepened in organizational practice. Garvey's mastery of performance shines through in the most impressive UNIA parades in August 1920 and August 1922 in New York, the latter of which launched the Third International Convention of the Negro Peoples of the World. As part of a spectacular *mise en scène*, hundreds of people marched the streets of New York City in full regalia. As Ford-Smith points out, these parades were at "once a fiction and a threat" and they opened performative spaces that "allowed for multiple maneuvers among the movement's subjects" (25).

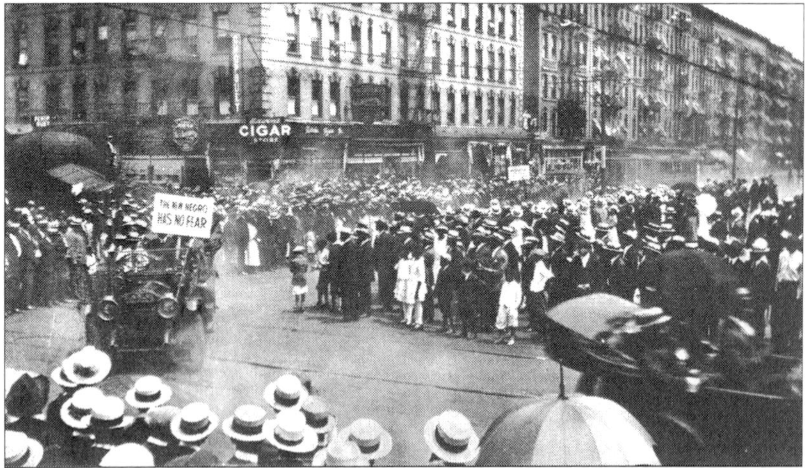

Figure 2: UNIA parade, organized in Harlem, 1920s (© Schomburg Center).[4]

---

4   Schomburg Center for Research in Black Culture, Photographs and Prints Division, The New York Public Library.

A mix of entertainment and politics in public space also character-ized Garvey's cultural practices in Jamaica. Inspired by the rich black entertainment scene of the Harlem Renaissance, he founded the Edelweiss Park Amusement Company at 57 Slipe Road in King-ston in 1931. InterAmerican flows brought Harlem-style variety shows to the Caribbean island. Performance practices, styles of va-riety, and names such as that of the nightclub Dreamland were bor-rowings from Harlem nightlife. Garvey's concept of black agency fully embraced cultural production as an important political tool. The mission of the Amusement Company was to propel black cul-tural production on the island. The Company's task included the management of the facilities and cultural sections of the UNIA, and to present artistic work and seek out local talent (Hamilton 1987, 92). Edelweiss Park was the site where much of the cultural work took place in Kingston. It consisted of a two-story house, a number of outbuildings, an attached spacious yard, and, most importantly, an outdoor amphitheater that could hold an audience of several thousands, refurbished for the 1929 UNIA convention in Jamaica.

The Amusement Company project was truly transcultural, com-bining amusement park with variety shows. American popular cul-tural industries, often in the style of Harlem Renaissance perfor-mances, set the variety shows apart from established theater tradi-tions in the Caribbean. Black-face minstrel shows which had emerged in the northern U.S. in the antebellum years, vaudeville practices, and elegantly staged chorus lines in the style of black mu-sical cabaret from Harlem found their way into Jamaican entertain-ment (Reid 2018, 37–38).

As Reid points out, "Relying on glamour and spectacle on the one hand, and social satire, comedy, exaggeration, and repetition on the other, variety performers drew in and transformed multiple in-fluences from both 'high' and 'low' culture" (2018, 37–38). The acts comprised a wide range of cultural and artistic practices – in-cluding recitations, dances (acrobatic, classical, and jazz), musical revues, minstrel shows, comedy shows, carnivals, plays, garden par-ties, choral concerts of spirituals, religious services, classical recitations, and orchestral concerts. The idea was to reach a large public and thus shape the public sphere through cultural practices in open air space. For further transmission of variety programs, amplified "radio broadcasts" were installed to reach those who could not be present. A panorama of largely but not exclusively afrodescendent musical genres and styles shaped a variety show program that syncretized jazz, mento, and glamorous song and dance routines. The charleston, the black bottom, the rumba, and tap were all part of the regular program (33–34).

In parades and variety shows, the UNIA offered performers a set of modes of production and distribution. It arranged opportunities to occupy and redefine public space through cultural practice and to communicate with a large audience to advance the anticolonial struggle. While the parades generally followed a more rigid military pattern, with men wearing military uniforms and women donning nurse dresses, the performers of variety shows added diversity and gender as well as class consciousness to the anti-colonial struggle. Many performances undermined colonial cultural tastes to create others based on new class and gender evaluations.

Through often contradictory interAmerican processes of borrowing and transforming influences from Caribbean festival tradition and American popular culture, black and black-identified performers reappropriated public space to create a rich spectrum of popular narratives and new spectacles with social visions beyond the control of white coloniality, and even outside the orthodoxies of the UNIA's mainly patriarchal black nationalism. Performances opened spaces for women in real world politics. For example, different women took center stage in the UNIA movement such as Amy Jacques Garvey, Garvey's second wife, who was involved in the international and national UNIA leadership. She helped build and expand the movement at the same time as she took a strong stand against male domination of the movement. Louise Little, a working-class Trinidadian immigrant wife of a U.S.-born black minister and UNIA member, Earl Little, joined and created UNIA chapters throughout the Mid-West. She played an active role in the

UNIA as a grassroots believer, member, organizer, and leader who wrote reports of meetings and organizational activities for *The Negro World* (Walton 2008, 8).

Performances in the UNIA movement were characterized by flexibility, parody, and excess. Exploring and employing the effervescence of performance in public space, Garvey and his followers succeeded in expanding the subversive power of cultural production. A multitude of performance styles in the parades, but even more so in the variety shows, created a sense of possibility (cf. Burton 1997). The combination of critique, parody, acculturation, and assimilation was constantly in flux and bound to change from context to context. The high visibility in public space provided cultural agency for "plural projects of resistance across a range of sites and subject positions" (Reid 2018, 41).

The emergence of "The New Negro" and rethinking "black self" in relation to public space

The attention to the self's relation to hegemony, public space, and public sphere in the cultural work of Garvey and the UNIA also characterized the artistic and intellectual work in the Harlem Renaissance at large. The Harlem Renaissance, also called the New Negro Movement, formed an important black contribution to new American aesthetics. The "New Negro" seemed to be the perfect metaphor for a society and culture at a moment of rupture, change, and transition. While the Harlem Renaissance cherished many artistic collaborations between poets, painters, photographers, musicians, and communal grassroots movements, for many, the "New Negro" entity was first of all a "mood, or a sentiment" in which black cultural workers were acknowledged as equal partners in the world of cultural production (Powell 2002, 42). It was an important part of an intensifying process of self-reflection, and a propelling force for individual and communal creative expression in smaller and larger public settings.

Garvey's level of self-reflexivity showed primarily in his use of the spectacular in public space. His parades drew on the importance of both the mask and performativity in black cultures. Importantly, his appropriations of public space happened with his and his followers' deep awareness of colonial history and the trauma of oppression and exclusion it involved. At the same time, Garvey's use of and performance in public space involved a spectacular showing of pride and strength. Established in modernity as a term to describe the relation of the self to the social, "reflexivity" gained strong prominence in the literary and artistic expressions by black writers and intellectuals. American pragmatism shaped the understanding of the concept in the 1920s and 1930s, when reflexivity was comprehensively defined by George H. Mead as "the turning back of the experience of the individual upon [oneself]" (1934, 134). In late modernity, Sara Delamont explained reflexivity as "a socially scientific variety of self-consciousness" (1991, 8). Critics like Margaret Archer have developed the concept further by introducing the idea of "internal conversation" (2007, 8). The latter notion theoretically reflects the permanent self-confrontation of the individual and its dialogical interaction with an ever-changing social and cultural environment.

While Anthony Giddens's theory of reflexive modernity remains current in studies of the self, social, and their interrelations (cf. Giddens 1991), more recent postcolonial and decolonial thinkers oppose the Western and Eurocentric conceptualization of the rational self as well as the Western-centered definition of social experience in Giddens's discourse. In theories such as Nicos Mouzelis's apophatic reflexivity (cf. Mouzelis 2010), special attention is paid to the emotional, spiritual, and therapeutic side of self-reflexivity. As Eugene Halton puts it, "Being human involves feeling, dreaming, experiencing, remembering and forgetting, and not simply knowing" (1995, 273). It is Hortense Spillers who pushed for new approaches to reflexivity in the feminist and postcolonial discourse of Black Studies of the late twentieth and early twenty-first century.

Badia S. Ahad reminds us of "Hortense Spillers's call for attention to deeper modes of self-reflexivity" (2010, 733).

To further reflect on a fundamental "twoness" (black self, "American" self) in African American cultural analysis, Spillers introduces her idea of "interior intersubjectivity" (1996, 713) as an interpretative strategy and practice of resistance. While her reflections emerged in the context of late modernity, as did those of Giddens, Delamont, and Mouzelis, they provide a point of departure to reach a better understanding of "The New Negro" as a comparative metaphorical construct within Harlem Renaissance identity politics in the 1920s, as well as a better understanding of the relations of black subjects to public space and sphere. "If by substitutive identities … we mean the capacity to represent a self through the masks of self-negation," she writes, "then the dialectics of self-reflection and the strategies of a psychoanalytic hermeneutic come together at the site of a 'new woman/man'" (711–712). Spillers's discourse emphasizes three key markers that illustrate the complexity of black identity formation and reformation in the 1920s: the mask, self-negation, and self-reflection. Equally important, though, is bell hooks's understanding of place-making during the Harlem Renaissance through which female and male agency became visible for both private and public creations of space (hooks's place-making). It is in the overlapping reflections about self and public space that the creative spirit of the Harlem Renaissance can be fully recognized.

The appropriation of public space, as well as the transformation of the public sphere, was central to cultural practices that redefined black identity politics. This makes sense given the exclusion from and segregation within social, cultural, and economic spaces that black populations in the Americas had experienced throughout history. Textual and performative reflections about the relation of self to public space and public sphere were thus essential to cultural and social practices of black artists and thinkers in the early twentieth century.

As an umbrella term for a new identity politics, the "New Negro" quickly gained widespread public attention. The term emerged from the progressive race rhetoric of thinker Booker T. Washington and black woman rights activist Fannie Barrier Williams in contributions for the black magazines *Voice of the Negro* and *Crisis* in the late nineteenth and early twentieth century, with illustrations done by John Henry Adams Jr. Maintaining original sociopolitical connotations, "New Negro" entered the discourses of aesthetic progress and racial redefinition with Alain Locke's *The New Negro: An Interpretation* and "Harlem: Mecca of the New Negro," a special issue of the magazine *Survey Graphic*. Both were published in 1925 and popularized the term in artistic, intellectual, and cultural market circuits (Powell 2002, 42).

"The Old Negro" versus "The New Negro"

The emergence of "The New Negro" as a powerful metaphor was the result of practices of comparing in intellectual, political, and artistic circles of the time and a new way of viewing black self and culture in relation to public space and sphere. The meaning of the term took shape against the backdrop of its metaphorically constituted other, "The Old Negro." Both terms were further differentiated along class, gender, and generational lines. Accordingly, as a metaphorical construction, both terms held the potential for multiple significations and were exposed to different performative, theatrical, artistic, and literary interpretations during the early decades of the twentieth century, particularly in the manifold cultural productions of the Harlem Renaissance. On various levels, "The Old Negro" signified what Butler and Athanasiou refer to as "the dispossessed" (cf. Butler and Athanasiou 2013) while, in different ways, "The New Negro" suggested agency and empowerment.

On a political level, "The Old Negro" stood for political conservatism and social accommodationism, while "The New Negro" represented renewal and change (Bernard 2011, 273). The basic metaphorical constitution of these *comparata* signals the complexity of a new, rather free-floating synthesis of "blackness." Comparisons between the "The Old Negro" and "The New Negro" inevitably involved questions of tradition and innovation. The terms also entailed drawing comparisons between imaginaries of African, African American, and Euro American cultures to undo long lasting paradigms of difference and hierarchy. With the new flows and exchange between Caribbean, African, and African American cultures, blackness gained even more complexity and richness, as reflected in a varied use of public space: from streets, to parks to marketplaces for aesthetics, politics, and trade.

The question of the self and how to relate to identity, the social, and the other was even more complex for the modern black subject. Writers like Countee Cullen and Jean Toomer wanted to transcend race, even refusing the label "black writer." On the other hand, Langston Hughes completely embraced his blackness. His poetry gave voice(s) to the conflicts involved in reflecting on what it meant to be a poet in Harlem of the 1920s, what it meant to be a *black* poet, and what it meant to manage the spaces between communities. Reflectivity signified looking at the self, but also at the black self's often "disenfranchised" and "dispossessed" positioning in comparison to others and his limited access to public space and history. After all, the publication of works by black authors still largely depended on white publishing policies and the priorities of white publishing houses (Bernard 2011, 269–271).

Reflectivity also involved a continuous comparing of the self with the floating metaphors of "The Old Negro," "The New Negro," and society at large, which meant white hegemony, censorship, and selection. The act of writing and subsequent comparisons took place from a peripheral or (invoking Spivak) "subaltern" positioning. In spite of the optimistic spirit of renewal, black writers had to manage the colonial baggage of anxiety, dispossession, displacement, and anger in their acts of writing, singing, and painting of "The New Negro." This varied spectrum of emotional complexity shaped their reflectivity, as well as the act of comparing beyond a pure cognitive understanding. There were (and still are) specificities of black culture that have been marked by a distinct difference to white mainstream culture. Even in the works of W.E.B. Du Bois, an African American intellectual educated at Humboldt University in Berlin and one of the bastions of Western thinking in the late nineteenth and early twentieth century, a spiritual reflectivity is highly noticeable. His works mark African American culture as a strongly spiritual culture, quite different from the white mainstream which is based upon rational principles. Practices like roadside preaching in Jamaica, street corner preaching in Harlem and preaching in and outside storefront churches from the Deep South carried these forms of spirituality into the public spaces of cities like Chicago and New York.

To explore black cultural immersion into public space and sphere, artistic and cultural practices during the Harlem Renaissance should be observed in a relational way: how the cultural actors related themselves to history, to a past and contemporary social context, and to the other (whiteness in general terms). The positioning of actors in the public was of key importance for the ways in which they did or un-did comparisons, articulating their relation to signifying practices beyond Euro-American standards, such as in the African, Caribbean, and African American cultural traditions. Practices of comparing occurred in local, national, and, most of all, transcultural networks (interAmerican and trans-Atlantic) and they reflected the black subject's relation to public space. They built on colonial and emancipatory processes and were fundamentally conflictive.

Colonial and peripheral practices of comparing: what is my position in public Space?

It is commonly agreed among historians and critics that practices of comparison played a central role in the processes of colonizing the New World (cf. Epple and Erhart 2015; Fauconnier and Turner 2002). Comparisons veiled under the guise of science and universal knowledge helped establish structures and hierarchies based upon white supremacy and racial discrimination. At the beginning of the twentieth century, this meant that, for the black subject in the Americas, by and large one still spoke from a peripheral locus of enunciation. For the black subject in the Harlem Renaissance (and in the Americas at large), practices of comparing were first of all a way to order one's own position – one's own place in society and in relation to hegemonic public space. These practices frequently included references of the self with the dominant structure, the public sphere, the canon, the established art world, or the successful music industry. They served as tools for self-positioning, self-reflection, and further self-empowerment. They also included dissident and trickster strategies based upon black oral cultures.

What differentiated them from mainstream practices of comparing is the high degree of reflexivity about the group and the self, which was at the core of black thinking during the Harlem Renaissance. In Alain Locke's manifesto of *The New Negro*, it is a local, national, and global consciousness of black history and cultures that provides a new sense of public space and sphere in terms of blackness and that Locke locates in the reflective quality of African American culture. In his thinking, "The New Negro" becomes the spearhead of a global black liberation movement with a double mission: "One is the consciousness of acting as the advance guard of the African peoples in their contact with Twentieth Century civilization; the other, the sense of a mission of rehabilitating the race in world esteem from that loss of prestige for which the fate and conditions of slavery have so largely been responsible" (Locke 1997, 14). Certainly, Garvey's parades in the streets of Jamaica and Harlem impressively performed this consciousness of black leadership. Similar to Locke's historical consciousness, Langston Hughes reflects on a long trajectory of black "high" culture in "The Negro Speaks of Rivers," linking African and Black-American cultures (Hughes 1995c, 257). In a self-reflexive way, he contemplates the freedom of the black writer and compares him to the vanguard, experimental, and ground-breaking group of artists and writers in his literary manifesto "The Negro Artist and the Racial Mountain": "We younger Negro artists who create now intend to express our individual dark-skinned selves without fear or shame …. We build our temples for tomorrow, strong as we know how, and we stand on top of the mountain, free within ourselves" (1995b [1926], 95). Hughes claims black cultures' audibility and visibility in public discourse. He concludes his manifesto with spatial metaphors that signal a new black presence in the public spaces in and around Harlem. Even more, though, with the biblical reference to the mountain he envisions a free black self who has the agency to reshape global public space according to a new inclusive vision.

Hughes's reference to the "top of the mountain" has biblical and secular connotations; it compares the black artist to the prophet Moses on the mountain and to John Winthrop and his futurist model of a city upon a hill. By comparison, Hughes relates the black self to larger theocratic and secular imaginaries of America, thus inscribing the black poet into an "American" modernist and progressive discourse. Through acts of comparing, writers and intellectuals like Locke and Hughes challenged the ruling geopolitics of knowledge from their peripheral positioning.

The mask and practices of comparing in African American cultural production

As a cultural and political movement, the Harlem Renaissance resisted fixed structures. The writers, activists, and intellectuals worked within networks and searched for new dialogical ways of interaction. In this way, the first Black Arts Movement developed a self-reflexive dimension in which identity, social structures, cultural expressions, and ways of being were discussed and questioned. By confronting the power hierarchies of the literary and cultural industry and discarding the colonial baggage and stigmatization of "black inferiority," these black thinkers and artists acted boldly, becoming inventive and playful to challenge the mainstream. "Masking" manifested itself as a central practice through which self-positioning, moving in public space, and comparative ways of thinking unfolded in the Harlem Renaissance. Already in 1895, Paul Laurence Dunbar had written his poem "We wear the mask," a reflection on the cultural dissemblance at the core of this practice. The poem gives voice to decades of black masking during times of conquest, slavery, and reconstruction.

> We wear the mask that grins and lies,
> It hides our cheeks and shades our eyes, –
> This debt we pay to human guile;
> With torn and bleeding hearts we smile,
> And mouth with myriad subtleties.
>
> Why should the world be over-wise,
> In counting all our tears and sighs?
> Nay, let them only see us, while
> We wear the mask.
>
> We smile, but, O great Christ, our cries
> To thee from tortured souls arise.
> We sing, but oh the clay is vile
> Beneath our feet, and long the mile;
> But let the world dream otherwise,
> We wear the mask!. (Dunbar 2018, n. pag.)

Dunbar's meditation on masking speaks to what African Americans have experienced from slavery, through Jim Crow, to the contemporary period. Psychological masking is a way to protect one's inner self and the thought system of one's group (cf. Hills 2010, 217). The practice of masking is shared by other colonized people, e.g. in the Caribbean. Frantz Fanon (1970) explained the whitening efforts among his countrymen in the Antilles through cultural displacement. Once the black subject starts moving among white people, he becomes self-conscious that he is measured by different norms than those in his community. Fanon's thought bears similarities with W.E.B Du Bois's "double consciousness" – an awareness of constantly looking at one's self through the eyes of the other (cf. Du Bois 1999).

This self-reflexive attitude fundamental to black thought in the Americas influenced the practices of comparing in Harlem Renaissance cultural production. In Harlem during the 1920s and 1930s,

African, Caribbean, and African American cultural production gained increasing presence in public sites and institutions. Masks as material artefacts occupied a special place in the community. Exhibitions of African masks, sculptures, and ornamentation were regularly mounted at the 135th street branch of the Public Library, as well as in the galleries of midtown and downtown Manhattan. To artists and intellectuals like Alain Locke and Aaron Douglas, African masks were not only pieces of ancestral legacy but also signs of the importance of Africa to the development of modernist art throughout the Western world (Hills 2010, 210). In reference to Pablo Picasso's *Les Demoiselles d'Avignon*, Henry L. Gates Jr. explains that "[t]he Cubist mask of modernism covers a black Bantu face. African art – ugly, primitive, debased in 1900; sublime, complex, valorized by 1910 was transformed so dramatically in the cultural imagination of the West" (1997, 163).

The mask became a touchstone for African American art from the Harlem Renaissance into the contemporary period. However, it is the *reinvention* of the mask as an abstract literary and artistic tool for *doing* and *undoing* comparisons, and for rethinking black cultures' position within and relation to public space, in the works painter Aaron Douglas and poets Claude McKay and Langston Hughes that marked the most distinctive challenges to white culture and power "from within."

Claude McKay, Jamaican poet and leading literary figure of the Harlem Renaissance, published "If We Must Die" in 1919 in the July issue of *The Liberator*. McKay wrote the poem in response to mob attacks by white Americans on African American individuals and communities during the race riots of the so-called Red Summer. The riots were the outcome of post-World War I social tensions in numerous cities throughout the United States and showed that public space could instantaneously turn into a combat zone over issues like racism and inequality. The return of African American soldiers from Europe and increasing competition in the job market lead to another violent racist explosion. The poem reflects the frequently haunted position of black people in public space, which is conceived of as a *mise-en-scène* battlefield and a large time-space continuum of violence, monstrosity, and racism. McKay uses the literary mask of the sonnet to address the violent tensions and challenge white norms and standards. Written in iambic pentameter, the poem consists of 14 lines with a complex rhyme scheme. It has three quatrains: the first with an a/b, a/b rhyme scheme, the second with c/d, c/d, the third with e/f, e/f, and a concluding couplet with g/g. The intricate and strict form mimics public order and control. The poem's opening line repeats comparative practices of the white supremacists comparing black people to "hogs." The poetic speaker echoes white racism. The comparisons shift from animals to humans as blacks become humanized: "Oh Kinsmen." … "like men." The comparisons go the other way in relation to white people, who are first referred to as hunters and later likened to "mad dogs."

McKay presents direct and implied comparisons; he masters the form of the sonnet but changes its content. The conventional themes of love, courtship, and romance in the sonnet tradition turn into a social, cultural, and political appeal. McKay focuses on oppression, negation, and violent resistance. His sonnet is a call to resist. On the level of reflectivity, McKay compares himself, through the mask of the Shakespearian sonnet, to the canonized writers of the Anglo-Saxon tradition. However, this comparison implies a reversal of power and the love it expresses is for a black brotherhood that transcends national boundaries. It is a call for black Pan-African nationalism, as the reference to "kinsmen" highlights. "The New Negro" in McKay's vision is a collective movement connecting multiple black cultures:

> If we must die – let it not be like hogs
> Hunted and penned in an inglorious spot,
> While round us bark the mad and hungry dogs,
> Making their mock at our accursed lot.
> If we must die – oh, let us nobly die,
> So that our precious blood may not be shed
> In vain; then even the monsters we defy
> Shall be constrained to honor us though dead!

Oh, Kinsmen! We must meet the common foe;
Though far outnumbered, let us show us brave,
And for their thousand blows deal one deathblow!
What though before us lies the open grave?
Like men we'll face the murderous, cowardly pack,
Pressed to the wall, dying, but fighting back!. (1995, 290)

McKay's poem recalls mob hunts of runaway slaves, lynching scenarios, and mob attacks on black protesters. It draws an image of public space for black people as fragile, threatening, and deadly. At the same time, his poem implores black subjects to take their stand in public and pursue social justice.

Langston Hughes's poem "I, Too" was first published in 1926. Similar to McKay, Hughes also chooses a masking strategy to challenge the white modernist discourse of Anglo-Saxon America. In the poem, practices of comparing work on the level of authorship, and citizenship and are embedded in a reflective mode. Hughes's title refers to Du Bois's notion of twoness and double consciousness, evoking black intellectual confrontation and interconnectedness with a multiplicity of public spheres. Declaring himself the darker brother, the black poetic voice claims blood ties, citizenship, and communal belonging. As the short poem unfolds, Hughes describes a ubiquitous scene of domestic racism, against which he sets an initial comparison. In free verse form, the black poetic voice of an apparent domestic servant addresses his master household. The comparison expressed through "the darker brother" is simple and powerful. "The New Negro" is conceived in communal, political, and aesthetic terms: "How beautiful I am" (Hughes 1995a, 257). But Hughes goes a step further, from familial/social/aesthetic comparisons to comparisons on the level of authorship. Writing through the mask of Whitmanesque self-celebratory expression and adopting for African American poetry Whitman's free verse style, Hughes compares himself to Whitman as a poet and citizen, the canonically acclaimed founding father of modern poetry. The domestic servant's poetic voice not only claims black equality, but celebrates the beauty of blackness in Whitman's style of self-embrace.

The Whitmanesque mask provides an authoritative and literarily defined public space for bold cultural and social claims. Hughes uses it to refer to the blackening of America through music from slavery to the Jazz age. "I, too, sing America" claims black authorship for Modern American artistic expression (Hughes 1995a, 257). At first glimpse, merely a simple intertextual reference to the famous opening of Whitman's "Song of Myself" (2018), the verb in the context of the Harlem Renaissance actually expresses a celebration of African American oral and musical culture. Hughes's textual practice of comparing lifts African American folk culture into the realm of modernist American literature and culture. His singing voice is as biblical as Whitman's, but his sources are spirituals, blues, and jazz. Underneath the surface of the Whitmanesque modern American utopia, Hughes inserts dissidence (laughter) and expands utopian ideals with a strong belief in social change.

Clearly, Hughes's choice of musical metaphor draws on the extended presence of black music in the American public in the 1920s. Through music transmitted by radio, records, and vaudeville and cabaret shows, black culture permeated many aspects of social life within and beyond black communities. While the poem references spatial segregation and exclusion in a half-domestic, half-public setting, singing the nation, as Hughes's poetic voice has it, places black cultural production right in the center of the hegemonic public sphere.

> I, too, sing America.
> I am the darker brother.
> They send me to eat in the kitchen
> When company comes,
> But I laugh,
> And eat well,
> And grow strong.
>
> Tomorrow,
> I'll be at the table
> When company comes.
> Nobody'll dare
> Say to me,

"Eat in the kitchen,"
Then.

Besides,
They'll see how beautiful I am
And be ashamed – (Hughes 1995a, 257)

These examples from Hughes and McKay reveal that the literary mask, at the level of form and voice, served multiple purposes. The mask provided a safe aesthetic space to claim mastery of knowledge and form in order to push the comparison of the self with the accomplished master in the field of cultural production. The abstract literary mask allowed the poet a tongue-in-cheek method to subvert and expand the acknowledged and canonized literary expression for his own aesthetic, cultural, and political claims. It also provided a superb medium for designating reflexivity on blackness as a public concern to all of society.

Strategies of "masking" and the use of literal masks had an equally powerful presence in the Harlem music and cabaret scene (double entendre), and especially in the visual arts. The painter Aaron Douglas was arguably the most prolific African American painter to use masks and develop masking strategies to counter white hegemonic visions of blackness. He also embraced the opportunity to present his painterly vision of blackness on the walls of public institutions. "The New Negro" in Douglas's work came in hybrid African American/African attire. His artistic inclinations included experimental modernist forms like Braque's and Picasso's cubism, Winold Reiss's modernization of folk painting, and African art (cf. Mehring 2016). Many black figures in Douglas's paintings show faces modelled on masks of the Dan people of Liberia in Africa, their personality concealed, silhouettes of strong bodies rendered abstractly. Douglas concealed individuality to let a collective narrative of history emerge. He adopted cubist dynamics of form and a modern, avant-garde style in general; this served Douglas as a painted mask to look beyond Eurocentric visions of modernity and compare contemporary black culture with African, particularly Egyptian, culture.

Commercially, the cubist mask opened a path into the American art world; he was subsequently commissioned to paint murals for the New York Public Library. The murals provided high public visibility and demonstrated that Douglas considered himself as capable of adapting African art as the European masters of cubism at the time, Picasso and Braque. Yet, Douglas was not paying homage to Western modernist art. He used the mask in cubist style to celebrate black art and history from ancient Egypt to Harlem. His mask and silhouette-like presentations of blackness merged together his figures from African and African American art history and folk art merge in mask and silhouette-like presentations of blackness. His painterly practices of comparing built on the *comparata* Egypt and Black America(s), not on the *comparata* Black America(s) and Europe. Douglas created a complex vision of "The New Negro," presented in *Aspects of Negro Life*, a series of four murals sponsored by the federal Works Progress Administration (WPA). *Song of the Towers* (1934) is arguably the most modern of the four.

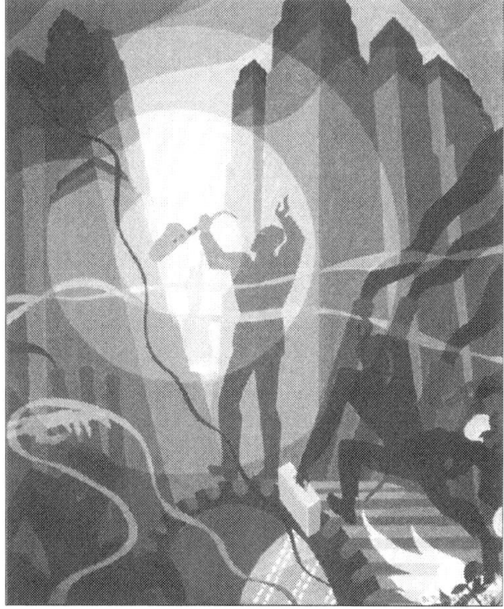

Figure 3: Aaron Douglas's *Song of the Towers*, 1934 (© Douglas Foundation).

The murals collectively outline black history from its African roots through the Great Migration; *Song of the Towers* tells a story of the conflicted black struggle with modernity. Complex and multi-layered, *Song* of *the Towers* relies on graphic designs as well as patterns of geometric shapes and, thus, speaks through the practices of cubist painting. Dominating the mural's center are concentric circles, framed by jutting rectangular prisms. Through this careful improvisation of various forms, Douglas unfolds a narrative that catapults the black figures into the whirlwind of modern, urban machinery. The mural unfolds a journey through various temporalities and public spaces reflected in an overall metropolitan setting. In a comparative, yet, relational way, cubist abstraction shows the dispossessed and the rising, the human and the machine, the left behind "Old Negro" and the rising "New Negro" in the center. By setting his abstract black figures in a mix of Cubist inspired dynamic forms, Douglas reflects the black origins of modernist art. The figures, however, are still struggling to claim their position in the setting of modern metropolis.

Song of the Towers (Douglas 1934) wistfully celebrates the triumph of black artistic expression in the Harlem Renaissance. Not only does the work demonstrate Douglas's mastery of Cubist modernism; the black musician in the center alludes to the musical blackening of Harlem and America during the heydays of Race Records in the 1920s. Nevertheless, the struggle against history, the wheel of modernization, and the towering presence of metropolitan architecture – the upward-gazing central black figure – suggests that a complete black arrival is still "a dream deferred" (Hughes 1990, 221). This interpretation is further supported by the contours of the Statue of Liberty, the quintessence of a public space open to all, which in the mural is removed in size and position. The mural intricately compares dream and reality, myth and history; the result is abstraction and ambiguity.

Like McKay and Hughes, Douglas displays mastery of form. Like other literary figures, he used the master form to present a self-reflexive discourse on blackness. His murals manifest diversity within blackness and relate different shades of blackness to a long trajectory of African diasporic history. The mastery of form gives Douglas the authority to speak for the modernist community, yet raises a racial critique on modernity.

In the state-commissioned mural *Song of the Towers*, Douglas cannily inserted a critical yet self-empowering black modernist vision. By comparing and relating different figures and stages of African American history with the emergence of the modern metropolis, he reveals the cracks within modernist American utopian design; he continues to push a concept of "the New Negro" that lies outside of Euro-American practices of comparing white versus black. His black figures demonstrate a difference within blackness in terms of history and identity. Africa and the African diaspora in the Americas serve as *comparata* reference points. Black spheres, according to Douglas, can only be perceived as multitudes.

Concluding remarks

Resulting from an editorial board meeting of the Harlem magazine *Fire!!*, Douglas penned an artistic statement in 1925:

> We are group conscious. We are primarily and intensely devoted to art. We believe that the Negro is fundamentally, essentially different from their Nordic neighbors. We are proud of that difference. We believe these differences to be greater spiritual endowment, greater sensitivity, greater power for artistic expression and appreciation. (cf. Douglas, qtd. in Kirschke 1999, 122)

Reflexivity characterizes Douglas's manifesto. The gaze is inward. It is a reflection on the black self, the black collective, and their relatedness. His comparison between black and white cultures is based on gradual difference, and he concludes with an affirmation of black superiority. Douglas's emphatic message signals a difference along the lines of emotion, spirituality, and aesthetics, while presenting a radical reversal of white supremacist paradigms (cf. Douglas 2002). The above statement from Douglas also shows that the emphasis on black differences as an essentialist strategy helped to challenge normative practices of comparing that attempt to give hegemonic order to the world. While "masking" strategies meant an appropriation of white master models, the performativity within it allowed for in-group reflectivity, a multitude of affirmative "New Negroes," and a chance for new comparative models within black cultures. This created an understanding of deep and complex connections between diverse black cultures and new affirmative visions of blackness in literary texts, in visual artistic expressions, and in black cultural practices in public space beyond colonial histories and racial baggage.

Works cited

Ahad, Badia Sahar. 2010. *Freud Upside Down: African American Literature and Psychoanalytic Culture*. Illinois: University of Illinois Press. Print.

Archer, Margaret S. 2007. *Making our Way through the World: Human Reflexivity and Social Mobility*. Cambridge: Cambridge University Press. Print.

Bernard, Emily. 2011. "The New Negro Movement and the Politics of Art." In *The Cambridge History of African American Literature*, ed. Maryemma Graham, 268–287. Cambridge: Cambridge University Press. Print.

Burton, Richard. 1997. *Afro-Creole: Power, Opposition and Play in the Caribbean*. Ithaca, NY, and London: Cornell University Press. Print.

Butler, Judith, and Athena Athanasiou. 2013. *Dispossession: The Performative in the Political*. Cambridge: Polity Press. Print.

Compton, Allyson. 2017. *The Breath Seekers: Race, Riots, and Public Space in Harlem, 1900–1935*. New York Hunter College Thesis. Print.

De Jongh, James. 1990. *Vicious Modernism: Black Harlem and the Literary Imagination*. New York: Cambridge University Press. Print.

Delamont, Sara. 1991. *Fieldwork in Educational Settings*. London: Falmer Press. Print.

Douglas, Aaron. 2002. "Letter Editorial *Fire!!*" In *Claiming the Stones, Naming the Bones. Cultural Property and the Negotiation of National and Ethnic Identity*, ed. Elazar Barkan and Ronald Bush, 289. Los Angeles: The Getty Research Institute. Print.

———. 1934. *Song of the Towers*. Mural Series *Aspects of Negro Life*. Schomburg Center for Research in Black Culture, New York.

Drake, St. Clair, and Horace R. Cayton. 1945. *Black Metropolis: A Study of Negro Life in a Modern Community*. New York: Harcourt, Brace & World. Print.

Du Bois, W.E.B. 1999 [1903]. "The Souls of Black Folk." *Bartleby.com*. https://www.bartleby.com/114/.

Dunbar, Paul. 2018. "We wear the mask." *Poetry Foundation*. www.poetryfoundation.org/poems/44203/we-wear-the-mask.

Epple, Angelika, and Walter Erhart. 2015. "Die Welt beobachten – Praktiken des Vergleichens." In *Die Welt beobachten: Praktiken des Vergleichens*, ed. Angelika Epple and Walter Erhart, 7–31. Frankfurt a. M.: Campus. Print.

Fanon, Frantz. 1970. *Black Skin, White Masks*, trans. Charles Lam Markmann. London: Paladin. Print.

Fauconnier, Gilles, and Mark Turner. 2002. *The Way We Think: Conceptual Blending and the Mind's Hidden Complexities*. New York: Basic Books. Print.

Ford-Smith, Honor. 2004. "Unruly Virtues of the Spectacular: Performing Engendered Nationalisms in the UNIA in Jamaica." *Interventions: International Journal of Postcolonial Studies* 6.1: 18–44. Print.

Gaines, Kevin K. 1996. *Uplifting the Race: Black Leadership, Politics and Culture in the Twentieth Century*. Chapel Hill/London: University of North Carolina Press. Print.

Gates, Henry Louis Jr. 1997. "Harlem on Our Minds." In *Rhapsodies in Black. Art of the Harlem Renaissance*, ed. Richard Powell and David H. Bailey, 160–167. Berkeley: University of California Press. Print.

——. 1987. *The Signifying Monkey: A Theory of Afro-American Literary Criticism*. New York: Oxford University Press. 1987. Print.

Giddens, Anthony. 1991. *Modernity and Self-Identity: Self and Society in the Late Modern Age*. Cambridge: Polity Press. Print.

Halton, Eugene. 1995. "The Modern Error: Or, the Unbearable Enlightenment of Being." In *Global Modernities*, ed. Mike Featherstone, Scott Lash, and Roland Robertson, 260–277. London: Sage. Print.

Hamilton, Beverley. 1987. "Marcus Garvey: cultural activist." *Jamaica Journal: Quarterly of the Institute of Jamaica* 20.3 (Aug.–Oct.): 21–30.Print.

Hill, Errol. 1992. *The Jamaican Stage, 1655–1900: Profile of a Colonial Theater*. Amherst, MA: University of Massachusetts Press. Print.

Hills, Patricia. 2010. *Painting Harlem Modern. The Art of Jacob Lawrence*. Berkeley: University of California Press. Print.

hooks, bell. 1991. *Yearning: Race, Gender, and Cultural Politics*. London: Turnaround. Print.

Hughes, Langston. 1995a. "I, Too." In *The Portable Harlem Renaissance Reader*, ed. David L. Lewis, 257. New York: Penguin Books. Print.

——. 1995b. "The Negro Artist and the Racial Mountain." In *The Portable Harlem Renaissance Reader*, ed. David L. Lewis, 91–95. New York: Penguin Books. Print.

——. 1995c. "The Negro Speaks of Rivers." In *The Portable Harlem Renaissance Reader*, ed. David L. Lewis, 257. New York: Penguin Books. Print.

———. 1990. "Montage of a Dream Deferred." In *Selected Poems of Langston Hughes*, 221. New York: Vintage Books. Print.

Johnson, James Weldon. 1930. *Black Manhattan.* University of Virginia: Perseus Books Group. Print.

Kirschke, Amy Helene. 1999. *Aaron Douglas: Art, Race, and the Harlem Renaissance.* Jackson: University of Mississippi Press. Print.

Locke, Alain. 1997. "The New Negro." In *The New Negro. Voices of the Harlem* Renaissance, ed. Alain Locke, 3–16. New York: Touchstone. Print.

Madison, Soyini D., and Judith Hamera. 2005. *The Sage Handbook of Performance Studies.* London: Sage. Print.

McClintock, Anne. 1995. *Imperial Leather: Race, Gender, and Sexuality in the Colonial Contest.* London/New York: Routledge. Print.

McCombs, Harriet G. 1985. "Black self-concept: An Individual/ Collective Analysis." In *International Journal of Intercultural Relations* 9: 1–18. http://dx.doi.org/10.1016/0147-1767(85)900 17-3.

McKay, Claude. 1995. "If We Must Die." In *The Portable Harlem Renaissance Reader*, ed. David L. Lewis, 290. New York: Penguin Books. Print.

Mead, George Herbert. 1934. *Mind, Self, and Society.* Chicago: University of Chicago Press. Print.

Mehring, Frank, ed. 2016. *The Mexican Diary. Winold Reiss between Vogue Mexico and Harlem Renaissance.* Trier: WVT, Tempe: Bilingual Press. Print.

Mouzelis, Nicos. 2010. "Self and Self-Other Reflexivity: The Apophatic Dimension." In *European Journal of Social Theory* 13.2: 271–84. Print.

Ogren, Kathy J. 1989a. *The Jazz Revolution: Twenties America & the Meaning of Jazz.* New York: Oxford University Press. Print.

———. 1989b. "Controversial Sounds: Jazz Performance as Theme and Language in the Harlem Renaissance." In *The Harlem Re-

naissance: Reevaluations, ed. Amritjit Singh, William S. Shiver, and Stanley Brodwin, 159–184. New York: Garland. Print.

Powell, Richard J. 2002. *Black Art: A Cultural History*. London: Thames & Hudson. Print.

Rampersad, Arnold. 1989. "Langston Hughes and Approaches to Modernism in the Harlem Renaissance." In *The Harlem Renaissance: Reevaluations*, ed. Amritjit Singh, William S. Shiver, and Stanley Brodwin, 49–72. New York: Garland. Print.

Raussert, Wilfried. 2000. *Negotiating Different Temporalities: Blues, Jazz and Narrativity in African American Culture*. Heidelberg: Winter. Print.

Reid, Marsha. 2018. *1917–2017 Public Space: Culture of Exclusion, Exclusion of Culture*. Middleton: Wesleyan University. Thesis. Print.

Robertson, Stephen. 2011. "Parades in 1920s Harlem." In *Digital Harlem: Everyday Life 1915-30*. https://digitalharlemblog.word press.com/2011/02/01/parades-in-1920s-harlem/.

Spillers, Hortense J. 1996. "'All the Things You Could Be by Now if Sigmund Freud's Wife Was your Mother': Psychoanalysis and Race." *Critical Inquiry* 22.4: 710–734. Print.

Walton, David M. aka Kalonji A. Butholenkosi. 2008. "A Re-Introduction to the New Negro Movement and Pioneers of Modern Black Radical Thought." Unpublished paper.

Whitman, Walt. 2018. "Song of Myself." *The Walt Whitman Archive*. www.whitmanarchive.org/published/LG/1891/poems/27.

Chapter II

Mexican Avant-Gardes and InterAmerican Flows: Redefining the Relation between Art Practice and Public Space in the 1920s and 1930s

> If the mural form takes its shape as a constituent of public space, and not only as a representation of it, then the question of mural form concerns the relationship between the mural image and other forms of public discourse. Rather than being a strictly aesthetic concern, the mural form becomes in this way a broader, cultural one. (Bruce Campbell)

> Public imagery opens political as well as introspective questions. It may be confrontational …. If art is part of the expression of a value system, then to question the dominant values of a society or culture is legitimate subject-matter for art. (Malcolm Miles)

Initially, the goal of the Mexican Revolution at the beginning of the twentieth-century was simply to overthrow the Díaz dictatorship. However, that simple mission brought about broad economic and social upheaval that heralded major developments in the twentieth-century Mexican experience. During the struggle, the Mexican people developed a sense of identity, nationhood, and purpose arguably unmatched by any other republic in the Caribbean and Latin America. By 1940, many reforms in Mexico's social, cultural, and economic fields were in place, and the goals of the revolution were institutionalized as guidelines for future Mexican development and policies. The protracted struggle of the Mexican Revolution, thought by some historians to have lasted nearly three decades, brought about conflict, crisis, and change in many spheres of Mexican society (Monsiváis 2010, 57, 115–213).

Against this tumultuous background, public art practice in the form of muralism helped create new communal visions, unfold new cultural and historical narratives, and redefine modernity through the lens of a cosmic (Vasconcelos 1950) and multi-ethnic Mexican identity (Azuela 2005; Monsiváis 2010, 62, 95). In the 1920s and 1930s, Mexico City turned into a hub for local, national, and international artists to engage with Mexico's cultural and ethnic diversity; to join the struggle for social, cultural, and political renewal; and to advance art's role as shaper of the social.

Mexico's first self-acknowledged artistic vanguard movement, *Estridentismo* [stridentism], took its leap of faith in 1921. In the final days of December, Manual Maples Arce, a young law student and poet, spent his nights plastering his provocative manifesto on walls all over Mexico City. In bold type and newspaper-style headlines, he mingled his artistic-political ideas with sundry entertainment, sports, and business announcements (Flores 2013, 1, 17). Subtitled as an "avant-garde sheet," his manifesto was a radical call for artistic and social innovation. With bitter attacks on the literary establishment and cultural bourgeoisie, Maples Arce launched his concept of an art of the here-and-now as a basis for rethinking the artistic, cultural, and social in post-revolutionary Mexico. Similarly, in July 1928, ¡30- 30!, a group of radical painters and artists including Díaz de León, Fernandéd Ledesma, Alva de Canal, Leal, and the Cuban art critic Marti Casanovas, made its fierce presence visible in colorfully crafted manifestos glued to public spaces around the Mexican capital (Flores 2013, 82–83).

Deliberately aggressive and offensive, the thesis statements from their manifestos attacked official culture and called for a true public art. Their critique did not stop short of caricaturing the most influential muralists of Mexican modernism: Diego Rivera, David Alvaro Siqueiros, and José Clemente Orozco. Its primary target, though, was the Academy of San Carlos, the first of its kind in the Americas, accusing it of abusing and wasting public funds. Already in the summer of 1911, the students of the Academy of San Carlos had circulated manifestoes in the streets and plazas of the Mexican capital to call for new approaches to art in society and education. With the onset of the Mexican revolution, many of them felt that the time was ripe for reconnecting art with public life. On July 24, 1911, the students congregated in parks and plazas and mounted a violent strike that lasted over nine months. They created their independent "*Academia libre*" and developed a new style painting in public: "*plein air* painting" (Flores 2013, 53). Their artistic and social actions brought about change in the direction and leadership of the Academy, and art returned to a larger public in the so-called open air schools.

The third manifesto of ¡30- 30! announced: "We are convinced that art is an occupation of social utility, put at the service of the multitudes, and an element of progress from the moment that it creates a balance between aspirations of beauty and the needs of the collective" (Lowe 1995, 36). Minister José Vasconcelos, the architect of the revolutionary state's educational policy, helped realize the group's vision by promoting the creation of monumental and didactic art to forge a Mexican national imaginary. From 1921 to 1924 he commissioned a variety of artists to paint murals on the walls of public buildings in Mexico City (Vasconcelos 1950, 23–24).

Vasconcelos granted the muralists artistic autonomy, asking only that they create a sense of Mexican identity through their art. *Estridentismo*, the ¡30- 30! movement, the open-air schools, and, with its long lasting outreach, the muralist movement commissioned by the Ministry of Public education (SEP) illustrated that public space was redefined by numerous actors in post-revolutionary Mexico. Public space was reinterpreted as a didactic and educational arena, an arena for developing new artistic expression in alliance with social change, and for rethinking the social through cultural and artistic practices. The avant-garde movements in Mexico were by no means one-sided, however. The very process of creating murals was conflictive. Rival artists and groups used public painting to manifest artistic concerns, dissidence, and disagreements with each other, sometimes with fellow painters of the same mural (cf. Flores 2013, 75–79). Murals were created by some and destroyed by others in a cultural and social battle for the appropriate cultural vision of nationhood and history. There were heated debates even over where to install the murals.

David Alvaro Siqueiros felt that the educational and governmental institutions selected as mural locations by the SEP were still too far removed from the streets and the people. Instead, Siqueiros favored marketplaces, plazas, and corners of highly frequented streets as public sites for art performance and exhibition. He argued that the muralist movement committed a fatal error by placing revolutionary images in public buildings and courtyards, where no masses of people ever passed (Siqueiros 2012, 36; Trueba, Villaurutia, Comisarenco Mirkin, and Neruda 2015, 85).

Diego Rivera, on the other hand, felt at ease creating his murals in public sites and close to centers of education and political power. Despite differences and tensions between the muralists, there was one thing they had in common: they believed that just as art helped shape public space, so too could it have a hand in shaping culture and society. Post-revolutionary Mexico City was an inviting laboratory for exploring intense links between artistic and political practice and may still be the unrecognized center in the Americas for modernist public art in the early decades of the twentieth century.

Among the international artists flooding to Mexico, photographers like Tina Modotti and Edward Steichen recognized in Mexican culture an enormous potential for vibrant artistic expression and a different modernity. Modotti's photograph of Mexico City's Zócalo, one of the most frequented public spaces in the Americas, portrays the public space as a contact zone. It reveals Modotti's closeness to the artistic *zeitgeist*, which understood art practice in public space as essential for reimagining social, ethnic, and cultural relations in post-revolutionary Mexico.

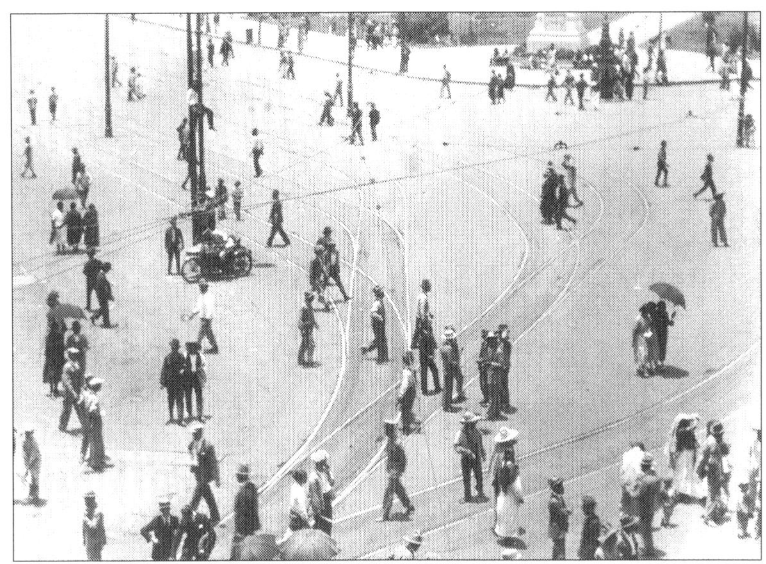

Figure 1: *Zócalo* (© Tina Modotti).

Modotti's photograph translates the multi-ethnic constituency of Mexican culture into a scene of modern urban life and mobility.

As Tatiana Flores writes, "Mexico City in the twenties and thirties offered a complex and stimulating panorama, as its artists experimented with a variety of proposals on what should be the future direction of art" (2013, 305). For many Mexican and international artists at the time, a unification of social and artistic vision was of utmost importance. The muralist movement became the first modernist movement in the Americas in which monumental paintings on public walls reflected identity, history, memory, and ideals of a nation in search of a new beginning after the Mexican Revolution (Raussert 2017). Beyond its elements of stylistic and thematic innovation for imaginary nation-building, it instigated strong debates about whose public was it, which public spaces were truly public, who defined public space and who fed the public sphere, and finally, who closed and who could trespass boundaries of public space. While the officially commissioned SEP (Ministry of Public Education) program was promoting a political aesthetic of imagining the nation, many of the participating artists developed their own individual vision of art and society, thereby challenging the spatial control and hierarchy of the new social order. With muralism a new vanguard impulse in the arts set in to reinvent the social through images exposed in public to a large audience. In the context of Mexican culture, traditionally rich in visual art and semiotics, the muralist movement's imagistic narratives provided eye-catching expressions of social change and utopian vision, paving the way for art on public walls and in public sites throughout the Americas in the decades to follow.

From South to North: Mexican muralist influences in the U.S. and InterAmerican dialogues

Many commissions brought Mexican muralist artists into the U.S. Diego Rivera received his first invitation to work in the U.S. as early as 1927. His two mural commissions were for the California School of Fine Arts (later renamed the San Francisco Art Institute) and for the Pacific Coast Stock Exchange. An increasing U.S. interest in Mexican artistic expression brought further commissions, and Rivera became a celebrated and controversial figure in the U.S. due to artistic mastery, his performances as a public statesman, and his leftist politics. His success was also a stimulus for more invitations to other Mexican artists to work in the U.S. and design public art projects. José Clemente Orozco created large murals in several public institutions like the New School for Social Research in New York City, Dartmouth College, and Pomona College. While David Alfaro Siqueiros worked predominantly in Los Angeles and New York City, many more Mexican painters produced their public art in cities throughout the United States. Muralists like Alfredo Ramos Martínez and Jean Charlot worked and taught in schools in the United States and spread the idea of public art practice as an important artistic as well as social tool. (Cándida Smith 2017, 74–76). Muralist art unfolded in the Americas through manifold transferences.

Among the U.S.-based artists and muralists coming into Mexico were many women. The sisters Marion and Grace Greenwood from New York took a pioneering role in learning muralist techniques in Mexico and bringing female muralist visions to Mexican culture. They were commissioned to produce murals in Taxco, Guerrero, Morelia, and other places. In the 1930s, they also worked in the U.S., supported by the U.S. Public Works of Art Project (PWAP) in 1933 and 1934, and collaborated in the context the Federal Art Project (FAP) in 1935 as part of the New Deal program. Collaborations and exchanges occurred between them and Mexico-based artists during these times. In dialogue with Pablo O'Higgins and Rámon Alva Guadarrama, the Greenwood sisters developed their artistic style, which was inspired also by the works of Rivera and Siqueiros (Mirkin 2017, 34–35, 46). Another artist from New York City, Ryah Ludins, was commissioned by Gustavo Corona Figueroa, rector of the *Universidad Michoacana de San Nicolás de Hidalgo*, to create a series of mural in 1932 and 1934 (50–51). Portland muralist Ione Robison spent several stays in Mexico, supported by a Guggenheim Fellowship, working as an assistant to Diego Rivera in 1929 (31).

Numerous artistic collaborations south and north of the U.S.-Mexican border fostered close interAmerican networks. José Clemente Orozco and Thomas Hart Benton worked together in the 1930s on murals at the Architectural League and also at the New School for Social Research in New York. At the same time, African American muralism took on the role of reinventing the social from a black historical perspective and artistic vision. Aaron Douglas's *Tower Series* remains one the most comprehensive redefinitions of blackness, black history, and black community in 1930s North America. There was also direct exchange between Mexican and African American muralism. This shows in African American artist Hale Woodruff's murals for Talladega College in Alabama, executed from 1938 to 1939, which marked the hundredth anniversary of the revolt of Mende slaves on the Spanish ship *Amistad*. Woodruff painted them in a highly expressive figural and monumental style, translating his experiences from working with Diego Rivera in

Mexico two years earlier into a vivid visual narrative of a revolutionary moment in black history. Like many murals commissioned by Vasconcelos and the SEP in Mexico City, these murals at Talladega College had a didactic and educational purpose – here to instruct black students about their ancestors' struggle for liberation.

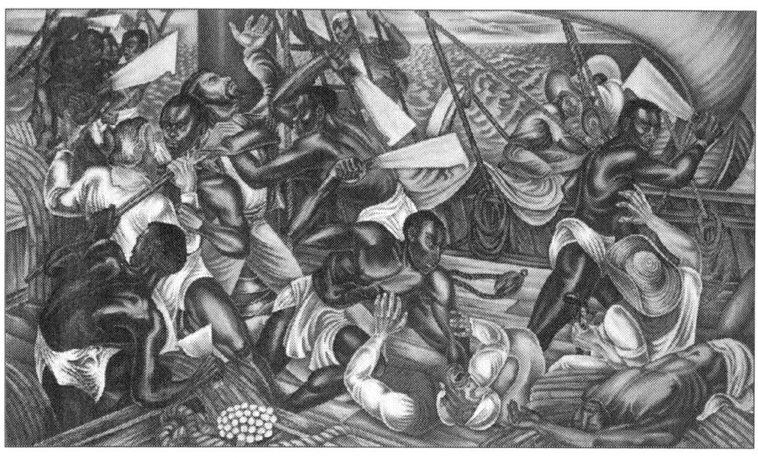

Figure 2: Hale Woodruff, *Mutiny on the Amistad*, 1939. Talladega College, Alabama (© Estate of Hale Woodruff/VAGA, NY).

Throughout the 1930s, woman muralist Ethel Maxine Albro executed many commissions under the Federal Arts Program in the U.S., including murals at Coit Tower and a mosaic at San Francisco State University. Many other talented but critically neglected female muralists like Helen Fornes and Dorothy Puccinelli were involved in those projects. Throughout her life, Abro would return to Mexico numerous times. There, Albro became an assistant to Rivera and studied with Pablo O'Higgins, with whom she also painted frescoes. Rivera's work became a major aesthetic and political inspiration for many more muralist projects in the U.S. in the 1930s, particularly the murals of Coit Tower. Addressing working-class living conditions, the Coit Tower panels represented the leftist artists' most startling moment of activism and cohesion in the U.S. This project constituted the largest collective federal project in the United States.

Herbert Fleishhacker, a San Franciscan instrumental to the building of Coit Tower, determined the tower's links with the Public Works of Art Project (PAWP). Victor Arnautoff and Bernard Zakheim, two leftist artists commissioned for this project, saw in it the opportunity to express their political beliefs.

The Mexican muralist movement undoubtedly awakened a new and different modernist consciousness at the intersection of art and politics, receiving widespread attention throughout South and North America (O'Connor 1986). The post office murals that emerged all over the United States during the Great Depression, which were designed to uplift the U.S. nation through visual imaginaries of national community, were another important example of cultural flows from South to North (Raussert 2003, 61–62). The influence of Mexican artists such as Rivera, Siqueiros, and Orozco, was unmistakable in these murals. Largely spurred during the Great Depression by President Franklin Roosevelt's ambitious New Deal programs, U.S. artists took part in competitions to create these murals in the post offices and other government properties. They were paid through public or private wages to paint murals for U.S. museums, hospitals, high schools, housing projects, colleges, music halls, and even ships and night clubs as well. While these murals were politically motivated like their Mexican models and celebrated the heterogeneity of U.S. American society, they tended to avoid representing harsh social realities like unemployment and homelessness.

With the Mexican muralists socialist and communist ideology also traveled to the U.S. Early in the 1930s, Rivera created "Detroit Industry and Machine Man" [La industria de Detroit u Hombre Máquina] in Detroit and during that time he was also commissioned to decorate the main wall of the Radio Corporation Arts building in Manhattan's Rockefeller Center. Rivera's explicit references to Marxist socialism and inclusion of Lenin's face in the mural outraged the Todd group directing the construction of Rockefeller Center, causing one of the most famous scandals in art history. While Rivera's *Hombre en la encrucijada mirando con esperanza y altura el advenimiento de un nuevo y major future* [Man at the Crossroads

Viewing with Hope and Grandeur the Emergence of a New and Better Future] was removed, New York's Museum of Modern Art still conserves a general design of it. Against all odds Rivera decided to stay in New York and use the Rockefellers' payment to paint murals free of charge at centers of communist militants in the city (Pliego Quijano 2013; García Sánchez 2004, 71).

As Rivera's case shows, aesthetic and political flows collided in the spreading of muralist art from South to North. Repeatedly, murals were destroyed or removed for both aesthetic and political reasons. David Alfaro Siqueiros came to Los Angeles upon his expulsion from Mexico in 1932 for radical political militancy; during his stay he taught classes on fresco painting and completed several murals. Siqueiros's most important mural in Los Angeles was *La América Tropical*. A radically political statement, it was executed along the exterior of the second floor of Olvera Street's Italian Hall, where the Plaza Art Center was located. The central visual and symbolic focus of the piece contained an indigenous subject, representing oppression by U.S. imperialism; the man is crucified on a double cross with an American eagle on top.

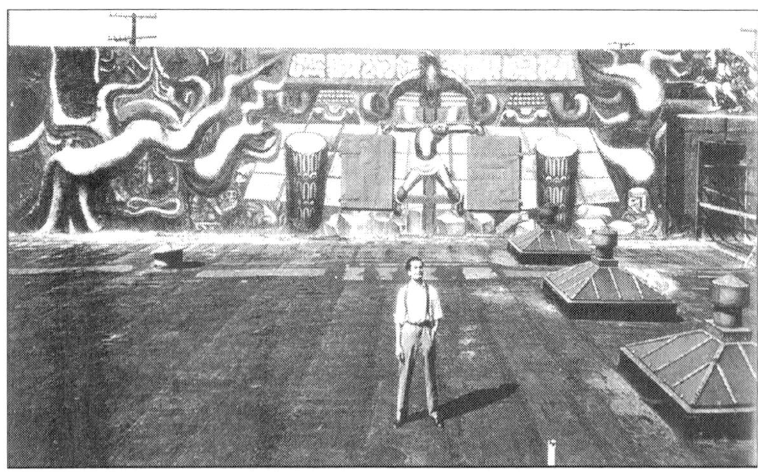

Figure 3: Siqueiros, *La América Tropical*, Los Angeles
(© America Tropical Interpretive Center).

In the background of the scenery, a Mayan pyramid is overrun by vegetation, while an armed Peruvian peasant and a Mexican farmer sit on a wall, determined to defend themselves. Siqueiros's mural became the embodiment of muralist art depicting the unequal power divide in the Americas. In executing this work, along with his other murals in Los Angeles, Siqueiros used mechanical equipment such as the airbrush for the first time. *La América Tropical* (1932) was also significant for Siqueiros's artistic development and for the development of muralism in public spaces. Most importantly, it was the first large-scale mural in the United States that created a public space by being painted on an ordinary exterior wall. The Los Angeles community responded to the mural with enthusiasm. A huge crowd attended the unveiling, and *Tropical America* garnered critical acclaim in both the United States and Mexico as one of the most important works ever produced by the Mexican muralist movement (Cándida Smith 2017, 82–83). Siqueiros's radical practice was taken up during the political and social upheavals of the Vietnam War and Chicano Civil Rights movement. *La América Tropical* acquired its most far-reaching significance by becoming the predecessor and prototype for activist Chican@ murals in the 1960s.

The ways muralist art traveled in the modernist period were multidirectional. Siqueiros was the major inspiration for muralist expansion and collaborations within Latin America. Conducting numerous workshops and collaborations, Siqueiros spread Mexican muralism and promoted the political function of public art throughout Latin America. He was convinced that art should be public, ideological, and educational. His murals contained images of the Mexican revolution – its goals, its past, and the current oppression of the working classes. They also expressed a story of human struggle to overcome authoritarian and capitalist rule. As in Rivera's work, the everyday people were ideally involved in this struggle. His murals depicted stories of revolutionary heroes who, being loosely based on Mexican history and mythology, could be easily transferred to different cultural and political contexts, as occurred during the Chilean and Nicaraguan muralist movements.

In 1943, Siqueiros traveled to Peru, Ecuador, Colombia, Panama, and Cuba. He delivered lectures championing mural painting and promoted his organizations Art against Fascism and American Art at the Service of the Victory of Democracy. In Chile, Siqueiros established fertile collaborations with Chilean artists such as Camilo Mori, Gregorio de la Fuente, as well as with Fernando Marcos in the Mexican School in Chillán. Siqueiros's presence and influence helped transform the art scene in Chile into a center for radical propaganda painting. Even more than the Mexican Renaissance, Chilean muralism embraced a collaborative spirit that enacted its communal ideology and advanced its artistic-political agenda.

The Mexican muralist movement was pivotal for the spread of public wall painting in the early decades of the twentieth century. In reviving and innovating the art of fresco painting, the Mexican muralists created the chief model for a widely followed return to mural painting. Mexican models figured prominently in cultural efforts to create new visual imaginaries of histories and cultures in South and North America in the 1930s and 1940s. They were also a formative influence on subsequent generations of public art in their emphasis on indigenous American cultural practice and values. They developed socially conscious themes and projected them in large scale in public places. Their art was designed for maximum public exposure and interaction. They succeeded in sparking public debate about social and political issues not only in Mexico but in the United States and Latin America as well. In retrospect, Mexican muralism and its extension north and south of Mexico came to signify "the social and political function of art" for the American art scene in the 1930s (Harris 1995, 35).

Muralism as public art practice

The following explanations take a more detailed look at muralism, focusing on the intersection of painterly practice and public space in the example of Mexican muralism. The significance of muralism as an artistic medium for rethinking public spheres lies in muralism's being a monumental and primarily two-dimensional art form designed for huge walls and high visibility. Etymologically the word "mural" goes back to the Latin *murus*, signifying wall. In Spanish "mural" has an additional relational dimension, with the word defined as belonging or relating to a wall. Frequently, murals are created in such a way that the mural and wall become inseparable. Some murals include a third dimension by integrating sculptures and other media, while others emphasize the performative act of creating a mural by removing it from the wall. A close proximity between murals and public sites accompanies their presence in art history. Thus, murals have a prominent place in the sphere of communal public art. Some express individual artistic expression, some are commissioned and censored by governments and institutions, some deliver social commentary and political messages, and some promote consumer culture (cf. Raussert 2020, entry 37).

Muralism in the twentieth-century Americas was the result of intense artistic exchanges in public art between the South and the North. While dialogue and transversal flows largely characterized the development of muralist art in the Americas, it is safe to say that Latin America, and Mexico in particular, took the lead in establishing muralism as a vital public art in the American hemisphere. Since muralism has developed mainly via artistic collaboration, such as took place in the above examples, it is also fair to claim that muralism contains strong interAmerican elements through the contact and patterns of influence between various artists from different regions of the Americas. Mexican muralism emerged in response to the social changes and reforms of the Mexican Revolution. Mexico was considered "a center for interdiscursivity that allowed the integration of aesthetic, ideological, social, and national issues to muralism as a platform throughout the Americas, which was capable of generating conflict and social tension" (Raussert 2020, entry 37). With the traveling of key figures such as Rivera and Siqueiros, artistic South-North and South-South flows frequently went hand in hand with the mobility and collaboration of artists, who demonstrated muralism's power to connect art with public space and foreground the artistic, communal, commercial, social, political, and larger public function of art in the Americas.

Uneven temporalities within larger frameworks of South-North and South-South transference characterized the expansion of muralism as a social and aesthetic art practice throughout the Americas. The emergence of Mexican muralism in the context of the Mexican revolution and its aftermath revealed the didactic, educational, and political dimensions of muralism, although one must acknowledge the rich diversity of muralism's subjects beyond immediate communal and political concerns.

The political and cultural outreach of Mexican muralism drew on a long history of public art practice in various cultures of the Americas. Muralism in the Americas can be traced back to various indigenous peoples in the Americas – the Chumash culture in the southern California region, for example. The Chumash continued their rock paintings and engravings until the early decades of the nineteenth century. Their works, which can still be seen at Painted Rock and in the Painted Cave State Historic Park in Santa Barbara, are characterized by geometric designs, and human and animal figures. They range from monochrome to multicolored representation (McDonald 2013, 25). Mural art in Teotihuacan, Cacaxtla and some of the Mayan cities has been influential in muralism on a global scale. The pre-Hispanic mural paintings present in different regions of Latin America did not directly influence the form, content, or techniques of Mexican muralism in its first decades. Rather, the links with pre-Hispanic worlds in modernist Mexican muralism were established mainly through allegorical representations that evoked a certain pre-Columbian era and culture. These links were established by way of legitimization through the past or affirmation of one's own.

Modernist muralism in Mexico: examples and analysis

On a technical level, the first murals were made encaustically; it was Jean Charlot who taught the muralists in Mexico City the fresco technique using Renaissance models. In the SEP (Ministry of Public

Education), an attempt was made to use calabash slime, under the assumption that it was a pre-Hispanic technique. The experiment failed, however. Nevertheless, the muralist movement in the 1920s started by figures such as Jean Charlot, Diego Rivera, José Clemente Orozco, and David Alfaro Siqueiros took full swing and marked the modernist beginnings of mural art in the Americas. These murals, commissioned and promoted by the Mexican government for their nationalistic, political, and social messages, are still displayed inside and outside public buildings in Mexico City (Schacter 2013, 98).

Benedict Anderson's assumption that print media such as the newspaper and novel have helped shape ideas of nation and national culture is still widely accepted. But while print media has no doubt played a decisive role in the recreation of national identity after the Mexican Revolution, the Mexican case illustrates that other media have gained prominence. Photography, cinema, and – arguably even more influential on an interAmerican scale – Mexican muralism took center stage in the 1920s. In particular, the murals of Rivera from his first mature phase in the SEP and his Mexico City murals that allegorically narrated Mexican history illustrate the power images have in an increasingly visual culture in the twentieth century.

They also meant an effective institutionalization of art in public as social and political commentary. Whereas European and U.S. American art critics at the time ignored the artistic and cultural achievements of Mexican muralism, art and cultural criticism in recent decades has acknowledged the avant-garde status of the mural art by painters such as Rivera and Charlot (Flores 2013, 32–45). Critics like Luis Cardoza y Aragón have emphasized that Mexican muralism occupies a status in art history similar to that of jazz in music history in that it marks an innovative and original contribution by artists from the Americas to the development of modern art (Cardoza y Aragón 1986, 185).

The murals created in the SEP and the National Palace in Mexico City in the 1920s showed that mural art was capable of providing an alternative historiography in terms of both form and content. Street art on a grand scale, they were seismographic indicators of what was happening artistically, socially, and politically (Stahl 2008, 8). Rivera, Charlot, and other Mexican muralists surrounded the people with their own culture and history in an attempt to create an all-inclusive image of a heterogeneous Mexican nation and a history that include pre-Hispanic, colonial, and modern times.

It is not surprising that Western critics like Clement Greenberg had difficulty including the Mexican muralists in the canon of twentieth century modernist and avant-gardist aesthetics (Rochfort 1993, 7). Rivera favored the figurative over the abstract, the panoramic over the purely experimental, and the communal over the individual. Most of all, he created an imaginary of an "indigenized" modernity in many of the murals he painted in the SEP, imagery that in the 1920s did not fit the scheme of progressive modern art history. Rivera's SEP murals expressed the vision of a new post-revolutionary Mexico that moved between related yet different utopian strands in the Americas.

While in the murals of the SEP Rivera dedicated himself primarily to a national vision, his urge to find ways to create a "Mexicanized" modernity that included indigenous and black cultures of the Americas paved the way for his Pan-American visions that overcame the North-South hemispheric divide in later murals. Rivera's penchant for utopian visions left him captivated simultaneously by the dream of a mass-producing capitalism in the making, and by socialism's claim to the attainability of a new revolutionary society (Rochfort 1993, 123). The SEP murals by artists like Rivera and Charlot embraced socially conscious subject matter. In addition, their work championed local culture "through references to pre-Columbian and folk traditions" (Flores 2013, 121). The murals of Rivera, Charlot, Orozco, and Siqueiros denounced social oppression while exposing the hegemony of European culture. Repeatedly, they addressed the neocolonial situation Mexico was in due to the pressures of capitalist imperialism from the North (121).

Rivera's eclecticism and creation of a new spatio-temporal unity meant also a redefinition of public space and public sphere, which was evidenced as far back as *Mécanicazión del Campo* and other murals of the early 1920s. In his muralist collages, the painter juxta-posed and fused various civilizations and cultures in Mexico (and the Americas at large). To inscribe the pre-Hispanic past and mod-ern indigenous subaltern into the national discourse of modernity, Rivera drew on montage and collage to express simultaneity and multiplicity in his vision of history. By championing the workers and farmers, he turned the common man and woman into the pro-tagonists of modernist fresco painting in the Americas.

Indigeneity and Mexicanidad:
murals and the vision of a new nation on public walls

Diego Rivera's mural art work in the context of the cultural and ed-ucational politics of the Ministry of Education (Secretaría de Educa-ción Pública or SEP) meant a redefinition of artistic practice in its relation to public space. His muralism embraced both individualistic thematic innovation and popular appeal. At the same time, his art practice signaled a redefinition of public walls as a matrix for an in-dividually defined historiography with inclusive social vision. Cer-tainly, Rivera's artistic vision was also embedded in intellectual ex-changes with José Vasconcelos and Manual Gamio. According to Vasconcelos's vision, the larger project of the SEP was to instill in all of the Mexican population the idea of a unified nation. The an-thropologist Gamio provided with *Forjando patria* [Forging the Na-tion] a seminal text for Latin American nation building. He offered several explanations why a national sentiment was lacking in Mexi-co, pointing to its large territory, class divides, and racial and cul-tural differences. As a potential remedy he recommended a national artistic expression that would reflect the mind, body, and soul of the people (Gamio 1992, 7).

For Rivera, public walls provided the ideal venue for exposing new national narratives. In particular, Rivera's early works created images meant to foster a distinct national imaginary. In sum, they inscribed Mexican history and culture into the discourse of moder-nity and suggested an alternative vision of modernity – one aestheti-

cally and politically rooted in the artist's conception of an indigenous Mexican identity. While his murals were commissioned to
thematically and aesthetically dress institutional public sites, his
content and narrative frequently followed his very subjective interpretations of Mexico's past and future, and of Pan-American connectedness beyond nationalistic sentiment.

Rivera's murals in the Ministry of Public Education
(*La Secretaría de Educación Pública*):
public walls and an inclusive vision of the nation

Diego Rivera's first chance to build a major mural program came in
1923. With the consent of José Vasconcelos, Rivera was given the
walls of the two great courts at the *Secretaría de Educación Pública*
(SEP) in Mexico City. From among the many artists and painters
working at the *Escuela Nacional Preparatoria*, Jean Charlot, Amado
de la Cueva, Xavier Guerrero, and Rivera himself were given minis-
terial assignments for corridor murals in the new headquarters of the
Ministry of Education. Rivera soon took the reins and by the summer of 1924 gained possession of nearly all the available wall space,
with the approval of the new minister in charge, Puig Casaurac. Access to and control over public wall space, as in Rivera's example,
was an essential step toward diffusing aesthetic and social visions
from a privileged position. Clearly, these public sites were still
framed by institutional authority and protection, and as Siqueiros
criticized, still too far away from the masses to have a true class-
transgressing input. Nevertheless, Vasconcelos's laissez-faire attitude toward artistic expression permitted Rivera and the other muralists involved to explore individual artistic visions of national
identity and history within the public arena.

Designed by architect Federico Méndez Rivas and built between June 1921 and July 1922, the SEP was the immediate result
of the Mexican Revolution. Designed and laid out to accommodate
the goals and functions of the reformed Ministry of Education, it
became the center of a new federal system of education that would

coordinate educational programs throughout the country. It replaced the previous system of independent state control (cf. Downs 1987, 241–242). This three-story building was built along a long axis that ran east to west from the view of the entrance point. The two courts were open and exposed to light from the sky. For Rivera and the others, the architectural setting thus supported an effective *mise-en-scène* for artistic expression on open air walls. The two courts were separated only by a crossover at the second and third levels of the building. Thematically Rivera decided to divide them into a Court of Labor, the smaller, square court, and the Court of Fiestas, the larger, rectangular counterpart (cf. O'Connor 1986). The mural decorations on the walls surrounding the smaller courtyard were unified by an unfolding theme of labor in Mexican communities. The eighteen panels on the ground floor were painted by Rivera with substantial help by Xavier Guerrero. Representing numerous aspects of manual and physical labor, the topics of these murals were based on the agricultural, industrial, and handicraft economies of various regions within Mexico (cf. Downs 1987, 243–244). Together they were designed to create a panoramic vision of the Mexican labor world.

It is important to note that Rivera's murals at the *Secretaría de Educación Pública* represented current political aesthetics within an architectural and pedagogical decorative program. His mural series in the new headquarters of Mexican education presented a cosmology of modern Mexico after the Mexican Revolution. Aesthetically, Rivera's work quickly surpassed the original patron José Vasconcelos's vision of combining classical traditions with indigenous cultural values. Indigeneity in particular was essential for Rivera's pursuit of a renewal of art within and from the Americas. As Rivera states:

> El arte Americano, si algún día puede decirse que existe, deberá ser el producto de una fusión entre el maravillose arte indígena que deriva de las profundidades inmemoriales del tiempo en el centro y el sur del continente … y aquél del obrero industrial del norte. (qtd. in Tibol and Rivera 1979, 27)

[American art, if one day it can be said to exist, would need to be the product of a fusion between the marvelous Indigenous art that stems from the immemorial depths of time in the Center and the South of the continent … and that of the industrial worker from the North] (author's translation).

The innovative potential that Rivera saw in the American art production lay precisely at the intersection of America's indigenous cultures and modernist aesthetics.

The huge spaces for art in public provided by the architectural design permitted Rivera to unfold a Mexican modernist vernacular in grand panoramic style. The innovative aspects of Rivera's murals are at least twofold. In his artistic practice he profoundly moved indigenous culture and "*el Indio*" to the forefront of a new "*mexicanidad.*" In addition, he created spatio-temporal collages that represented cultures and histories in multiplicity and simultaneity. As Rochfort points out, "In the Fiesta Courtyard, on every available wall space, between the entrances to the offices, even to the doorways, Rivera painted hundreds of figures, as though he was creating a vast portrait of the Mexican people" (1993, 57). In my reading, Rivera's mural democratized space for people and democratized people's relations in space. A general air of celebration permeates the mural sections *The Festival of the Distribution of Land*, *The Festival of the First of May*, and *The Market*. "The murals exude an air of revolutionary optimism and idealism, creating visual eulogies to the gains of the revolution with its new atmosphere of political liberation" (59), as Rochfort reminds us.

The compositions are made up of compacted groups of predominantly Indian figures. They reveal Rivera's attempt to create what he saw as an authentic, indigenous national image, his tiered arrangement of figures echoing "the pictorial method of the Aztecs and Mayans" before the conquest (Rochfort 1993, 59). The ground-floor murals in the Fiesta Courtyard express a "celebration of the life and traditions of the Indian peasant" (59).

> In sum, Rivera's mural program at the *Secretaría de Educación Pública* represents a cosmography of modern Mexico, presenting the life of the Mexican people in several allegorical series based on their histories, their struggles for social improvement, their achievements, and their popular festivals,

O'Connor explains, adding that "Rivera evolved a new visual dialect – an artistic vernacular based on Mexican realities and popular consciousness" (1986, 159). Similarly, Susana Pliego Quijano observes:

> Los murals de la posrevolución contribuyeron a generar una imagen colectiva de nación, exaltando la esencia de los mexicanos y plasmándola en edificios públicos importantes para el proyecto de Estado posrevolucionario; (2013, 61)

> [The post-revolution murals helped generate a collective image of the nation, exalting the Mexican essence and depicting it on public buildings important for the post-revolutionary State project]. (author's translation).

Her observation underscores the importance of public sites to the creation of new national imaginaries, as well as the importance of an alliance between politics and art to promote these images effectively. What muralists like Rivera, Reyes, and Siqueiros demonstrated through their art practice was that avant-garde art in Mexico sought a close link between aesthetic expression and concrete communal engagement.

A new spatio-temporal "mexicanidad" for the public sphere

It is indeed only in recent decades that critics have started to reconsider Rivera's work more explicitly in the context of avant-garde studies (Flores 2013). How Rivera challenges Western modernist aesthetics and the trajectory of Western modernity remains at the base of scholarly reevaluation. Rivera pursued a double positioning. As a self-declared public intellectual, he embraced the public role of politically engaged artist, defining himself as an avant-garde artist as well. Since he never saw them as separate entities, both forms of self-positioning could be seen as interdependent.

Public sphere and public space became equally important for Rivera's mission to create and spread new imaginaries of social and historical inclusion. By frequently putting the indigenous imaginary in the center of his artistic vision of an emerging Mexican nation, he challenged Western modernity with its concepts of teleological orientation and racial supremacy. He achieved this aesthetically by creating a simultaneous presence of multiple layers of time in his muralist assemblages.

The mural *Mecanización del campo* provides an illustration of Rivera's spatio-temporal imagination. While we have the rural peasant woman in the center of the mural extending the indigenous past into the present, we also have the presence of mythic time exemplified by the flying figure on the left. In addition, we see images of the revolution and its aftermath in the male figures on the right and the arrival of modern technology with the caterpillar approaching the figure in the center. The huge wall space provides the background in which several historical epochs coexist. The superimposed layers of time help create the imaginary of a history in which mythological and real time coexist (Achtner, Kunz, and Walter 1998). The visual constellation also juxtaposes images of stasis with those of mobility and change. In the mural, Rivera subtly fuses cubist elements – featured in his landscape, plane, and industrial section – with figurative and folkloric representation, the latter exemplified in the central female figure.

Perhaps for ideological reasons "Rivera preferred to hide his aesthetic bonds with Europe, and for a long time he didn't say anything about his experiments with Cubism" (Lozano 2004, 101). In his early works produced in Europe, he "made an advance by giving special importance to the iconographic charge of the objects represented" (103). As Lozano asserts, "The outstanding quality of these Cubist paintings from 1914 is the creative use of color and the all-encompassing sense of the composition, in which persons and objects acquire omnipresence, projecting their personality and meaning" (103). In *Mecanización del campo*, cubist elements served to create a complex narrative of an alternative modernity that emerged aesthetically and politically when Rivera turned the walls of public institutions into visual history books. His experiments with cubist forms allowed him to address time and space simultaneously, which in turn helped him rethink public space as a site for visually reimagining the nation, at a time when post-revolutionary Mexico was struggling to establish a coherent national vision.

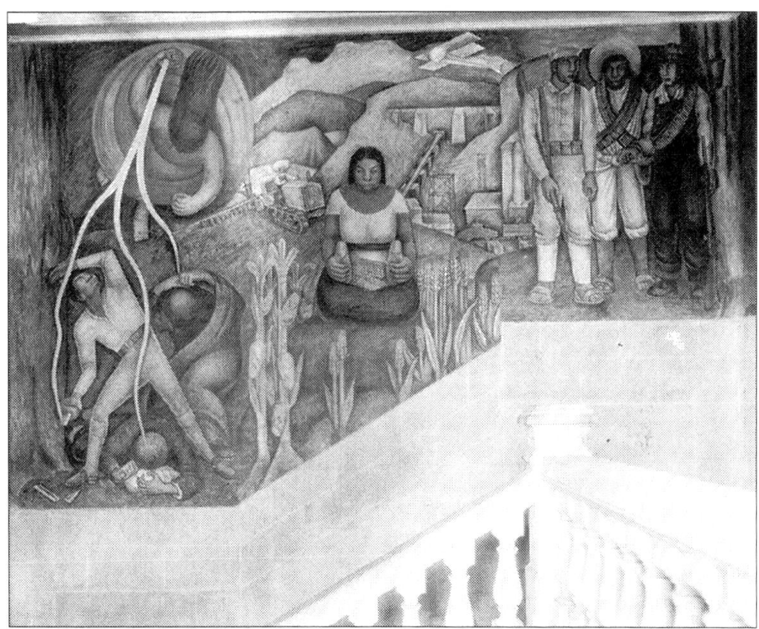

Figure 4: *Mecanización del campo*, in La Secretaría de Educación Pública, Mexico City (© SEP).

By focusing on the nationalist and socialist touches in Rivera's murals for the SEP, critics have overlooked the simultaneity and multiplicity in Rivera's painterly us of public walls. Not only did Rivera oscillate between his classical training, the avant-garde impetus, and his Mexican folk imagination; his works engaged in a dialogue with other modernities like the ones produced by the Harlem Renaissance and the contemporary murals by African American painters like Aaron Douglas, Charles Alston, Charles White, and Hale Woodruff. The latter three also adopted elements of the Mexican muralists' work into their own in the 1930s.

Inspired by Vasconcelos's vision of a new cosmic race, Rivera proudly performed his own hybrid identity as a "Mexican cosmopolitan" with Hispanic, African, and indigenous roots. Rivera "indigenized" and "blackened" Mexican modernity through a visual redefinition of public space. This process can be seen in the mass scenes that characterized many of his murals. Beyond its socialist appeal, for instance, the mass scene in the mural *Asamblea* visualizes an ethnically, racially, and culturally diverse Mexican imaginary through brush strokes of beige, red, blown, and black in the faces of the people. References to and distinct affinities with Afro Caribbean and South Pacific artistic expressions also appeared in his work. These cross-cultural references shine through in his SEP mural *El bano en Tehuantepec*. While working in the U.S., Rivera further developed the themes of red race and black race in his Detroit murals.

Mass scenes, multitudes in public spaces, and Rivera's vision of the nation

In the SEP murals, Rivera's initial focus was still on smaller groups of people. But even in these works an early shift from individual portrayal to communal depiction surfaced. Rivera fully displayed his preference for mass scenes in the murals that he painted for the National Palace. There multitudes populate his mural art and imaginatively inhabit the walls of the public institution. He wanted to capture communal life in all its contemporary facets. At the same time, he aimed at creating a pluri-ethnic, cosmic mosaic of history and national identity that included prehispanic and existing indigenous cultures. Politically, the Mexican Revolution and the mobilization of people in rural and urban settings certainly triggered his preference for mass scenery. Mass scenes took center stage as a commentary on the Mexican Revolution's power to mobilize. They also unraveled Rivera's conviction that changes in arts and politics would have to be negotiated in public space. Carefully crafted mass scenes gave expression to multitudes and evoked collective consciousness.

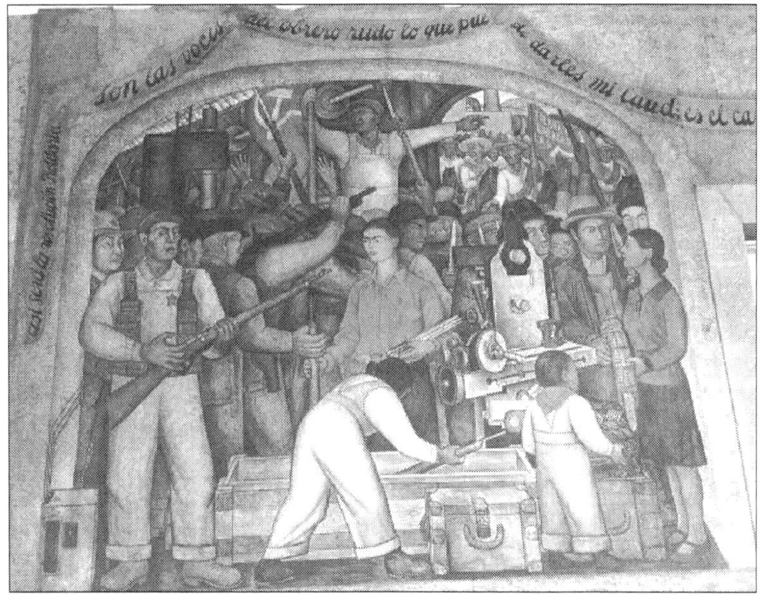

Figure 5: Diego Rivera, *Asamblea*, in La Secretaría de Educación Pública, Mexico City (© SEP).

In addition to his public statements about art and identity, Rivera imagined a new *"mexicanidad"* through his images. According to Benedict Anderson, "in fact, all communities larger than primordial villages of face-to-face contact (and perhaps even these) are imagined. Communities are to be distinguished, not by their falsity/genuineness, but by the style in which they are imagined" (1991, 5). Imagined communities, and thus the process of nation-building, was facilitated by print media such as the newspaper and novel. In the case of Mexican nation-building, I argue that visual media in the public space occupied a central role. Both, muralism and later Mexican cinema, were vital to creating images of Mexico at home and abroad.

The 1920s, SEP murals demonstrated that art practice in public was capable of providing an alternative historiography in terms of both form and content. Images have the power to speak directly and publicly, beyond language. These SEP murals were at the time clearly didactic and taught history through a new, visual sign system emphasizing the everyday presence of diverse cultural and historical trajectories (cf. Banerjee 2005, 297).

Collage as muralist expression: *Tejedores* and *El Trapiche*

Rivera's view of Mexican mural art was original from the beginning. Although he did not call himself a montage or collage artist, he saw muralism as an avant-garde mode of expression. Elements of collage and bricolage (Benjamin 1982; Lévi-Strauss 1964) enter Rivera's work, bringing together multitudes. I agree with Flores, who writes:

> Art historians adopted the term "Mexican School" to describe the visual arts and exalt the achievements of a select group of individuals, *los tres grande*s: the muralists Diego Rivera, José Clemente Orozco, and David Alfaro Siqueiros. The relation of art with politics tended to be overemphasized or simplified, leading to stereotypes that equated post-revolutionary Mexican art with nationalism or socialism, disregarded its avant-garde characteristics, and overlooked its global scope and outreach. (2013, 3)

Rivera himself, as cited by Tibol and also by Luis Cardoza y Aragón, attributed to Mexican muralism a pioneer role in democratizing the world of modern art:

> Por la primera vez en la historia del arte de la pintura monumental, es decir, el muralismo mexicano, cesó de emplear como heroes centrales de ella a los dioses, los reyes, jefes de Estado, generals heroi-

cos, etcetera; por primera vez en la historia del arte, repito, la pintura Mexicana hizo héroe del arte monumental a la masa, es decir al hombre del campo, de las fábricas, de las cuidades, al pueblo. (qtd. in Tibol and Rivera 1979, 27; Cardoza y Aragón 1986, 187)

[For the first time in the history of art of monumental painting, that is, Mexican muralism, it ceased to employ gods, kings, heads of state, heroic generals, etc. as central heroes; for the first time in the history of art, I repeat, Mexican painting turned the mass into the hero of monumental art, that is to say, those who work the lands, or in the factories, in the cities, the people] (author's translation).

In this manifesto Rivera celebrates the common man and inscribes himself in a larger tradition of democratic renewal and liberation from European aristocratic hierarchies in the Americas. He embraces an avant-garde role for himself and his fellow muralists by declaring the Mexican muralist movement an innovative force that challenged the tradition of fresco painting. In addition, he emphasizes a new spatio-temporal concept that, according to him, marks Mexican muralism as unique in art history:

También por primera vez en la historia, la pintura mural ensayó de plastificar en una sola composición homogénea y dialéctica la trayectoria en el tiempo de todo un pueblo, desde el pasado semi-mítico hasta el future científicamente previsible y real. (qtd. in Tibol and Rivera 1979, 27)

[Also for the first time in history, mural painting tried to plasticize in a single homogeneous and dialectical composition the time path of an entire nation, from the semi-mythical past to the scientifically foreseeable and real future] (author's translation).

In his rhetoric, Rivera characteristically distances his aesthetics from those of his European predecessors. Still, he references modernist techniques like montage (Benjamin 1982) and bricolage (Lévi-Strauss 1964) when he paraphrases them as "homogeneous composition" to describe his own style. His eclectic compositional style and his layering of spaces and times, shape the multilayered representation of history and culture for instance in murals like *Méca-nización del campo*.

After his return from Europe, Rivera saw himself confronted with various, at times overlapping, civilizations and cultures in Mexico (and the Americas at large). To inscribe the prehispanic past and the modern indigenous subaltern into the national discourse of modernity, he chose simultaneity and multiplicity, avoiding subordination. Rivera's use of the various Mexican pasts served to mobilize the subaltern indigenous. By visualizing the indigenous and prehispanic past within revised modernist representational forms, he created an overall impression of simultaneity, continuity, and change.

As Flores puts it, "The SEP murals by Charlot and Rivera questioned the relevance of modernism in Mexico by juxtaposing formal elements from European avant-garde art to socially conscious subject matter and championed local culture through references to pre-Columbian and folk traditions" (2013, 121). Flores further argues, with reference to Rivera, that "the murals denounce social oppression while exposing the hegemony of European culture" and what Rivera saw as "Mexico's neocolonial condition" (121). While other Mexican avant-garde artists like Maples Arce embraced urban modern life and technological innovation, Rivera in his 1923 murals embraced rural Mexico and images of the revolution. Despite his turn toward greater flatness in general, some of the SEP murals, like *Tejedores* and *El Trapiche*, illustrate Rivera's revisionist modernist aesthetics, exposing unequal modernities (Canclini 1995, 41–42, 206–207).

In *El Trapiche*, for instance, the perspective creates an idyllic illusion; Rivera's figures are devoid of agency and self-determined identity. With a nod to Flores, I read the loom in *Tejedores* as an artistic representation of the modern machine. Rivera enters a temporally multilayered space when he inscribes modernist imagery into the local nativist tradition of weaving. Rural and urban production gets superimposed and interconnected. The loom's lines resemble the wires of telegraph and telephone poles, insinuating the manual workers into a larger industrialized and modernized production system. With the aesthetic modernization of the loom Rivera unfolds a *long durée* view of labor exploitation and confinement. The dark bodied workers appear "trapped by the loom" (Flores 2013, 119). On the one hand, they are sign of the colonial past; on the other, given the mechanized loom imagery, they stand for the workers of Mexico's neo-colonial present. It is depiction of local culture in the revised shapes of modernist aesthetics that marks Rivera's art as innovative. While being keenly aware of his social and educational mission, like contemporaries Charlot and Leal, Rivera never ceased to experiment with formal and representational techniques.

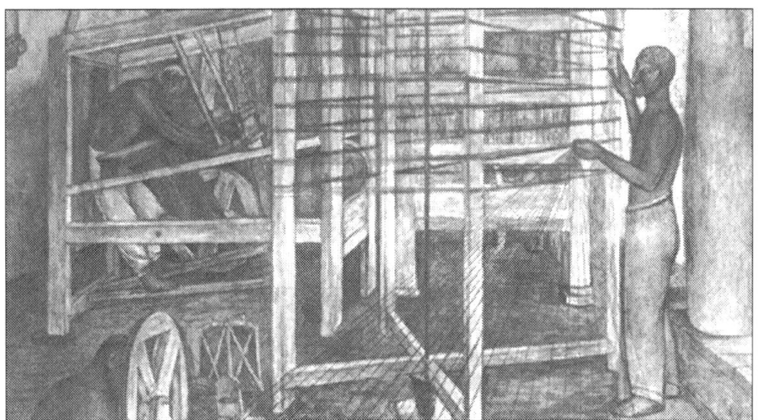

Figure 6: Diego Rivera, *Tejedores*, in La Secretaría de Educación Pública, Mexico City (© SEP).

My above reading of *Tejedores* with respect to modernist aesthetics finds an echo in Hector Jaimes's assessment:

Los "ideales estéticos" de Rivera no estarían determinados por la ideología, sino por un sentido alegórico y vanguardista que recorre su obra … el espíritu vanguardista de Rivera supera cualquier determinación estrictamente ideológico-marxista de su obra. (2012, 12)

[Rivera's "aesthetic ideals" would not be determined by ideology, but by an allegorical and avant-garde sense that runs through his work … Rivera's avant-garde spirit surpasses any strictly ideological-Marxist shaping of his work] (author's translation).

As Flores has it, "Rivera identifies forms associated with modernity within the local tradition" (2013, 119). In sum, Rivera radically modernized Mexican folk traditions and folklorized modernist aesthetics. Through form and content Rivera revealed Mexico's neocolonial situation after the Revolution and depicted the Indian peasant as the subaltern on the rise within that situation.

Consciousness of coloniality

Another important example of Rivera's treatment of coloniality is his mural *El Trapiche*. Here, Rivera used a perspectival spatial technique reminiscent of Renaissance painting. The spatial arrangement parodically presents "a window onto the perfect world" (Flores 2013, 120). The workers appear in a choreography that suggests movement in harmony – and, at the same time, a chain gang. Dedicating this mural to the sugar industry, Rivera alludes to slavery and exploitation. The mural depicts different steps in the sugar production. The theme is coherent, yet, form and message clash. As *El Trapiche* demonstrates, Rivera experiments with master narratives of the visual arts by creating a revisionist modernist collage of work scenes that create simultaneity as well as a profound critique of coloniality. The collage brings together various locations involved in the sugar production. Their simultaneous presence points to the entanglement of the indigenous peasant workers in colonial sugar production. It is the indigenous image embedded within a new spatio-temporal collage that creates the other modernity in Rivera's work.

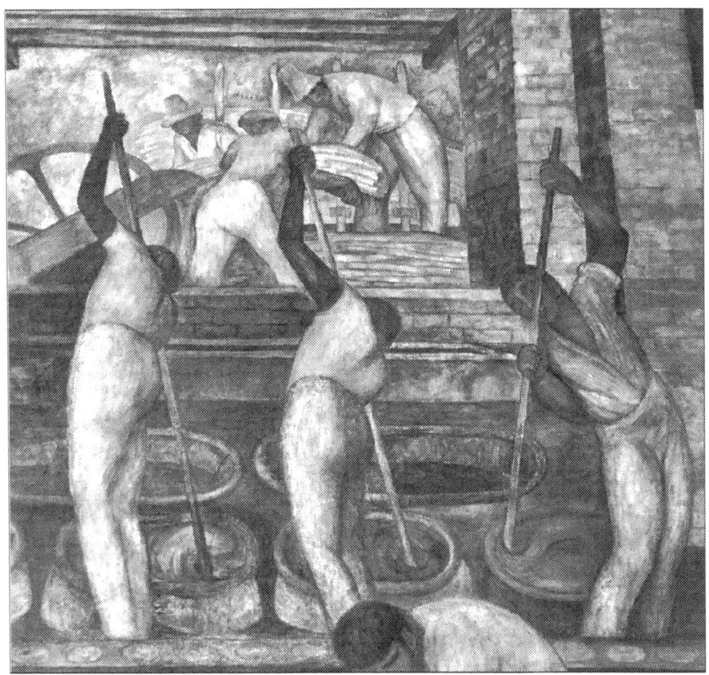

Figure 7: Diego Rivera, *El Trapiche*, in La Secretaría de Educación Pública, Mexico City (© SEP).

Pan Americanism and muralism

Rivera saw great potential for innovation in American muralist art production, insofar as it could place itself at the intersection of America's indigenous cultures and technological modernity. The *Pan-American Unity* Mural at San Francisco College represents the most complex montage in Rivera's work in terms of the superimposition of temporalities and spatialities of preindustrial and industrial cultures. His mural synthesized utopian strands of thought in the Americas to achieve an all-inclusive pan-American vision of past and future (Lozano, Arteaga, and Robinson 1999, 1–12).

Arguably, Rivera's *Pan-American Unity* exposed a previously unseen panoramic vision of interconnectedness and interdependence in the Americas beyond radical visions of Marxist struggle and Monroeist hegemonic thinking. Interestingly enough, the mural was the result of another interAmerican collaboration, as Rivera was assisted by the African American artist, designer, and cultural worker Thelma Johnson Streat in the piece's creation. And it appears to be Rivera's most ambitious work in bringing together precolonial, colonial and modern aspects of American cultures.

This panoramic mural created for the Art in Action exhibition at Treasure Island's Golden Gate International Exposition in San Francisco in 1940 brought muralism from the Americas to a high degree of international attention. In addition, it exemplified muralism's power to redefine hemispheric thinking in the Americas, which had its roots in Monroism and Bolivarism. Pan-American discourse had lost currency when the mural was created. While always sparking debate, it had flourished in the early decades of the twentieth century. "By 1915 we can see a singular, even strange phenomenon developing: national leaders were encouraging a utopian vision of the future relation of the world's peoples," Cándida Smith points out (2017, 16). Arguably, Rivera's mural marks one of the last panoramic artistic attempts to capture this hemispheric spirit. James Monroe and Símon Bolívar had provided two conceptual starting points whose tension with each other continues to be negotiated two centuries later (Parks 2017, 92–96). In 1823, Monroe presented what we know as Monroe Doctrine (1823) to the Congress in Washington, DC. He argued that the Western hemisphere was exceptional and off limits to colonization by European nations – in effect so that the U.S. could exert its own influence throughout the region. The Monroe doctrine eventually came to dominant hemispheric thinking in the Americas in the twentieth century.

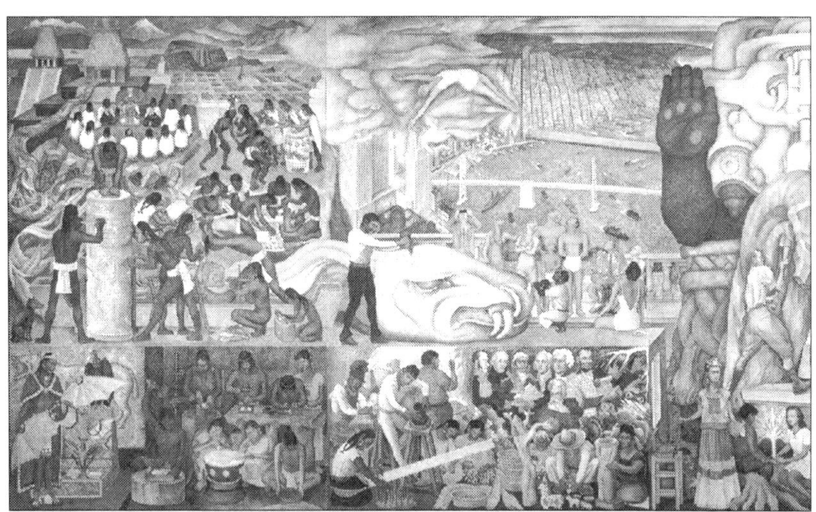

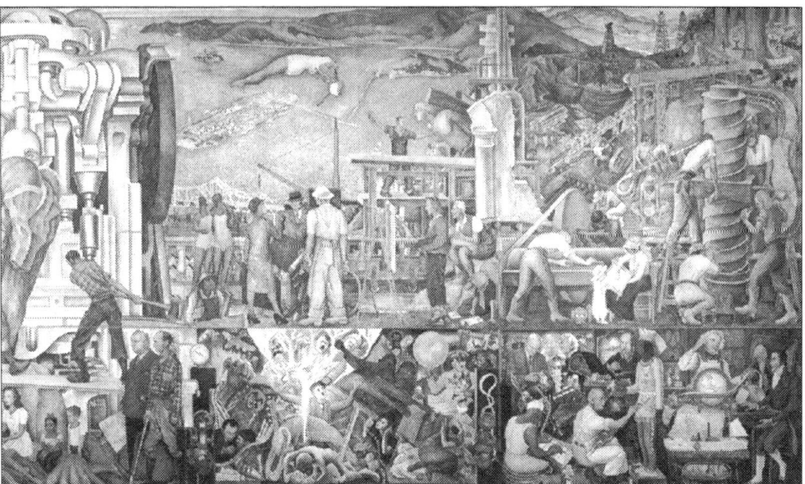

Figure 8: Diego Rivera, *Pan-American Unity*, San Francisco, 1940
(© San Francisco College).

(The graphic was divided for reasons of better visual representation.)

The other pole of hemispheric thinking was found in Bolívar's Congress of Panama from the year 1826. Bolívar, who was skeptical of the U.S. and its claims of alliance and friendship, envisioned a transnational bonding among the former Spanish colonies in Latin America. Monroe and Bolívar differed greatly in their relation to coloniality (Parks 2017). Even a century later, José Vasconcelos, in his ponderings on *mestizaje* and cosmic race, still saw in them the antipodes for hemispheric thinking in the region. According to him, "Bolivarism [is] the Hispano-American ideal of creating a federation with all the peoples of Spanish culture" (1935, 7). In contrast, "Monroism [is] the Anglo-Saxon ideal of incorporating the twenty Hispanic nations into the Nordic Empire, through the politics of Pan Americanism" (7). As Stephen Parks points out,

> Though the term "Pan Americanism" has fallen out of mainstream usage, until the mid-twentieth century it was the most common way of talking about hemispheric relations. It was even granted its own holiday in 1930, when the White House declared April 14 to be "Pan American Day," an occasion which U.S. school children observed for decades after by learning about the shared cultures and traditions of the Americas. (2017, 94)

When Rivera collaborated with Thelma Johnson Streat on the mural in San Francisco, he did so against the background of a largely U.S.-centered way of imagining the Americas. Rivera's vision, however, attempted to mediate southern and northern visions of the hemisphere.

His mural *Pan-American Unity* negotiates the two utopian strands we encounter in the Americas and creates a more comprehensive imaginary of "America." Outside Latin America, the term "America" frequently recalls images of U.S. America only, but both the English and the Spanish term have historically functioned as signifiers in respect to notions of utopia and independence in particular. As Quijano and Wallerstein see it, the differences between South and North America lie within utopian conceptualizations: North America's "utopia of social equality and liberty" and Latin

America's indigenous "utopia of reciprocity, of solidarity, and of direct democracy" (Quijano and Wallerstein 1989, 556–557). While in the murals of the SEP Rivera dedicated himself primarily to a national vision primarily, his yearning to conceive of a more inclusive modernity paved the way for his Pan-American visions overcoming a North-South divide in murals like the one in San Francisco. Susana Pliego Quijano asserts that Rivera explored new frontiers with which he associated hopes for human progress (2013, 59).

Concluding thoughts

The Harlem Renaissance, Garveyism, and the Mexican avant-gardes of the early twentieth century provided interAmerican examples of redefining modernity through cultural practice. As public intellectuals, figures like Marcus Garvey and Diego Rivera used public space to transform the social and the historical through radical cultural and artistic practice. Their powerful use of art practice in public sites established public space as a modernist arena for rethinking the social and political. Their relational redefinitions of public space with regard to self and nation, individual and community, and subject and hegemon opened up new ways to conceive Pan-African, Pan-Mexican, and Pan-American visions of cultures and histories silenced by Western hegemonic discourse. Thus, they created multiple public spheres against the grain. Taking to the streets, public places, and public institutions, they developed performative and representational skills that were in dialogue with but went beyond contemporary Western avant-garde practices, in that these movements fomented social and cultural visions of difference *and* inclusion. While they predominantly worked within the urban grid patterns of Kingston, Mexico City, and New York (Harlem) and within institutional frameworks, they transformed the hegemonic conception of public space through performance and art practice. In some instances they did so temporarily, while in others they transformed public buildings and spheres permanently.

Works cited

Achtner, Wolfgang, Stefan Kunz, and Thomas Walter. 1998. *Dimensionen der Zeit: Die Zeitstrukturen Gottes, der Welt und des Menschen*. Darmstadt: Primus Verlag. Print.

Anderson, Benedict. 1991. *Imagined Communities. Reflections on the Origin and Spread of Nationalism*. New York: Verso. Print.

Azuela, Alicia. 2005. *Arte y Poder. Renacimiento artístico y revolución social en México, 1910–1945*. México: El Colegio de Michoacán-Fondo de Cultura Económica. Print.

Banerjee, Mita. 2005. *Race-ing the Century*. Heidelberg: Winter. Print.

Benjamin, Walter. 1982. "Der Autor als Produzent. Ansprache im Institut zum Studium des Faschismus in Paris am 27. April 1934." In *Gesammelte Schriften*. Band 2, Teil 2, ed. Rolf Tiedemann and Hermann Schweppenhäuser. Frankfurt a. M.: Suhrkamp. Print.

Campbell, Bruce. 2003. *Mexican Murals in Times of Crisis*. Tucson: University of Arizona Press. Print.

Canclini, García. 1995. *Hybrid Cultures: Strategies for Entering and Leaving Modernity*. Minneapolis: The University of Minnesota Press. Print.

Cándida Smith, Richard. 2017. *Improvised Continent. Pan-Americanism and Cultural Exchange*. Philadelphia: University of Pennsylvania Press. Print.

Cardoza y Aragón, Luis. 1986. "Diego Rivera's Murals in Mexico and the United States." In *Diego Rivera: A Retrospective*, ed. Cynthia Newman Helms, 185–192. Detroit: Arts Institute of Arts. Print.

Downs, Linda. 1987. "Secretaría de Educación Pública: Mexico City." In *Diego Rivera: A Retrospective*, ed. Cynthia Newman Helms, 241–251. Detroit: Arts Institute of Arts. Print.

Flores, Tatiana. 2013. *Mexico's Revolutionary Avantgardes: From Estridentismo to ¡30-30!*. Yale: BW&A Books. Print.

Gamio, Manuel. 1992. *Forjando patria*. México, D.F.: Porrúa. Print.

García Sánchez, Laura. 2004. *Diego Rivera*. México: Instituto Nacional de Bellas Artes y Literatura. Print.

Harris, Jonathan. 1995. *Federal Art and National Culture. The Politics of Identity in New Deal America*. New York: Cambridge University Press. Print.

Jaimes, Hector. 2012. *Fundación del muralismo mexicano. Textos inéditos de David Alfaro Siqueiros*. México, D.F.: Siglo XXI. Print.

Lévi-Strauss, Claude. 1964. *El pensamiento salvaje*. México, D.F.: Fondo de Cultura Económia. Print.

Lowe, Sarah. 1995. *Tina Modotti Photographs*. New York: Abrams. Print.

Lozano, Luis Martín. 2004. *Diego Rivera y el cubism. Memoria y Vanguardia*. México D.F.: Instituto Nacional de Bellas Artes. Print.

Lozano, Martin, Augustín Arteaga, and William H. Robinson. 1999. "Introducción." In *Diego Rivera, Arte y Revolución*, ed. Martin Lozano, Augustín Arteaga, and William H. Robinson, 1–12. CONACULTA, The Cleveland Museum of Art, Ohio Arts Council, México. Print.

McDonald, Fiona. 2013. *The Popular History of Graffiti. From the Ancient World to the Present*. New York: Skyhorse Publishing. Print.

Miles, Malcolm. 1989. *Art for Public Places: Critical Essays*. Winchester: Winchester School of Art Press. Print.

Mirkin, Dina C. 2017. *Eclipse de Siete Lunas: Mujeres muralistas en México*. Ciudad de México: Artes de México. Print.

Monsiváis, Carlos. 2010. *Historia Mínima deLa cultura Mexicana en el siglo XX*. México: El Colegio de México. Print.

O'Connor, Francis. 1986. "The Influence of Diego Rivera on the Art of the United States during the 1930s and After." In *Diego Rivera: Retrospective*, ed. Cynthia Newman Helms, 157–183. Detroit: Arts Institute of Arts. Print.

Parks, Stephen. 2017. "Sites of Pan American Thinking: A Methodology of Place. In *The Routledge Companion to Inter-American Studies*, ed. Wilfried Raussert, 92–105. London/New York: Routledge. Print.

Pliego Quijano, Susana. 2013. *El Hombre en la Encrucijada. El Mural de Diego Rivera en el centro Rockefeller*. México, D.F.: Trilce Ediciones. Print.

Quijano, Anibal, and Immanuel Wallerstein. 1989. "Americanity as a Concept, or the Americas in the Modern World System." *International Sociological Association* 1.134: 549–557. Print.

Raussert, Wilfried. 2020. "Muralism." In *The Routledge Handbook to Culture and Media in the Americas*, ed. Wilfried Raussert, Giselle Anatol, Sarah Corona Berkin, José Carlos Lozano, and Sebastian Thies, entry 37. London/New York: Routledge. Print.

———. 2017. *Art Begins in Streets, Art Lives in Streets*. Bielefeld: kipu. Print.

———. 2003. *Avantgarden in den USA. Zwischen Mainstream und kritischer Erneuerung 1940-1970*. Nordamerikastudien; 18. Frankfurt a. M./New York: Campus Verlag. Print.

Rochfort, Desmont. 1993. *Mexican Muralists: Orozco, Rivera, Siqueiros*. San Francisco: Chronicle Books. Print.

Schacter, Rafael. 2013. *The World Atlas of Street Art and Graffiti*. London: Aurum Press Limited. Print.

Siqueiros, David Alfredo. 2012. "Conferencia sobre arte pictórico mexicano sustentada el 12 de febrero de 1935, en el Sálon de Actos de la Escuela Nacional de Medicina." In *Fundación del muralismo mexicano. Textos inéditos de David Alfaro Siqueiros*, ed. Héctor Jaimes, 36. La Cuidad de México: Siglo XXI Editores. Print.

Stahl, Johannes. 2008. *Street Art*. Berlin: Ullman. Print.

Tibol, Raquel, and Diego Rivera. 1979. *Arte y Politica*. Madrid: Editorial Grijalbo. Print.

Trueba, Lara, José Luis Xavier Villaurutia, Dina Comisarenco Mirkin, and Pablo Neruda. 2015. *Libros Pintados: Murales de *la Cuidad de México*. La Cuidad de México: Artes de Mexico. Print.

Vasconcelos, José. 1950. *Discursos, 1920–1950*. Mexico City: Ediciones Botas. Print.

———. 1935. *Bolivarismo y Monroísmo: Temas Iberoamericanos*. Santiago, Chile: Biblioteca América V. Print.

Web sites

http://www.olvera-street.com/-Siqueiros-Mural/-siqueiros-mural.html.

http://afgj.org/nicanotes-murals-nicaraguan-revolution.

https://americanart.si.edu/artist/hale-woodruff-5477.

http://hcl.harvard.edu/collections/digital_collections/chile_murals.

http://latindictionary.wikidot.com/noun:murus.

https://library.brown.edu/create/modernlatinamerica/chapters/chapter-10-chile/moments-in-chilean-history/chilean-protest-art/.

Chapter III

The Body as Public Sphere:
Taking Theatre, Performance, and Music
to the Streets in the Turbulent 1960s and 1970s

Context

Politicizing, dramatizing, socially re-contextualizing, and sexualizing the body, art practices in the 1960s powerfully positioned the body as public site in a public space. By staging and performing the body in its social, artistic, and sexual dimension, art practices redefined the relation between colony and hegemony, subject and public space, between domestic and public politics, between man and woman, and between youth culture and mainstream society. In retrospect, one may state that performances of the 1960s and early 1970s rediscovered and reinterpreted the body in public space as the primary source for performing utopian concepts and anti-colonial ideas of social protest and change. Such an assessment requires differentiation. Although the critical focus on nakedness as an avant-garde shock technique certainly has become commonplace in performance criticism, other aspects of staging the corporeal need to be further explored. With art practices in the 1960s, it is important to consider that the body was no longer primarily a trope-making agent through costume, mask, and role playing. Instead, the body signified through its corporeal presence in action. As such it continues to fulfill representational functions. Yet, it is not an a priori meaning or conception that the corporeal embodies (Raussert 2003a, 434–435).

Staging human bodies in public spaces became an important way for artists to shape new social visions. When we consider that Michel Foucault (1979) understands the body as site of political control and power, and that docile bodies in his analysis are the result of control and surveillance in public sites and institutions, it becomes all the more understandable that artists took to the streets to reclaim control over public spaces. Both, the individual body in action and the mass scene performances became models for worldwide political protest during the 1960s. Especially in its presence in public spaces, the artist's body could assert its role as an innovative agent in theatre, dance, and performance arts with an immediate impact on community and social relations.

Most of all in the U.S. but also in other parts of the Americas, theatre, performance art, music, and dance took to the streets to occupy public sites such as street corners, plazas, and parks to perform community-building, to express individual and collective dissent, to support individual political causes and social movements, and to liberate public space from military control, police surveillance, state control, and mob violence. Bodies functioned as agents in performances, performed in public sites and served as media for rethinking social relations. Through their performance in streets, parks, and plazas they took on a central role in reinventing the social and in rethinking public space in relation to contemporary cultural and political discourses: the media-centered global village utopia by Canadian visionary Marshall McLuhan; anti-colonial, anti-imperialist, and anti-racist struggles in the U.S., Latin America, Asia, and Africa; and the iron curtain separating communist and capitalist world orders (McLuhan 1967, 8; 1962, 3).

In the U.S., the American New Left was activated by the Civil Rights Movement, the Vietnam War, and campus democracy; in Canada, the major issues were postcolonial nationalism (in Anglophone Canada and Quebec) and U.S. American control of the Canadian economy and cultural production. In Latin American countries, new left movements were activated in resistance to totalitarian structures from within and to imperialist influence from the North.

Art practices reaching into public space expressed the desire to create imaginaries for the leading utopian metaphor of the global village, and to come to terms with fractured realities that challenged McLuhan's utopian argument that an interconnected global village was emerging as a consequence of new electromagnetic discoveries. These fractured realities manifested themselves differently in the

South and the North due to different political systems and cultural contexts. Flows between artist communities and collaborations between artists in the South and North represented attempts to overcome Cold War divides based upon ideological, political, and economic lines. In addition, these artists also had to confront their own different positioning as creative agents in their respective societies. Geopolitical divides between North and South also needed to be mediated in the act of exchange and collaboration. While exchange, contact, flow, and encounter provided a realm for developing shared visions, they also made artists aware of the limited access to public space and the difficulties involved in crossing boundaries and borders due geopolitical differences and hemispheric divides – the Cuban Missile Crisis providing the most dramatic example of this.

An interAmerican lens reveals that art practices in the 1960s and 1970s demonstrated a profound interest in claiming public space(s) and performing the social anew throughout the Americas. As the turbulent 1960s in the Americas remind us, public space was framed by bourgeois, working-class, and ghetto zones. It was also controlled by militarily marked territories, as well as by different levels of access and denial due to differences in class, race, ethnicity, gender, and national origin. These aspects also show that the promising metaphor of the global village for some simply meant struggling for access to the next neighborhood, while for others ways it opened the way for rethinking the world as a new *cosmopolis*.

Performances in public space attempted to break down the division and segmentation in public space. They explored how spaces were constructed or deconstructed, where space performances took place, and to what purpose. While New York, San Francisco, and Los Angeles were hotspots for radical theater practices in the U.S., radical theater also developed in Mexico and Argentina, as well as in the *favelas* in Rio de Janeiro. InterAmerican links emerged in the performances of the Living Theatre in the *favelas*; in Allan Kaprow, Marta Minujín, and Wolf Vostell's joint happening between New York, Buenos Aires, and Berlin; and in the performances of Black Power through funk, soul, and dance in New York, Panama, Columbia, and Brazil. The Black Power performances intensified their interAmerican exchange and expansion, especially in the 1970s (Steinitz 2019). They also surfaced in the context of Cuban revolutionary practices and in their impact on the politics and aesthetics of the Black Panthers in the U.S. Socialist Cuba also became a safe place for those black activists and artists who wanted to escape from the illegal activities of J. Edgar Hoover's Counter Intelligence Program. Between 1967 and 1968, dozens of Black Panther activists went into exile in Cuba. Among them were movement leaders Eldridge Cleaver, Huey P. Newton, and Assata Shakur (Benvenutti 2015, 133; Rojas 2016, 190–192)

Theater that broke the fourth wall and took to the streets was a leading art practice in the late 1960s and early 1970s, especially in the U.S. As Bradford Martin emphasizes, "The heightened social tensions and political crises of the sixties catalyzed public performance as a newer, more symbolic, but also more immediate way of 'doing politics' than conventional political protest" (2004, 5). Public performers of the sixties across the nations fostered the development of a common performative language and hoped to bring this vocabulary to a wide range of activist endeavors and political goals, from Civil Rights, to personal liberation, to democratization of art-world institutions (5–6).

With the growth of the anti-Vietnam War movement, a heightened sensitivity to anti-colonial struggles, and a growing presence of the political left inspired by the Cuban Revolution, performance practices occupied artistic, social, and political niches. Angela Rothman reminds us that American protest against the establishment grew between the years 1967 and 1968. Due to the moving power of "dramatic aspects manifested in theatrical methods," many examples of protest theatre emerged (2016, 2). Among them were the street performances by the San Francisco Mime Troupe, the Festival of Life by the Yippie movement at the Chicago Democratic National Convention in 1968, the indoor and outdoor performances of *Paradise Now* by the Living Theatre, and even a Broadway cast production of the musical *Hair*.

All engaged in mass scenes for collective performance; in addition, they referenced and used public space for reflecting the social and disseminating new communal visions. In the U.S. the 1960s marked a period of intense domestic conflict. Activists and performance artists "embraced theatrical revolutions of radical theater as visible forms of protest" (Rothman 2016, 5). The San Francisco Mime Troupe drew on "guerrilla theatre" to rebel against theatrical conventions as well as social and political institutions. In *Paradise Now* the Living Theatre promoted revolutionary ideas of non-violent anarchism to subvert a non-committed, complacent, capitalist society. The Yippie movement expressed its distrust of hierarchy and authority, performing theatrical protest in Chicago during the city's Democratic National Convention. And the actors in the Broadway cast of *Hair* broke conventional theater norms and pursued interactive forms of communication with the audience. "Group participation as a theatrical and popular form of socio-political collective action" characterized the performative arts toward the end of the 1960s (2).

As concerns their relation to public space, the San Francisco Mime Troupe chose parks and streets for their performances to launch a grassroots guerrilla revolution. While the Living Theatre performed mainly inside buildings, their actuation of revolutionary anarchism would eventually leave the doors and enter the real world. In Brazil the Living Theatre also performed in streets of *favelas* in collaboration with local artists and activists (Rosental 2011). *Hair* was designed to instigate a mass protest against the Vietnam War and to define the peaceful revolutionaries against the Broadway establishment. The Yippies in Chicago 1968 embraced spectacle and festival culture in streets and parks to perform in rebellion against the Democratic National Convention. Referencing the revolutionary statement of the Living Theatre's *Paradise Now*, Rothman sums up the performative essence of theatre in the 1960s: "the streets belong to the people" because "the theater is in the streets" (2016, 25).

Happenings across the Americas:
taking theatre and body performance into the streets

In the U.S., artists like Allan Kaprow developed happenings as performative expressions that reinvented the relation between private and public space. In Mexico, Chilean artist Alejandro Jodorowsky created his world of panic, a series of happenings to arouse a sense of crisis in the spectators and call them to action (Medina 2006, 98). His one-time events and interventions called *efímeros pánicos*, or panic ephemerals, included artists, poets, dancers, and people from the street. They involved simultaneously occurring individual and collective actions that reached out into public space. As Alan W. Moore phrases it,

> The radical politics of the New Left, the radical students who emerged during the 1960s Civil Rights and anti-Vietnam struggle, was theater, a spectacle of change, conceived and enacted in the loud, dynamic terms of conflict that the medium of television, a cousin of theater, required. (2011, 27–28)

The theatrical modes evolved by visual and performance artists in the late 1950s and early 1960s were taken up by political movements. Happenings, spectacles, and other public performances served as models for protest marches and mass demonstrations. Boundaries between artist performance and political protest became porous. "The political demonstration as a form of mass performance was carefully considered by radical activists of the day" like Daniel Cohn-Bendit.

Television introduced new forms of mediatizing politics and expanded the range of public spheres. Media images from the Cuban Revolution to the assassinations of John F. Kennedy and Martin Luther King turned an extended and mediatized public space into an arena of political information and conflict. Against this background, art practices embraced the spectacular in public sites to make themselves seen and heard in this intensified web of new media images. Television expanded the urban grid as public space and provided a new frame for information that reshaped public space and the public sphere on a national scale. From Vietnam protesters to heavily mediatized bodies of assassinated intellectual and political leaders, from the tribal presence of naked bodies in music festivals like Woodstock in the U.S. and Ávandaro in Mexico (Zolov 1999) to the political staging of naked bodies in happenings by Victor Jodorowsky, Carolee Schneemann, Yoko Ono, and Yayoi Kusama, the body exposed in public space became an instrument for redefining aesthetics and the importance of aesthetics for rethinking the social.

Kusama's activism in Wall Street and on Brooklyn Bridge in 1968 stands *pars pro toto* for artistic models of political protest in public. Painting "polka dots" on naked bodies combined with political messages on banners, Kusama expressed her anti-patriarchal and anti-war sentiments in public sites of high visibility and political and economic importance. Her painted bodies served as antidotes to the mediatized images of wounded and dead bodies from warfare and political assassinations. The naked and painted body exposed publicly became the aesthetic antidote to the national flag. Her anti-war naked happenings and flag burning practices opposed imperialism and colonialism, and her artistic staging of bodies demanded a rethinking of social norms and relations. Causing public scandal, her artistic provocation reached a climax when she offered her own body as love-and-peace-making agent in a letter to President Richard Nixon. She read the text aloud in front of the New York Board of Elections in 1968. In her appeal, she offered to have sex with Nixon in exchange for the end of the Vietnam War: "Truth is written in spheres with which I will lovingly, soothingly, adorn your hard masculine body. Gently! Gently! Dear Richard. Calm your manly fighting spirit!" (Kusama 2011, 35, Brody Devere 2008, 53).

Kusama's example shows that art and spectacle coincided in 1960s activism. Drawing on Wall Street as a metonym of global capitalism, she staged various performances in and near Wall Street. In "The Anatomic Explosion," a short naked performance piece, she performed inclusive communal imaginaries right in front of the Stock Exchange (Brody Devere 2008, 56) with a diverse multiethnic and multiracial group of dancers and performers. Kusama's performances revealed the essence of protest – the human body in public space, channeling the vast potentialities of human freedom, dignity, and love. However, her celebrations of new social relations, while certainly emerging out of a deeply felt crisis, also expressed the artist's profound desire for publicity and success. Immersion in public space seemed to open venues for a range of objectives: high protest visibility and artistic as well as economic success.

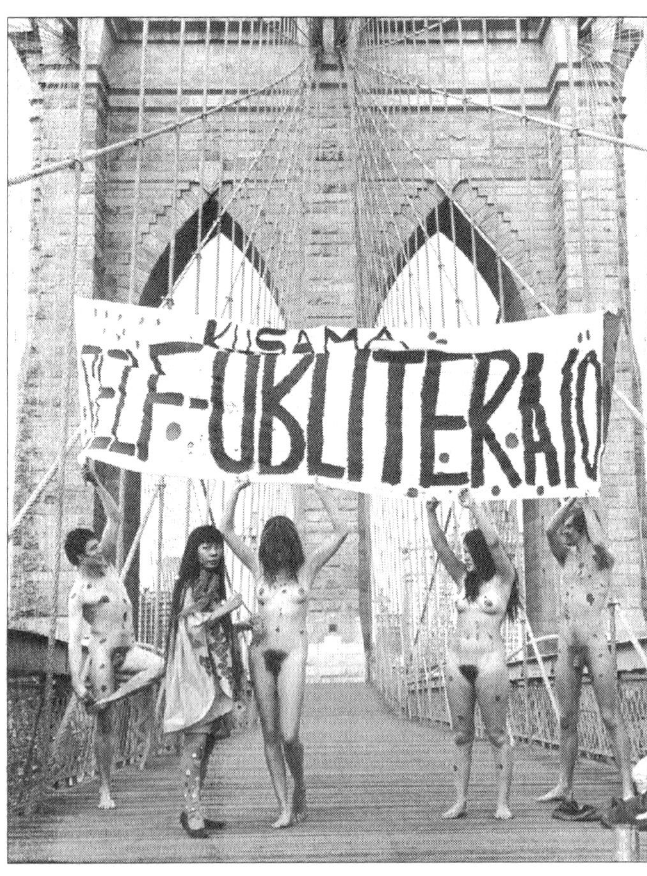

Figure 1: Yayoi Kusama, *anti-war* naked happening, Brooklyn Bridge, New York, 1968 (documented by Shunk-Kende; © Shunk-Kende).

Kusama's "polka dots" on human bodies were her painterly expressions of collective movement. These dots could unfold their meaning only in their simultaneous presence on the body and within a group of bodies (Brody Devere 2008, 56–57).

As the turbulent decade called for new artistic and social strategies to counter and reflect crises, artistic action by and on the human body became of the essence. For many artists and activists, spectacle culture appeared to be the most efficient strategy to multiply and diversify public spheres. Many of the performances expressed a yearning for publicity and a sincere protest against imperialist, racist, and sexist politics. Spectacle promised high visibility and an at least temporary presence in large public spaces. In addition, it allowed for collaborative and eclectic approaches to artistic practice. As mix-media events, happenings in the 1960s became a global articulation of new social visions. Darko Suvin provides us with a tentative definition of happenings as "a genre of theatre spectacle, using various types of signs and media organized around the action of human performers in a homogenous and thematically unified way, and a nondiegetic structuring of time and space" (1995, 294–295).

Important to Suvin's definition is his reference to "theatre" on the one hand and "spectacle" on the other. The fact that he fuses both terms suggests a fundamentally heterogeneous composition of this medium. Even if Suvin's choice of the term "spectacle" does not appear to be true of all happenings, and could be replaced by "ritual" or "everyday practices" in some instances, his approach illustrates how difficult it was to place happenings within art history and artistic categories. Happenings were fundamentally art in action and equipped with an eclectic openness.[1]

----

1   In order to find more precise criteria to artistically describe the "Happenings," one does well to go back to Michael Kirby's research. In his introduction to the illustrated anthology *Happenings,* he draws on various sources that have contributed to the development of "Happenings" in America and New York in particular. Starting from a classification of the "Happenings" as a form of theater, clear influences from the visual arts

InterAmerican exchanges and collaborations:
Marta Minujín, Allan Kaprow, Alejandro Jodorowsky,
and the Living Theatre

InterAmerican flows that spread the newly emerging performance cultures between North and South also brought forth collective collaborations. In 1966, Argentinian artist Marta Minujín, in collaboration with American artist Allan Kaprow and German artist Wolf Vostell, conceived of *Three Country Happening* and contributed to this international project the work *Simultaneidad en simultaneidad* [Simultaneity in simultaneity]. With her contribution, she reflected on the social significance of a newly technologized public space and mediatized public sphere. Incorporating an address to selected audience members – transmitted by newspaper, telephone, telegram, and local television and radio stations – *Simultaneidad en simultaneidad* put on display Minujín's profound interest in the effects of mass media and social interactions on individual creativity and institutional critique. She was a key figure in Argentina's happening scene, and her collaboration with Kaprow was only one of several dialogues between North and South in the performance scene of the 1960s. Artists such as Minujín, Edgardo Giménez, Dalila Puzzovio, Carlos Squirru, and Susana Salgado analyzed the premises of North American pop art and happenings while rigorously developing their own innovative synthesis of popular culture and performance. Minujin was hailed as "a Latin Answer to Pop" (Spencer 2015, n. pag.).

A key figure for exchange and dialogue between the happening scene in Latin America and the U.S. was Oscar Masotta, Argentine writer, intellectual and happening artist. In close dialogue with

---

can be recognized. Thus, it is striking that numerous "happenings-artists" of the 1950s and 1960s were initially active in the field of painting and sculpture. The Reuben Gallery in New York was the primary venue for these transitions. Artists like Robert Whitman, Claes Oldenburg, A. Kaprow, and Jim Dine exhibited their works in galleries before devoting themselves to performance art (cf. Kirby 1965, 10–11).

Minujín, he propagated and analyzed the happening and pop art scene in Argentina. Several trips to the United States in January and April 1966 and January 1967 brought him in direct contact with U.S. happening and pop art practices. In 1967, Masatto published *El Pop Art* and *Happenings*, two books that represented both a dialogue with New York's performance scene and a critical affirmation of Buenos Aires' unique alliance between pop art and happening culture (Spencer 2015).

A radical blurring of lines between pop art and happenings characterized the avant-garde scene in Argentina. Minujín's work was exemplary for these boundary-crossing processes. In the early 1960s, she moved from producing expressionist canvases and assemblages of cardboard boxes to pop art sculptures. Simultaneously, she began to produce vibrant environmental installations and happenings (Spencer 2015). Her explorations of transnational developments in performance art, spanning happenings and Fluxus activities in the U.S. and *nouveau réalisme* in France, provided the basis for a public art practice that easily moved between pop art and vanguard modes of expression. Minujín's direct participation in and contribution to transnational routes of exchange blurred clear distinctions between the local and the global, indicating a shared interest in urban beachcombing in cities such as New York, Buenos Aires, and Paris, yet, at the same time her artistic work gained distinct expression and meaning at each different geopolitical urban site.

Minujín's first happening in Buenos Aires towards the end of 1965 debuted live on television as part of the program *La campana del cristal* [The Glass Bell]. Influenced by McLuhan's media theories, her early embrace of television culture opened up a new public space for art practice and artistic vision. Minujín began the above performance, which she also referred to as *Cabalgata* [Procession], by putting layers of paint onto a canvas that previously had been installed in the television studio. To add more spectacle, Minujín arranged for horses to enter the performance space with tins of paint attached to them. With the movement of the horses, more paint dripped all over the floor. Finally, she released a large amount of balloons, which a group of muscle men she had hired for the show proceeded to burst. Designed to create a public scandal, the performance lead to chaos. In the end, the show's host desperately tried to halt proceedings and get Minují off the air. Although deliberately confusing, the basic trajectory of *Cabalgata* was to merge art with a larger life world. While Minují initially posed as artist in front of an upright easel, her presence became "gradually engulfed and replaced by a fracas of animals, people and balloons" (Spencer 2015, n. pag). Artistic practice turned into a public media spectacle, exposing art's power to rebel and agitate.

Minují's appropriation of a television show not simply as a venue for an event but a medium in its own right occurred in dialogue with Kaprow's vision of the expanded field that pop art could occupy in reshaping art and the social. Particularly in the use of new media like television, Minují and Kaprow challenged and even collapsed the geographic borderlines of artistic practice and production. Art attained a grander outreach into local and global networks and began to encounter in the new media an expanding public space that provided opportunity for new aesthetic practices and social involvement. One of Minují's lasting achievements was to see in television performance an extended practice in making art a public event. As high media coverage and audience response in Argentina showed, she managed to develop a fusion of pop art and happening into spectacles of public interest through which one could challenge normative concepts of the public sphere and the art world simultaneously.

Equally involved in interAmerican as well as transatlantic dialogues with artists from Latin America, the U.S., and from Europe, Alejandro Jodorowsky's art events nourished radical and provocative artistic uses of public space in Mexico. Alejandro Jodorowsky's ephemeral for *Canto al océano* [Song to the Ocean] (1963), staged in Mexico City, embodied his ides of "Panic theatre" (1965b). The fundamental idea was to take theater out of the theater and return it to public social life. Upon the invitation of his friend and fellow experimental filmmaker, Gelsen Gas, Jodorowsky was commissioned to present a temporary work for the unveiling of abstract painter Felguérez's mural, *Canto al océano*, at the Bahía recreation center.

The event coincided with the opening of a public pool, which made it all the more promising for Jodorowsky to bring theatrical action into a public site. Jodorowsky's work, as Decker describes it, represented a multi-media event that consisted of many actions taking place simultaneously (Decker 2015b). Jodorowsky himself repeatedly returned to the center of the action. Felguérez's abstract mural was revealed near the pool's changing rooms. Integrating the pool as public site into the event, Jodorowsky installed a series of floating balsawood platforms upon which members of a local ballet company performed improvised ballets. In the changing rooms that were semi-public spaces themselves, Jodorowsky placed several semi-nude or nude couples. Repeatedly during the *efímero*, the doors opened and closed, exposing the couples as they engaged "in sexual and otherwise salacious activities" (1965a, 12–13).

The spectacle was rendered even more sensational by a helicopter accident. Originally conceived as transportation for Jodorowsky, who wished to descend upon the scene by rope from the helicopter, the helicopter fell to pieces, which in turn formed part of the mise-en-scéne. Jodorowsky still entered the scene as master of the event and joined various groups of the performing artists. His pleasure to expose the human body in public space got complemented by scenes in tubs filled with ketchup and noodles. Dancers went in and out of these tubs covering their bodies with traces of food. The whole scenery was complemented by the unveiling of a mural represented a surrealist critique of the dominant Mexican School of Art. As Decker points out with reference to contemporary art politics in Mexico,

> The significance of the government's emphatic selling of abstraction, and individualism as the future of Mexican art, against the background of growing political tensions and social revolution, ignited Jodorowsky's political side enough for him to frequently confront this issue in the *efímeros*. (2015b, 74)

Reciting literary selections from Lautréamont in which the latter addressed issues of religion, morality, and iconoclasm, Jodorowsky made clear in his performance that individual action and expression are political and that the acting body requires presence in public space in order to diversify public spheres on a larger scale. Decker reminds us, "The ephemerals were truly political acts. They directly attacked religion, Mexican nationalism, and political corruption in the public and cultural sphere" (2015b, 52).

From the very first ephemerals to later events, Jodorowsky brought the public in to the performance and the event into the public. His preliminary ephemerals were called *Panic fiestas* and were conceived as a "fusion of *fiesta* and show" (Jodorowsky 1965b, 5), his objective being to dissolve the theater altogether. Indeed, all strata of society were invited: prostitutes, actresses, intellectuals, artists, politicians, and actresses to create a true encounter of the social with itself (García 2005). The event served as an observatory of how individuals of different sexes, classes, and races reacted in the midst of an "explosive cocktail party" full of chance encounters and exchange (Decker 2015a, 62). For Jodorowsky, this meant transgressing social boundaries, taking the common man out of his comfort zone, and turning him into a "panic man" – setting the stage to make him an active social agent who could claim his individual place in public space and the public sphere (79).

The Living Theatre in Brazil
and the Judson Dance Theater in New York

Large groups of bodies on stage, moving from the stage into public spaces, and performing and manifesting bodies became a major representative force in the 1960s. This holds true for radical bourgeois theatre practice in North as well as South. Part of *favela* performative traditions, street events marked creative expression and social protest in Brazil, despite the surveillance of them by municipal governments. In the U.S. performances of the Judson Dance Theater and the Living Theatre in New York developed various strategies to represent the public on stage and to bring art into public spaces.

Like the public emergence of mass demonstrations and marches in the context of the Civil Rights, The Black Panther, and the anti-Vietnam War movements, the staging of large groups in theaters and public places like Washington Square expressed a desire to develop new co-operative and communal forms of performing, working, and living (Banes 1977, 118–119). Looking at the Americas and even the globe, it is fair to argue that no performative collective has more famously brought art into the public realm than the Living Theatre. In contrast to working-class street art performances in Brazil's *favelas*, the performances of the Living Theatre were part of radical bourgeois theatre practice. It is the fusion of both traditions that the Living Theatre practiced for a short time in Brazil, and then around the globe after having been set free again from Brazilian prison. Creating theatre and street performances based on ritual, gesture, and movement was one way to perform community and bring political messages into public spaces while avoiding the surveillance of the military regime.

The fleeting presence of street performance and non-verbal work provided a way to occupy different public spaces without falling victim to the regime's censorship. The concept of creation favored a collective and public approach. Field research done in the *favelas* documented by recordings of interviews with the poor, workers, and peasants, and the notes they took down, became the material for collectively choreographed performances. Teaming with young Brazilian activists and intellectuals like Troya and Ivan Araujo (Rosenthal 2011, 65) facilitated the Living Theatre's access to the Brazilian communities. Likewise, this reunion it fostered public desire to participate in the performances. The range of performance locations chosen was impressive. Performances were held in hospitals, churches, schools parks, cemeteries, bus terminals, railroad tracks, docks, and mines.

The idea was also to move out to the villages and the countryside where the farmers and migrants dwelt. In the first of the *favela* projects the theme was the master-slave relationship, which had a clear local reference point given Brazil's history of slavery. The decolonial vision of the Living Theatre expanded this to an all-American, if not global, constellation of humanity. The enslavement meant a fundamental human condition. As with *Paradise Now*, the choreography was designed to create emancipatory moments. The master-slave pairs of the *favela* project reenacted poses of oppressor and oppressed slowly taking off blindfolds and facing each other.

The strong outreach of theatre and public performance led to the imprisonment of Brazilian and U.S. members of the Living Theatre. The military regime wanted to put a stop to these performance practices that repeatedly claimed new public spaces as venues. On July 1st 1971, the house in Ouro Preto in which the group stayed got searched and the company was put in prison. A new dimension of public awareness resulted from the group's arrest. A global outcry over the imprisonment and Brazil's repressive politics was raised by an international alliance of activists and artists. A public relations campaign produced hundreds of petitions. In Minas Gerais, Brazil media coverage made the Living Theatre the talk of the town. Further street art and worldwide protest events increased the pressure on the Brazilian regime. After 71 days, Brazilian President Emílio Garrastazu Médici had no choice but to free the prisoners (Rosenthal 2011, 66–67).

That U.S. American and European members of the group were treated with certain protection while their Brazilian cellmates were exposed to torture by the Department of Political and Social Order, revealed inequality on a local and global scale. The Brazilians had neither public presence nor the sufficient media awareness to escape imprisonment unharmed. These national differences, which would be eliminated in the work of the *favelas* project, surfaced with a vengeance. The Brazilian prisoners' treatment revived the social conditions of the streets and homes of the *favelas*. The work in the streets and the regular dinners that the Living Theatre group shared with the poor and homeless in the *favelas*, according to the Brazilian activists involved, represented the biggest threat to this social and political system based on class hierarchy.

The growing inequality between North and South and in different Latin American countries was manifested drastically in the happenings around the Living Theatre in Brazil. With media presence, the building of a global support network was possible. Still, Marshall McLuhan's global village was shown its limits. New media like television and computer technology had transformed the public spaces, helping to create new and larger networks. The access to these networks remained a privilege, and new hierarchies fed on old ones in the struggle to control the access to the public in urban material life and the media.

The Living Theatre was expelled from the U.S. after public performances of *Paradise Now* and further imprisonments after numerous public performances of the Favela Project in Brazil. Both cases sharpened the group's awareness of public space as a crucial battleground for self-expression, social change, and coexistence. The Brazil experience and the group's collaborations with the poor denizens of the *favelas* inspired the group to ground their work further in the streets. They also began to question their commitment to bourgeois radical art when they compared their own privileged position with the situation of artists and activists in Brazil facing military oppression. The Brazilian experience shaped the ensuing years of performing. The experience of living and performing at the intersection of class and power in direct communication with the poor and dispossessed shaped new sensibilities toward social realities. Returning to the U.S., they continued with community-based performances until the support of National Endowment and Mellon Foundation grant ran out. A return to festival performances and theatre and performing for the radical middle and upper class was eventually imposed upon the group by financial bottlenecks (Rosenthal 2011, 74–75).

In sum, the Living Theatre's work has been central for a redefinition of the relationship between art and public space. Like the Judson Dance Theater, it emerged in the heart of New York City.

Both groups shared a utopian American faith in community. However, for artists such as Judith Malina, Julian Beck, Deborah Hay, Yvonne Rainer, and Carolee Schneemann, community had to be reinvented in times of crisis. Blurring boundaries between participants and observers, art and politics, performance space and public space, work and play, they redefined the stage as part of a larger public space and developed stage devices and stage actions that allowed them to perform various shades of communal set-ups. Repeatedly, the artists involved left the stage setting to mingle with the public and left closed space to stretch the performance into the midst of public life. The evolution of Judson Memorial Church – located on Washington Square South – as a preeminent venue for downtown artists promoted boundary-breaking performance art and pioneering dance styles crucial to dance history; it also fostered the convergence of art and social activism, celebrating a multi-ethnic and diverse society.

Actions like the People's Flag Show, scheduled to run at the church in 1970 as a response to flag-desecration laws, resulted in public controversy with the arrest of some participating artists. Among the leading artists was Yvonne's Rainer whose "no assumed space" concept underscored the radical with spatial confinement. Initial meetings were held at Yvonne Rainer's studio, then at the Judson Memorial Church. Throughout the early 1960s, nearly two hundred works were presented by the collective. Members of the Judson Dance Theater participated in performance and multimedia art instillations – happenings that took place around the city, thus producing and supporting a mobile performance culture. Like the mass demonstrations and marches of the Civil Rights, Black Nationalist, Chican@, and anti-war movements, artistic reclaiming of public space integrated mass scenes as a means to infuse theatre practices with ritual structures. Artists like Yvonne Rainer and Deborah Hay choreographed group spirit and solidarity in close alignment with the political movements at the time (Raussert 2003a).

The Living Theatre embraced similar strategies. In the performance of *Paradise Now*, arguably their most impacting collaboration, mass scenes turned into a prevalent performative mode. The climax of the performance involved a breaking of spatial boundaries both horizontally and vertically. Describing one of the performances, Biner points out, "The actors, accompanied by willing spectators, would climb to a window of the Carmelite Cloister – a section of ruined wall – and after taking several deep breaths throw themselves into the air like birds taking a flight" (1972, 210). Further into the performance, in the action section labeled "The Street," the performers spilled out into the audience, mingling with them and leading them from the Carmelite Cloister scene into the streets, performing bonding practices with and between total strangers.

From ritual via art practice to a matrix for social action: Allan Kaprow's "18 Happenings in 6 Parts/The Script"

Happenings in the 1960s were admittedly an effervescent and ephemeral art. Nevertheless, they created important matrixes for a new social dimension of art by transforming ritual into art practice as a basis for social action. Allan Kaprow's "18 Happenings in 6 Parts/The Script" (1966) luckily provides us with a script and Samuel R. Delany with a spectator's report, both of which enable more profound description and analysis. Happenings acted out the process of rethinking the social by relating the performing body with public space. As both texts show, Kaprow's happenings were exemplary for many performances in the 1960s. The first event staged in New York, revealed already in 1959 the close adherence to the symbiosis of body, ritual, and event so central to public performances. A radical attempt to break down the fourth wall, Michael Kirby's performance of Kaprow's happening exposed the artistic reconceptualization of bodies in space. Delany's perceptive views of the event as an audience member highlight the dialogical structures at work between performers and spectators.

The Kaprow script already reveals that the body as a transformative element would play a central role in the different segments of the happenings. Bodies appeared directly or in costumes; Kaprow referenced naked bodies, painted bodies, and bodies in everyday summer and winter clothes; and the bodies were further transformed by various slides projected onto them during the course of the event (Kaprow 1966). Above all, the dimension of change as arising from the dynamics of exchange and repetition was emphasized. This structure found its expression, on the one hand in the different movements of the actors involved – "boy shakes at pole, girl gets up … walks up and down bouncing ball, … they suddenly do a frenzied Charleston" – on the other hand, in Kaprow's experiments with the idea of the private and public body as a place of memory (62; 58).[2] It is interesting to note that Kaprow did not rely on the tattooed body as such. Instead, he projected constantly changing slides on the body; that is, specified signs as an expression of memory were transformed into a processual state. Likewise, the projections reflected the changing positions of the bodies in and to public space.

As far as the aesthetic dimension is concerned, Kaprow's script shows that the body was presented as active and receptive at the same time. On the one hand, bodies were active agents that painted, walked, and moved things. On the other hand, they served as recipients of sound and light signals. As the stage assignments have it, "Two persons standing in front of the screen receive the image of several slides shown on them and the screen: stripes in red stripes in black stripes in pink: all different" (Kaprow 1966, 57). The body as an art object and its counterpart in everyday life stood side by side in Kaprow's concept of performance.

For Kaprow, art practice, the body, and public space were relational. And art practice was the realm of mobile spatial boundaries.

---

2   For a convincing study of the body as a place of memory and as an identity-creating medium for the example of American sailors, cf. Newman (1996).

His vision was one of perpetual change. In the performance slides changed "from all purple with white dot in center to all black with purple dot in center to word 'often'" (1966, 57). Viewing art practice as constantly moving and changing and not separating art practices from cultural practices of the everyday, Kaprow provided models of how to use art as a tool for social change. Embracing a view of culture and history as processes, he envisioned space as well as a changeable dimension. His references to moving and changing sites in his agenda for happenings reveal his belief in the transformability of public space. How eminently important processes were for Kaprow's performances emerges from his conception of happenings:

> The line between art and life should be kept as fluid, and perhaps indistinct, as possible …Therefore, the source of themes, materials, actions, and the relationships between them are to be derived from any place or period except from the arts, the derivations, and their milieu … The performance of a Happening should take place over several widely spaced, sometimes moving and changing locales … Time, which follows closely on space considerations, should be variable and discontinuous … Happenings should be performed once only … It follows that audiences should be eliminated entirely …. The composition of a Happening proceeds exactly as in Assemblages and Environments, that is, it is evolved as a collage of events in certain spans of time and in certain spaces. (Kaprow 1995, 197–205)

Interestingly, the synchronous and spatial juxtaposition of the individual parts in "18 Happenings in 6 Parts" were based on the principle assembly, but the perception remains fragmented. In retrospect, spectator Delany speaks of "the work's unseen totality" (1990, 82). As his commentary clarifies, an overall impression remained closed to the observer. Even if the images projected onto the screens provided a certain connection between the different rooms of the performance, the viewer was denied simultaneous insight into all the action sequences in the performance space. This underscores that both the timeline and the traditional boundaries of a theatrical performance were broken. Thus, for Delany, the beginning and the end of what is happening was unclear to the viewer. He describes his immediate reaction to what is seen and experienced: "For all its immense framing in wood and polyethylene, the actual work was even difficult to locate as to its start, content, style, or end" (183). However, not only the temporal, but also the spatial dimension of the happenings denied the participants in the audience the experience of an aesthetically closed work because the viewers were divided into different rooms and viewing directions.

Per Kaprow's script, "People will sit in the chairs whose arrangement causes them to face in different directions" (Kaprow 1966, 54). Kaprow's objective was to move away from the stage structure of a conventional theater and occupy an almost unlimited space for performing the social anew. "To my way of thinking," he wrote, "Happenings possess some crucial qualities that distinguish them from usual theatrical works, even the experimental ones of today" (1993, 17). In particular, he placed emphasis on context and site: "The most intense and essential Happenings have been spawned in old lofts, basements, vacant stores, natural surroundings, and the street, where very small audiences, or groups of visitors, are commingled in some way with the event, flowing in and among its parts" (1993, 17).

Kaprow's happenings performed a space expansion that had both local and global significance. In addition to a horizontal extension that signaled transcultural processes, a vertical expansion of the space was also possible. Kaprow's play with the idea of shifting space is evident in the following remarks:

> Even greater flexibility can be gotten by moving the locale itself. A Happening could be composed for a jetliner going from New York to Luxembourg with stopovers at Gander, Newfoundland, and Reykjavik, Iceland. Another Happening would take place up and down the elevators of five tall buildings in Chicago. (1995, 198)

Through the expansive spatial distribution, the presuppositions of the receptive acts are differentiated from the subordinating acts in "18 Happenings in 6 Parts." The spatial setting makes a totality claim impossible with respect to the perception of events *a priori*. At the same time, the audience is made interested in learning more about what is not directly experienced but fragmented. Delany, in his retrospective analysis, describes elements of the scattering and multiplication of perception:

> During the brief performance, while we sat in our room, now and again from one of the other chambers we could hear the sound of a single drum or tambourine beat – or at one point, laughter from one of the isolated groups when something in another point went (presumably) not quite according to plan. (Delany 1990, 181)

Boundaries of the receptive acts were blown up in the conventional closed space; yet, by awakening the curiosity about what was missed, an intensification of the interaction among the viewers occurred, although this can indeed be implemented after the end of the performance. "There was much palpable and uneasy curiosity about what was happening in the other spaces, walled off by the translucent sheets" (182), comments Delany, referring to conversations among the participants after the completion of the performance. Obviously, the not-experienced synchronicity of events activated the imagination of each spectator and encouraged the imagination of the fragmentary experience. Thus, the separation of artist and recipient in the conventional theater was also abolished. The communicative and interactive aspects of art made more complex the relationship between artist and recipient, as well as the relationship of the viewers among themselves. In this way, happenings became a way to rethink not only public space but also the relations within public space as fractured, fragmented, yet changeable. The practice of rethinking social relations was favored by a basic, flexible alignment of the happenings. Thus, there is no definition of the place or duration of the performance within the scope of action art.[3]

---

3   The concentration, however, lies in the moment. Daniel Charles captures the role of performance in the American context: "Every performance in American sense is characterized by vividness: its configuration of the presence in *hic et nunc*" (1989, 25, author's translation).

The number of people involved, and the techniques, media, and materials used also changed from one happening to another, from one performance to another.[4] In the viewer's encounter with the happenings, a tightrope walk developed between individual experience and a generally recognizable experience of archetypal nature. The presence of the actors (or artists) was essential for individual experience; real space and real time pointed to a familiar situation that was easily accessible to a larger group of people. By preserving real space and real time within the framework of the art of action, happenings and other forms of performance brought about a fundamental paradigm shift in terms of the mechanisms of the art work, overturning conventions enshrined in academies, museums, and galleries.

Art into everyday life: body politic and the political body

The reintroduction of art into everyday life, which had already been attempted by the Dadaists and Surrealists, was taken further in the experiments of the performance arts striving for new concepts of ethnic and cultural cohesion in the United States. In the 1950s and 1960s, numerous centers and forms of cooperation emerged as real existing communities of male and female artists – one thinks of Black Mountain, Greenwich Village, East Village, the Judson Dance Theater, Kaprow's circle at Rutgers University, the City Lights District, Umbra Workshops, etc. – which up to this point had been the most intense manifestations of artistic collaboration in the USA. These groups also participated in transcultural dialogues with artists from Latin America and Europe. Not infrequently, actors and the public formed a kind of community; this applied in particular to the early phase of the happenings in the USA, as well as in Argentina and Mexico. Thus, numerous comments point to a certain degree of

---

4   "A performance does not intend to produce a durable material product, but the creation of a unique, ephemeral event that can be perceived with the senses," states Jappe (1993, 10).

recognition between actors and spectators and prove the need to create new forms of communication and interaction within art.[5] Sally Banes combines the process of individualistic artistic experience with the desire for cohesion in a purely aesthetic dimension:

> To create community seemed to demand the presence of a body politic, not only in the metaphoric meaning of a consensual community, but literally in the sense of a political body – a person rendered political by physically taking a part in the life of the collective enterprise. (Banes 1993, 37)

For a society that places a premium on the individual's right to self-realization, the artistic experiments in cooperation represented a countermovement to the isolation of the artist in American history of art and literature, challenging the U.S. ideology of individualism. In performances in Mexico, Argentina, and Brazil, individualistic performative expression predominantly served as a critique of outworn communal and social norms and standards.

In this respect, the question arises as to how aesthetic procedures were used in order to embed art in an active community atmosphere. The fact that both the aesthetic and the everyday dimensions of action took on the form of ritual sequences in many performances showed that the everyday happenings were enhanced to create a sense of community. Movements of the everyday life were not only equated with artistic actions; they were also celebrated. The cutting and pressing of oranges in Kaprow's happening ("He cuts ceremoniously an orange and squeezes it into its glass" [Kaprow 1966, 65]) received the same aesthetic justification as the act of painting ("SOLEMNLY HE PAINTS" [55]). Kaprow, Jodorowsky, Minujín, and other happening artists were not interested in transforming experience into specific artistic forms, but rather allowing aesthetics and life to happen in an alternating and seamless flow.

Art in 1960s performance culture was not considered an aesthetic form that comes from experience, but one that expresses ex-

---

5   Cf. Delany's perception of the audience (1990, 182).

perience directly and vividly. Happenings strove for a principle of simultaneity so that experience and expression occurred as simultaneous events. This reorientation of consciousness from a linear, teleological way of thinking to a holistic understanding was evidenced by the reception and transformation of Oriental, African, and indigenous temporal concepts by performance artists in the Americas. The ritualization of action was usually done through the means of repetition, as Kaprow's explanations in the script illustrate: "An artist dressed in white duck sneakers and dress shirt sits on a red stool in the center of the enclosure and lights NINETEEN WOODEN MATCHES blowing them out in turn slowly without great movement" (1966, 55).

Not only is the single action repeated, but its slowness is also emphasized. In this way, receptive perception is directed to the action itself and not to a symbolic or extended meaning-creating context.

The same effect happened at the linguistic level because, according to Kaprow, words should not only assume metaphorical or symbolic functions. Thus, the actors articulated "words which should convey a ritualistic yet non-sensical feeling" (Kaprow 1966, 61). In their radical expression, happenings took on a nonverbal character, which strictly separated them from traditional theaters and moved them closer to body performance art and the absurd theater. When language was present, different structures could be recognized but they were largely non-diegetic, that is, not intended to describe action. Thus, the teleological orientation of language use dissolved. Kaprow's aesthetic goal was an elementary experience of language and action, of art and everyday life, in which acoustic, optical, and sensory perception were equally involved. For a cultural context, the process was a ritualization of all elements involved, because at the social level, the ritual functioned as community-building and community-promoting.

A ritualization process is commonly understood to mean the liberation of a form of behavior into a ritual. As has been shown, happenings in the 1960s represented a variety of intersections where

ideas met different cultures and media. These encounters were characterized by their closeness to ritual and activated the idea of exchange as an independent social, aesthetic, and cultural form. Thus,
public space as well as the public sphere could be reinvented by
building on tradition. It is above all Richard Schechner, who in his
theoretical analysis of performance art repeatedly points to the close
connection between performance art, ritual, and playful practices of
tribal cultures:

> The avant-garde is apparently a rule-breaking activity. But actually,
> experimentation in the arts has its own set of rules. Think about it:
> the ordinary technological environments most of today's Americans
> live in and with – cars and planes, appliances, TV and stereo, etc. –
> have changed much more radically over the past seventy years than
> have the concerns or techniques of the avant-garde. Performance ac-
> tivities all along the continuum – from play through ritual – are tra-
> ditional in the most basic sense. (1994, 11)

Due to the adaptation of traditional ritual practices by avant-garde
performance artists, Schechner concludes, "I think we will find that
the new theater is very old, and that our localized urban avant-garde
belongs next to worldwide, rural-tribal tradition" (40). Since rituals
have manifested themselves in all cultures, they represent a transcultural phenomenon. They have a particularly significant effect in
tribal cultures. In order to establish awareness of their importance in
Western society, many of the avant-garde artists needed/included
this in their art. Their turn toward ritual expressed longing for orientation and change, and was influenced by primitivism. As a result,
urban art took over functions traditionally performed by ritualistic
dance, play, and action in older tribal cultures.[6] A view of art prac-

---

6   Rituals and forms of pre-Columbian influence play an especially im-
     portant role in the American context. With the shift of the avant-garde
     centers from Europe to America in the early 1940s, there was also a
     change in primitivist influences. While the European avant-gardism and
     modernism were mainly oriented towards African predecessors, the
     American avant-garde scene was a reflection of cultural forms whose

tice emerged that associated artistic activity with human action and interaction beyond boundaries. This also illustrated that performance arts envisioning new social relations and communal ties could spread throughout the Americas in spite of different political systems among the countries.

By interlacing with the aesthetic, the interactive effect of ritual in public space was also transferred to the artistic process. Certainly, with the emphasis on simultaneity and the expansion of space in the happenings, theories of presentation were debated; but at the same time, the border between world and art, public and private space were questioned, and a relationship of congruence was brought into focus. On a temporal level, the artistic action left the fixed timeline of a closed performance and opened up to the temporal flow of everyday life. Interference and discontinuity were accepted as part of the creative process. Such acceptance spurred democratic, utopian visions that, on the basis of the artists' interaction with each other and with the public, located the design of new forms of coexistence in the immediate communal experience of the performance. Through the interactions of the artists from the Americas with artists from

---

history and traditions were connected with the American continent. Nationalistic and artistic ambitions were united insofar as the avant-garde performed a cultural demarcation from Europe and was based on its own traditions. Numerous avant-garde artists discovered values in pre-Columbian cultures that were not bound to a specific cultural context. Thus, the focus on the writings and works of artists like Barnett Newman or Jackson Pollock was mainly on the universal meaning of forms and structures of archaic cultures. While the surrealists' interest in the mentality and spirituality of primitive cultures was named by many American avant-garde artists as influential, the latter distanced themselves from Freudian elements, which were reflected in the close association between the primitive spirit and the individual psyche in surrealism. On the other hand, artists like Newman, Pollock, and Gottlieb emphasized the importance of primitive art for the expression of a collective unconscious, which moved more accidently than consciously into the proximity of Jung. For the role of primitivism in the visual art of the 1940s, cf. Varnedoe (1984, 620–621).

Europe and Asia, the arts practiced foremost in the USA in the 1960s and their proximity to community-promoting rituals were of tremendous transcultural importance, since the American ideas also penetrated the art world and social imaginaries in Asia and Europe.[7]

Black bodies, black voices, black performances in public space

Black culture in the 1960s became a hotbed for performance and protest in public space. As George Yúdice has commented, it was the Civil Rights and Black Power movements that developed the power of performance for the political (Yúdice 2003, 40). A mixture of grassroots activities like the actions of the Freedom Singers and the artistic black literary and poetic avant-garde emerging around the bebop and free jazz scene presented an explosive cocktail capable of reaching out to diverse sections of the black population and American society. One of the significant cultural acts happened in the spring of 1964 when LeRoi Jones, Charles Patterson, William Patterson, Clarence Reed, and of other black artists opened the Black Arts Repertoire Theatre School in Harlem (Neal 1968, 29–30). Not only did they produce a number of plays, including Jones's *Experimental Death Unit # One*, *Black Mass*, *Jello*, and *Dutchman*; they also initiated a series of poetry readings and concerts. High artistic quality and radical political content characterized these events.

---

7   On this point, cf. Sally Banes's *Greenwich Village 1963* (1993). In Fluxus, she sees a performative realization of an American utopia in an urban space and, with a view to the idea of community by Ken Friedman, describes the effect of Fluxus as follows: "When Fluxus went creeping from state to state with festivals and philosophy … year after year, it wasn't American because it went through *America*, it was American because it embraced America largesse, pioneer neighborliness and frivolity" (65). Regarding the proliferation of American avant-garde, one can think of the performances in Europe and Asia of John Cage and Merce Cunningham Dance Company in the 1960s and the international presence of LeRoi Jones, Ornette Coleman, and John Coltrane.

Most importantly, the Black Arts Repertoire Theatre took black culture out of the theater into the streets.

In accordance with its radical cultural ideas, the Black Arts Theatre presented performances in various public sites and streets of Harlem (Sell 2008). For over three months the theatre brought concerts, plays, and poetry readings to the community. As Neal puts it, they presented "plays that shattered the illusions of the American body politic, and awakened Black people to the meaning of their lives" (1968, 30). Beyond Harlem, Black Art groups spread to Oakland, San Francisco, Los Angeles California, Detroit, Philadelphia, New Orleans, and Washington D.C., bringing art practices to public sites in these cities. Many university campuses from the West Coast to the East Coast witnessed the rise of the Black Arts movements in the mid-1960s. In Watts, Los Angeles, after the riots in 1965, Maulana Karenga formed a Black Arts movement that gave collective voice to black art practice in public space (33–34).

For the Black Arts movement the theatre, next to music, represented the potentially most social of all art forms. For LeRoi Jones it provided a way to reflect social relations by staging black bodies in public space. His play *Dutchman* (1964) marked his transition from vanguard to black nationalist artist. Set in a New York subway, the play translated Black Arts theatre convictions that performances should reflect, reach, and change public spheres. The piece was based on cultural difference and racial hatred, and it mixed elements of European avant-garde theater (particularly the theater of the absurd developed by Beckett and Ionesco) with African American forms of performance: dance, minstrel show, and rapping (Raussert 2003b). Jones stages the black body as a radical critique of culture by associating that body with Eros and Thanatos, clearly pointing to intracultural, interethnic, and racial tensions in the United States and the Americas at large. In the context of a dramatization of the encounter between the white woman Lula and black middle-class man Clay in the New York subway, the moral-ethical dimension of the history of the Old Testament is assumed to be gender specific, and especially culturally and racially specific.

Through the role assignments of the characters – white woman, black man – LeRoi Jones plays with a variety of cultural processes and tensions that shape the relationship between different ethnic groups in the United States. Cultural rejection and ethnic discrimination in the form of anti-Semitism and racism permeate the at times grotesque and bizarre conversation between the two protagonists. Classification and stigma are based on ethnic distinctions, whereby irony, humor, and historical facts are mixed for polemical purposes.

While both characters repeatedly resort to stereotypical perceptions of ethnic difference, thereby cementing cultural boundaries, Jones continually integrates aesthetic elements that demonstrate the actual complexity of intercultural encounters in the United States. By connoting the minstrel tradition, Lula's dancing and singing inserts spotlight the processes of cultural borrowing and intercultural exchange among ethnically differentiated groups in the United States. But Lula's action also reveals the power hierarchies at work within cultural exchange. The encounter that leads to Clay's verbal rebellion and his consequential killing by Lula stages the urgency of black collective struggle against oppression. The idea of black brotherhood is introduced with the final words of the play, when the black conductors greet the newly entering black passenger with "Hey brother!" Beyond its mythical and historical allusions, the underground as public space turns into the very terrain for social conflict and potential change.

The desire to bring theatre to the people and turn public sites into a battleground for social and racial justice also motivated readings by poets, frequently in collaboration with jazz musicians such as Ornette Coleman and John Coltrane. And public space became a central trope for poetic discourse to call black people to action. In Jones's poems, such as "Form is Emptiness," rhythm, expressive power, and thematically prominent religious figures express a religious-transcultural vision in a sonic and visual way.[8] In the mid-1960s, his vision increasingly connected with a transnational awareness that united Africa, America, and the Caribbean in Jones's consciousness of a global black cultural heritage. In this phase, Jones's incorporated intensified anger and aggressiveness into his poetic discourse, in the face of white oppression. "Black Art" (1969) stages the envisioned revolution, referencing public space in horizontal and vertical dimensions (alleys, airplanes). The poem is written for performance in public as a direct address to an audience soon to be united in the struggle against colonialism, racism, and oppression:

> ... We want poems
> like fists beating niggers out of Jocks
> ... We want poems that kill.
> Assassin poems, Poems that shoot
> guns. Poems that wrestle cops into alleys
> and take their weapons leaving them dead
> ... Knockoff
> poems for dope selling wops or slick halfwhite
> politicians .... Airplane poems, rrrrrrrrrrrrrrrrrrr
> Rrrrrrrrrrrrrrrrrr ... tuh tuh tuh tuh tuh tuh tuh tuh tuh
> ... rrrrrrrrrrrrrrrrrr ... Setting fire and death to
> whities ass. (Jones 1969, 116)

In "Black Art," poetry is associated with physicality and force; poems become public weaponry. Jones locates action in the poem itself. Within his lyrical understanding, the poetic text becomes an

---

8   Cf. French (1980). French describes the aesthetic implementation of LeRoi Jones's artistic intentions in "Form of Emptiness" as follows: "Baraka has succeeded in marshalling together his basic themes in order to emphasize his aesthetic preferences – religion and magic as ritualistic forms of spiritual and social wholeness, the magical, pre-technological nuances of the chant as antirationalistic sound, and the idea of poetry itself as sound. And the blending of these themes results in an integrated structure that is coherent and symptomatic of the poet's deliberate sense of design – at the very moment in which the poem, as a whole, rebels against the idea of formal design for its own sake" (126–127).

agent – "poems that shoot guns." Textual sections also feed ono-matopoeically on a convergence of phonetic expression and action. Text sections like "rrrrrrr" and "tuh tuh tuh tuh" act like an acoustic reproduction of aircraft and machine gun noise. On the one hand, they are a direct expression of an energy pushing for change, which Jones attaches to the lyric text itself. On the other hand, they em-phasize the close link between lyricism and performance in Jones' understanding of poetry. Günter H. Lenz emphasizes the communi-cative aspect of this connection:

> In conceiving of his poetry as process, as performance, Baraka in his powerful readings dramatizes, acts out poetry as a communica-tion with music, with musicians, and "poetrymusic" as a communal experience with and provocation of, the audience. (1986, 225)

"Black Art" calls especially for a transnational feeling of black uni-ty at the level of cross-cultural communication:

> Let Black People understand
> that they are the lovers and the sons
> of lovers and warriors and sons
> of warriors. Are poems & poets &
> all the loveliness here in the world
> We want a black poem. And a
> Black World.
> Let the world be a Black Poem
> And Let All Black People Speak This Poem
> Silently
> Or LOUD. (Jones 1969, 117)

The world is imagined as a black *cosmopolis*, and the poetic refer-ence to speaking loud signals the desire to make the black cause heard around the globe. Poetic performance is a public and political act.

Keeping in the spirit of public presence and revolutionary change, many vocal poet-activists emerged in the Black Power and arts movement during the 1960s. Poets like Sonia Sanchez, Nikki Giovanni, Etheridge Knight, and Don L. Lee created the "Broadside

Quartet" of radical young poets. Their work focused on the black struggle for liberation from racial and economic oppression, with poets like Sanchez using the language of the streets to spread the gospel. Sanchez was among the first poets to blend ghetto impressions with lower-case letters, slashes, dashes, hyphenated lines, unconventional spelling, sudden abbreviations, and further untried uses of language and structure to reinterpret the poem as a public act, investigating for whom and how it should be performed. The urban street talk made her poems powerful reflections on art practice in public space and strong appeals to rethink the discourse of public spheres.

As Haki Madhubuti notes in *Black Women Writers, 1950–1980: A Critical Evaluation*, Sanchez respected the power of urban street talk and was responsible more than any other poet for "legitimizing the use of urban Black English in written form" (Madhubuti 1984, 421). Poets like Nikki Giovanni used the radio to broadcast poetry and political mission statements. Her early poetry grew out of her response to the assassinations of such figures as Martin Luther King, Jr., Malcolm X, Medgar Evers, and Robert Kennedy, and the urgency she felt to raise awareness of the plight and the rights of Black people. She gave her first public reading to a packed audience at Birdland, the famous New York City jazz spot in 1970, and has continued since to engage in poetry as a public act. As she recollects,

> So I started doing late night radio. WWRL was one of the first – and I was saying *"Black Judgment, Black Judgment* is coming. Come on down to Broadway, to Birdland." Sent out invitations, went to churches. It was fantastic because we had about five hundred people. Sunday. (Giovanni 2004, n. pag).

To reach a large public and to enter all domains of the public sphere was of the essence for the artists of the Black Arts movement. The public performance of poetry gained further strength in the decades to follow. In the 1970s and 1980s, poets like Ntozake Shange and Jayne Cortez continued the tradition of musically accompanied poetry performance. Cortez developed her performance skills as director of the Watts Repertory Theatre Company in Los Angeles between 1964 and 1970. Later she turned the public performance of poetry into chant-like events with the support of her band, The Firespitters.[9]

Black art practices became key patterns for social and political protest in public in the 1960s. With an even greater outreach than the Black Arts groups, the Freedom singers and freedom songs during the Civil Rights movement brought black musical tradition with new political messages into the streets all across the South and into urban centers up North and out West. As Bernice Johnson Reagon remembers, "Rhythm and blues based songs were generally sung on street corners, in offices of Movement organizations, in jail and in secular gatherings" (1980, 14). In addition, religion-inspired songs were performed in mass meetings, marches, and movement activities across the South.

Already during the Montgomery Bus Boycott from December 1955 to December 1956, mass meetings were held with public speeches and singing to hold the community together and keep the protests going. Black student protests at segregated lunch counters were accompanied by continuous singing in public. When they were beaten and put in jail they continued their musical performance. Likewise, when Freedom Riders were stopped and jailed in Mississippi, they kept on chanting in prisons such as Parchman Penitentiary and Hinds County jail (Reagon 1980, 16). As Civil Rights workers continuously moved from town to town, and as their word and image traveled far via television and radio, they effectively disseminated the music and messages of the Civil Rights movement.

Musical art practice from churches and streets impacted the mainstream music business as the movement's musical outpouring of folk, gospel, and topical songs reached the top of popular charts in the U.S. during the 1960s. These songs were rooted in Black musical traditions from the Americas. In songs like "Oh Freedom,"

---

9 https://www.modernamericanpoetry.org/poet/jayne-cortez.

"Freedom Now Chant," and "Calypso Freedom," call-and-response patterns were used and chorus structures implemented in which singers repeated the word "freedom" as counterline to the solo part (Reagon 1980, 4). Thus, the songs involved more chanting to move the masses during gatherings and marches. "Calypso Freedom" exemplified the interAmerican exchange between black cultures in the Caribbean and the American South. The song was based on a traditional Caribbean song popularized by Harry Belafonte as "The Banana Boat song" in the 1950s. These songs translated a desire for freedom and equality and provided a performance style ideally suited for community-building.

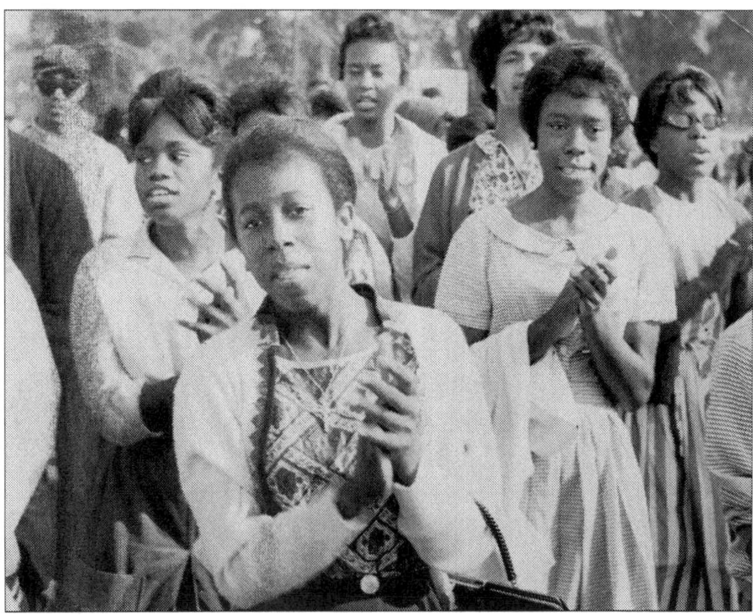

Figure 2: Freedom singers at rally, 1964, unidentified photographer, Amistad Center (© Amistad Center).

As the Civil Rights movement morphed into the Black Power movement, music continued to play a key role in black struggle and identity politics. It also became a powerful vehicle for reaching a larger public. Independent black radio and Motown guaranteed a rich dissemination of black music. Soul records by black artists like Ray Charles, Sam Cooke, Jackie Wilson, and Smokey Robinson started conquering the national charts and reaching white audiences (Steinitz 2019; Guralnick 1986).

Attaining high visibility and audibility in the streets was key to the community-building politics of the Black Power movement. Standing tall in leather jackets and berets, parading in the streets, at times with guns loosely over their shoulders, the Black Panthers used iconic visibility in public space to establish and secure black urban structures, including food and medical supply for the community. From their very beginning the Panthers' soul musicians celebrated black power in the wake of the Civil Rights movement and the assassination of Malcolm X and Martin Luther King. Black sound and iconic Black Power images in streets, parks, and other public sites created a strong black presence in public sites in cities like Detroit, New York, and Oakland.

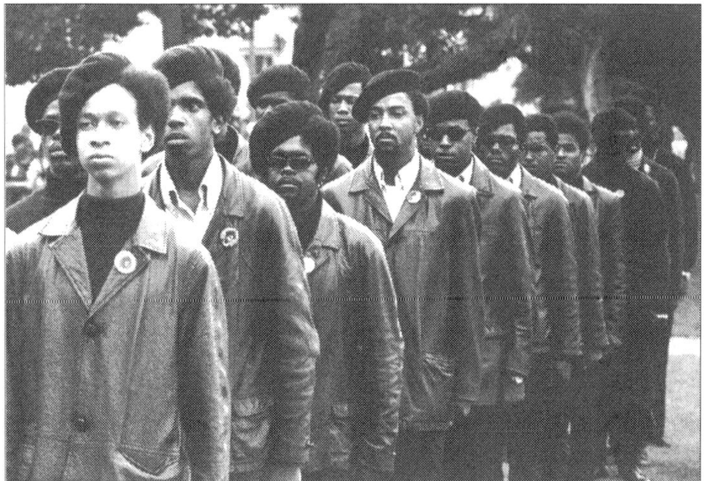

Figure 3: Black Panthers on parade during a Free Huey rally in Oakland, 1969 (© Stephen Shames, 2016).[10]

---

10   Cf. Shames and Seale (2016).

Musical celebrities like James Brown, Marvin Gaye, Curtis May-field, and Gil Scott-Heron wrote songs and music around some of the key messages of the movement. Soul and funk was the style of the black awakening and musically carried the message to black Americans. In the 1960s and 1970s, the Civil Rights and Black Power movements and their cultural manifestations in public space provided key references for the articulation of antiracist discourses and the construction of what Howard Winant has called "hemispheric blackness" (2012, ix).

InterAmerican flows of black music, iconic images, dress codes, and political symbols helped created a strong affirmation of black presence in public space in varying degrees throughout the Americas. In the Anglophone Caribbean, the impact of black politics and culture from the U.S. was tremendous. As a result, a Caribbean Black Power movement emerged (Quinn 2014), and local music genres like calypso, ska, and reggae manifested their indebtedness to African-American music (Fared 1998; Steinitz 2019). But soul and funk also traveled to black communities in Columbia, Brazil, and other countries. Preceding the emergence of reggae and hip-hop as global youth cultures, the transnational diffusion of soul music in the 1960s and 1970s was a transcultural phenomenon that exemplified, in the words of Livio Sansone, the "globalization of blackness" (2003, 1). As Steinitz puts it, the diffusion of soul and funk represented a key moment within "an ongoing process of cultural transfer between highly mobile afro-diasporic communities in which black popular culture from the U.S. occupied a prominent position as major focus of identification" (2019, 99).

InterAmerican flows also characterized the relationship between the Cuban revolution and African American radical thinkers. During the Black Power movement, the African American organization that arguably established the closest ties with Cuba was the Black Panther Party for Self-Defense (BPP). The BPP had a strong leftist leaning and was inspired by the Cuban revolution (Benvenutti 2015, 133). Most of the black radicals who supported the Cuban revolution in the 1960s were fond of Che Guevara's *foquismo* and considered guerrilla tactics a viable response to daily racial oppression (132). These tactics included an infusion of images, symbols, and ideas into a larger public sphere. Guevara, whose legendary revolutionary struggles touched North, Central, and South America and Africa, was a tremendous inspiration to revolutionaries all over the world during the anti-colonial era following World War II. Representations of Guevara also served well as an ideological and imagistic model. Guevara's iconic image with beret made him the embodiment of successful revolution and powerful resistance. Together with bebop style of dressing from the 1950s, black counterculture Guevara's revolutionary posture inspired the Black Panther's uniform and parade look. As black urban guerrillas, the Black Panthers also translated Cuban models of community-building and media flow for their appropriation of local politics and aesthetics in cities like Detroit, New York, and Oakland. For performance of ideas and style in public, the Cuban poster designs from the Cuban revolution provided creative models for politically charged Black Power aesthetics in the late 1960s.

The visual arts in Cuba drew from a longer history of linking aesthetics and performance with social commitment. During the Cuban Revolution the visual arts continued to provide visual representations of social visions. Graphic design turned into an expression of revolutionary art. Poster art in particular fulfilled "the role of forums and spaces for public dialogue, debate and negotiation of the concept of the common good in a changing geopolitical landscape" (Story 2018, 6). As critic Story points out,

> The visual arts were at the forefront of the shift in cultural orientation, and its international projection. Already by 1965, a clear revolutionary art form, graphic design, had begun to emerge within the Revolution. Its vehicle of choice was the poster and this art form was particularly supported due to its rapid ability to respond to events. (7)

Similarly, posters as aesthetic expressions of the Black Power (Arts) movement served well to respond to social crisis and inform the community rapidly about events, gatherings, and political actions.

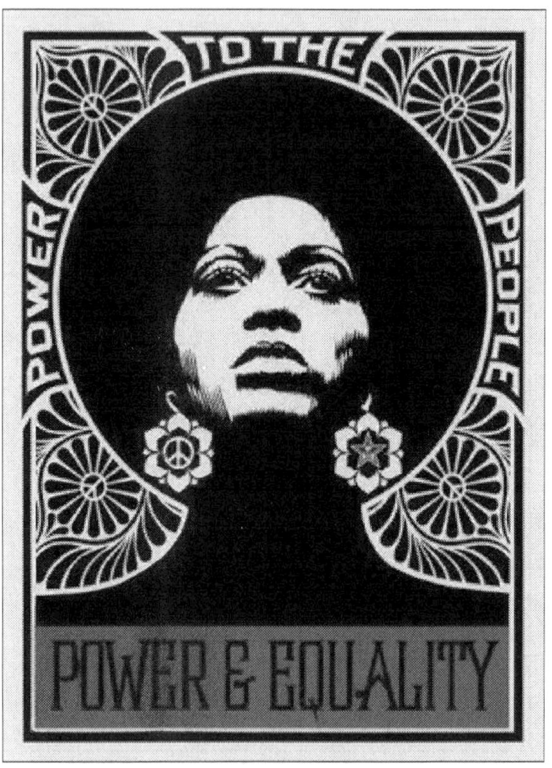

Figure 4: *Power & Equality* from Guity Novin's online history of graphic design.[11]

---

11   http://guity-novin.blogspot.com/2012/08/chapter-60-posters-in-social-protests.html#BP.

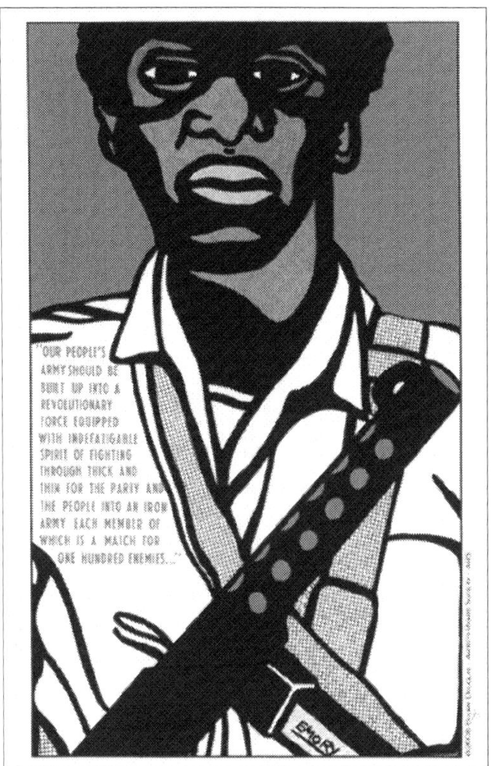

Figure 5: *Our People's Army* from Guity Novin's online history of graphic design.[12]

The visualization of black protest in public sites reached a climax in 1967 with what was presumably the first black mural in public space in Chicago. *Wall of Respect* was an outdoor mural done for the community by a collective of artists that included Chicago muralist William Walker and other painters, designers, and photographers (Alkalimat, Crawford, and Zorach 2017, 3–7). Rather than creating a historical outline of black cultural and political achievements, *Wall of Respect* did not follow chronology in its arrangement

---

12   http://guity-novin.blogspot.com/2012/08/chapter-60-posters-in-social-protests.html#BP.

of key figures of black culture. Rhythm and blues and jazz musicians like Aretha Franklin, Billie Holiday, and Miles Davis; political activists such as Harriet Tubman, Marcus Garvey, Malcolm X, and Stokely Carmichael; and literary figures such as poet Gwendolyn Brooks; public celebrities such as boxer Muhammad Ali; and religious leaders such as Elijah Muhammad ranged side by side on the mural. In their different social spheres and historical times, these figures had expressed their affirmation and pride in black cultures. So all the figures depicted on the wall spoke in their own way to the activism of the Black Power movement that had spread to Chicago by 1967. In the center of the composition was Malcolm X, throned as a key figure for having served as the foundational inspiration for the Black Panther Party with his call for the separation of black and white worlds. While the mural was destroyed in a fire and the building's consequent demolition in 1971, it is still considered the instigating piece of public art that launched Chicago black and Chican@ muralism in the late 1960s.

Chican@ theatre in streets, on flatback trucks, and in union halls

Central for interAmerican forms of theatre in public in the U.S. were the works of *El Teatro Campesino*. Since its inception, *El Teatro Campesino* and its founder and artistic director, Luis Valdez, set the aesthetic and political standards for Latino theatrical production in the U.S. It was a theatre that emerged directly from the social conditions of farmworkers on the West Coast, the majority of whom were of Mexican or other Latin origins. Founded in 1965 during the Delano Grape Strike of Cesar Chavez's United Farmworkers Union, the company *El Teatro Campesino* wrote and performed "*actos*" or short skits on flatbed trucks in streets as well as on stages in union halls. These works were conceived as dramatic expressions of the people for the people (Broyles-Gonzalez 1994), written explicitly for performance in public with a straightforward appeal to workers and the larger public. The company demonstrated a high degree of mobility and took the *actos* on tour to dramatize the plight and cause of the farmworkers. Hence, they frequented different public sites in various towns and cities to raise translocal social awareness. The company also unfolded a hybrid conceptualization of theatre synthesizing various cultural and religious traditions. Borrowing from Aztec and Mayan sacred ritual drama, nineteenth-century Spanish missionary drama, and European commedia dell'arte, *El Teatro Campesino* fused various communal theatrical traditions in their occupation of public space for social protest and communal network building. A major force for linking the social with the theatrical, the company received national recognition when it was given an Obie Award in 1969 for "demonstrating the politics of survival" and Los Angeles Drama Critics Awards in 1969 and 1972. The political panorama of *El Teatro Campesino* expanded and included a wide range of issues between the years 1967 and 1972, including racism, the Vietnam War, and education. The theatre was also the propelling force for an "the explosion of Chican@ arts," especially in the forms of public murals (Barnet-Sanchez 2012).

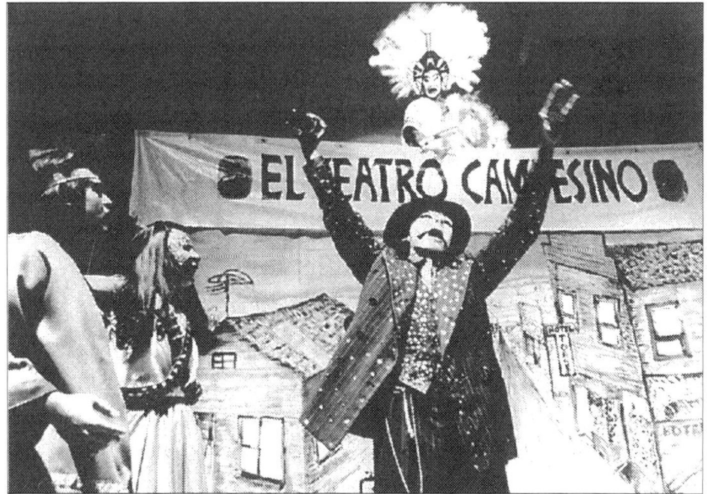

Figure 6: *El Teatro Campesino*, November 16, 1970
(courtesy American Theatre).

Chican@ muralists built on the inspiration provided by Siquieros's *La América Tropical* (1932), which was the first large-scale mural in the United States that created a public space by being painted on an ordinary exterior wall. This practice was taken up during the political and social upheavals of the Vietnam War and Chicano Civil Rights movement. *La América Tropical* acquired its most far-reaching significance by becoming the predecessor and prototype for activist Chican@ murals in the 1960s. Chican@ muralism continued Mexican muralism's impact on the American art scene in the 1930s by expressing the social and political function of art during the turbulent period of the 1960s and 1970s.

Building on earlier South-North flows, *El Movimiento*, the Chicano Movement fighting for Latino integration and equal rights, gained momentum in the U.S. in the 1960s. As an important aesthetic voice, the Chicano Art Movement represented attempts by Mexican-American artists to establish a unique artistic identity for Mexican Americans in U.S. Chican@ art. They were influenced by post-ideologies, pre-Columbian art, European painting, and Mexican-American social, political, and cultural issues. The movement challenged dominant social norms and stereotypes for the sake of cultural autonomy and self-determination. Issues addressed by the movement included the awareness of collective history and culture, restoration of land grants, and equal opportunity for social mobility. Throughout the movement and beyond, Chican@s used art to express their cultural values as social protest or for aesthetic purpose (Goldman and Ybarro-Frausto 1991; Jackson 2009). The art evolved over time, illustrating current struggles and social issues. In addition, it provided Chican@ youth with a sense of cultural identity and shared history. Chican@ art defined itself as a public forum for calling attention to "invisible" histories and people, depicting them in a unique hybrid form of American art.

Chican@ muralism drew much influence from prominent muralists from the Mexican movement. Nevertheless, it distinguished itself from Mexican muralist traditions by keeping production by and for members of the Chican@ community; their murals represented alternative histories on the walls of the *barrios* and other public spaces, and did not depend on government funding that might land them in museums or government buildings. In addition, similar to the creative process of *El Teatro Campesino* productions, Chican@ mural art favored collective work, including collaborations between multiple artists and community members. Ownership of a mural was frequently given to the entire community. The murals' significance was their accessibility and inclusivity, appearing in public spaces as a form of cultural affirmation and popular education. While most muralists were male, important female muralists emerged in the Chican@ movement, including Celia Herrera Rodriguez and Rosalinda Montez Palacios.

Concluding thoughts: performing and writing the body in/as public space or the new grid of the global village has fractures

The 1960s were characterized by an obsession with space. The space race between Russia and the U.S. and the first footprint on the moon in 1969 marked its off-planet climax. Youth cultures desired to leave behind the urban grids of surveillance and control to live new experiences of shared cultures in music festivals like Woodstock in rural settings. Artists across the world sought to break through the iron curtain of cold war politics. Protest and performance cultures in the streets transformed public space into conflictive yet promising spaces of cultural renewal from within the grid. While McLuhan's "global village" design (1962) promised a technologically-based utopian future for the planet, warfare in Vietnam, militant oppression under Latin American totalitarian regimes, and the race war in the American South and cities like Detroit in 1967 revealed deep social divides in the Americas.

As the various examples of theatre and performance arts in the 1960s Americas show, public spheres were multiplied, public space was contested, and streets were sites of political struggle and resistance – a struggle for inclusion as well as difference. McLuhan's global village utopia inspired transcultural, transethnic, and transnational communication. While artists like Kaprow and Minujín embraced its technocractic cosmopolitan design in their transcultural art practice, poets and artists from the Black Arts movement, the Chican@ movement, and the Mexican and U.S. American counterculture such as *la Onda* and the Beat poets took countercultural opposition to technocractic and colonialist ideas of progress and control and provoked resistance to their artistic visions of community.

Poetry for the Beat Generation, Black Arts poets, and writers from *La Onda* was text, spectacle, and performance in one (Zolov 1999). Public readings created ritualistic experiences of sharing poems, visions, and dreams, and transformed poetry into a communal experience and practice. Referencing the poetic body politics of Walt Whitman and Charles Olson, poets like Allen Ginsberg, Jack Kerouac, Lenore Kandel, Sonia Sanchez, José Augustin, and Amiri Baraka (Jones 1969) rethought the body's relation to public spaces and spheres. In their writings, the body turned into seismograph of cultural, ethnic, racial, and sexual politics. The body became a channel for the mediation of religious, economic, artistic, and erotic desires controlled or denied by the mainstream. In contrast with the hegemonic bodies placed on public pedestals, these performing bodies redefined public space as grassroots, democratic, porous, flexible, and communitarian.

Happenings and the body especially crystallized as key elements for the development of the theatre and performance arts. Critic Michail Bakhtin theorized that the representation of the physical is closely linked to the idea of social change and cultural renewal. The body, in his view, points beyond the limits of the individual to the strange and distant, thus suggesting a connection between the individual and a larger, even global community. According to him, the grotesque forms of the body dominate the artistic discourse of the non-European people as well as the folklore in Europe, emphasizing in both cases the fundamental processual nature of bodily presence: "The grotesque body is a growing body. It is always in the process of being built, in creation" (Bakhtin 1990, 16). Since the body for Bakhtin is the genesis and also the site of interaction with the world, he emphasizes those parts of the body that characterize it as open and crossing boundaries: abdomen, phallus, mouth, and anus (16–17). Obviously, communicative aspects are important to Bakhtin: "All of these prominent body parts are determined by overcoming the boundaries between body and body and body and world in the course of an exchange and a mutual orientation" (17). From temporal components, which directly connect the body to the event as a moment of change, he introduces the act of conception, birth, and death.

In the mainstream of many societies in the Americas, the body was still considered strictly private up to the 1960s, and dealing with it was often characterized by prudery in both public and artistic media (Banes 1993, 193–204). Moreover, for many artists, the isolation of the body in a private sphere was symbolic of a society that put a premium on the well-being of the individual and hardly considered the idea of community. Bakhtin's thoughts of the body and social change read like a basic script for a new orientation in theatre and performance practices in the 1960s. It also reads as inspiration for Allen Ginsberg's body poetics in relation to public space and the public sphere.

It is perhaps Ginsberg's poetic expression that best captures the intricate relation between artistic practice, the human body, public space, and the social in the 1960s and the hopes that were attributed to public performance. Following Walt Whitman's body metaphor in poems such as "Song of Myself" and "I Sing the Body Electric," he developed a poetic discourse that transmuted physical struggles between apocalypse and utopia into a transcultural and transreligious vision of a world that promised a renewal of human relationships. While Eastern philosophy and religion were influences from afar, his stays in Mexico provided him with cosmic vision from a society that was geographically close yet, as the Beat poets perceived, profoundly heterogeneous as well as different. The design of cosmic togetherness in Ginsberg's writings and public performances was defined through the body and its heterosexual and homosexual physical associations. As they were in 1960s' performance arts in general, feeling and the touching of bodies were key tropes in his poetry, serving to provoke the emergence of new communitarian identities. For many artists, it was not the idealized monadic body, but a publicly exposed, even grotesque, body that would pave the way for renewed social relations.[13] In many lines of Ginsberg's poem "The Change: Kyoto-Tokyo Express," this open portrayal of the corporeal is evident: "I am that I am I am/man & the Adam of hair in my loins" (Ginsberg 1982, 59–60).

For Ginsberg, the physical is the matrix of the erotic, the social, and the spiritual. Similar to the perception of his own body, divinity is described as a grotesque four-limbed body, which stands out in Ginsberg's appeal to the divinity in "The Change: Kyoto-Tokyo Express": "Come great God back to your only image, come to your many eyes and breasts, come turn thought and motion up all your arms" (Ginsberg 1982, 61).

In his conception of multiple divinities, it is also a divine instance that gives social approval to sexuality beyond heterosexual normativity and thus opens venues to imagine new communities and social patchworks. In "Wichita Vortex Sutra," the transgression of boundaries explicitly affects the transcendence of traditional concepts such as nation, culture, and God. Ginsberg's prophetic discourse is based on a transcultural group of prophets who, in their catalogues of juxtaposition, recall Whitman's poem:

> I call all Powers of imagination
> to my side in this auto to make Prophecy,
> all Lords
> of kingdoms to come
> Shambu Bharti Baba naked covered with ash
> Khaki Baba fat-bellied mad with the dogs
> Dehorahava Baba who moans Oh how wounded, How wounded

---

13 For more on the distinction between the grotesque and monadic body by Bakhtin, cf. Benthien and Wulf (2001, 14–16).

Citaram Onker Das Thakur who commands
give up your desire ...
William Blake the invisible father of English visions
Sri Ramakrishna master of ecstasy eyes ...
  Preserver Harekrishna returning in the age of pain
Sacred Heart my Christ acceptable
Allah the Compassionate One
Jaweh Righteous One
All Knowledge-Princes of Earth-man, all
ancient Seraphim of heavenly Desire, Devas, yogis
& holymen I chant to –
Come to my lone presence
into this vortex named Kansas,
I lift my voice aloud,
make Mantra of American language now,
I hear declare the end of the War!
Ancient days' Illusion!
and pronounce words beginning my own millennium. (Ginsberg
1982, 126–127)

Ginsberg conceptualization of American language is a transcultural one drenched in mysticism. His chant-like repetitions, which he drew from Black American and Eastern traditions, illustrate the performative basis of his poetry: "Holy! Holy! Holy! Holy! Holy! Holy! Holy! Holy! Holy! Holy! Holy! Holy! Holy! Holy! Holy!" (27).

Ginsberg produces a linguistic density and performative intensity which underlines the belief that utopia is here and now. Conventional categories of time and space are continually broken in "Footnote to Howl." Eternity, time, and moment merge in a kind of poetical ecstasy: "Holy time in eternity holy eternity in time ..." (1982, 28). Furthermore, Ginsberg resolves the separation between private and public spaces and declares national and international metropolises sacred: "Holy New York Holy San Francisco Holy Peoria & Seattle Holy Paris Holy Tangiers Holy Moscow Holy Istanbul!" (28). The fact that Ginsberg does not interrupt the list of cities with commas, dashes, or exclamation marks suggests the metaphorical global cohesion of geographically distant cities. Poetry for and in public space was a medium for Ginsberg to celebrate the interconnectedness of a multitude of public sites and the interdependence of different, at times conflictive, public spheres.

Performing and protesting in public, artists in the 1960s and 1970s developed practices for redefining the relations between subject and subject, subject and world. According to Stuart Hall, "we all write and speak from a particular place and time, from a history and a culture which is specific" (1990, 222). While this rings true for a citizen who locates himself, in the Aristotelian or Platonic sense, in one specific polis or city, one may question Hall's assumption in discussing the positioning of poets and performance artists who in the 1960s consciously broke open spatial closure – be it that of the theatre stage or the community's boundaries – and of artists who created events, happenings, and performances that took place in multiple locales simultaneously.

Television, space travel, and satellite information all suggested a new wave of cosmopolitanization. However, the ways in which these artists looked at the world broke down the global village ideal into local presence, struggle, emergency, and crisis. By reaching out into the streets, they challenged the abstract and distant utopian design of the new grid, the "global village." The experience of the Living Theatre in Brazil revealed that artistic protest and political struggle in the streets was riskier in some places than others in the Americas. Many of the performance artists critiqued the potential danger of non-committal views from above. While their artistic practices explored the possibility of public space as a social and aesthetic site beyond fixed geopolitical territories, beyond the diametrical oppositions of inside and outside, centre and margin, one of their major contributions was to point out the cracks in contemporary technology – and technocracy-based models of social relations. (Roszak 1995, 3–41). Their artistic practices emphasizing the human body in its relation to public space became a model for social action and political activism.

Works cited

Alkalimat, Abdul, Romi Crawford, and Rebecca Zorach. 2017. "Introduction." In *The Wall of Respect: Public Art and Black Liberation in 1960s Chicago*, ed. Abdul Alkimat, Romi Crawford, and Rebecca Zorach, 3–7. Evanston, Ill.: Northwestern University Press. Print.

Bakhtin, Michail M. 1990. *Literatur und Karneval: Zur Romantheorie und Lachkultur*. Frankfurt a. M.: Fischer. Print.

Banes, Sally. 1993. *Greenwich Village 1963: Avant-Garde Performance and the Effervescent Body*. Durham: Duke University Press.

———. 1977. *Terpsichore in Sneakers: Post-Modern Dance*. Hanover: Wesleyan University Press. Print.

Barnet-Sanchez, Holly. 2012. "Radical Mestizaje in Chicano/a Murals." In *Mexican Muralism: A Critical History*, ed. Alejandra Anreus, Leonard Folgarait, and Robin Adele Greeley, 246–251. Berkeley, CA: University of California Press. Print.

Benthien, Claudia, and Christoph Wulf. 2001. "Einleitung: Zur kulturellen Anatomie der Körperteile." In *Körperteile: Eine kulturelle Anatomie*, ed. Claudia Benthien and Christoph Wulf, 9–26. Reinbek: Rowohlt. Print.

Benvenutti, Alberto. 2015. "African American Radicals and Revolutionary Cuba from 1959 until the early Black Power years." In *Discourses of Emancipation and the Boundaries of Freedom*, ed. Leonardo Buonomo and Elisabetta Vezzosi, 129–137. Selected Papers from the 22nd AISNA Biennial International Conference, EUT Edizioni Università di Trieste. Print.

Biner, Pierre. 1972. *The Living Theatre*. New York: Horizon Press. Print.

Brody Devere, Jennifer. 2008. *Punctuation: Art, Politics, and Play*. Durham: Duke University Press. Print.

Broyles-Gonzalez, Yolanda. 1994. *Teatro Campesino: Theater in the Chicano Movement*. Austin: University of Texas Press. Print.

Charles, Daniel. 1989. Trans. Peter Geble and Michaela Ott. *Zeitspielräume: Performance Musik Ästhetik*. Berlin: Merve. Print.

Decker, Arden. 2015a. "The Panic Man. Shock and Alejandro Jodorowsky's Panic Theory." *Contemporary Art in the Americas* 3. https://terremoto.mx/article/the-panic-man-shock-and-alejandro-jodorowskys-panic-theory/.

———. 2015b. *Los Grupos and the Art of Intervention in 1960s and 1970s Mexico*. New York: Graduate Center, City University of New York. Print.

Delany, Samuel R. 1990. *The Motion of Light in Water: East Village Sex and Science Fiction Writing: 1960–65*. London: Paladin. Print.

Fared, Grant. 1998. "Wailin' Soul: Reggae's Debt to Black American Music." In *Soul – Black Power, Politics, and Pleasure*, ed. Monique Guillory and Richard C. Green, 56–74. New York: New York University Press. Print.

Foucault, Michel. 1979. *Discipline and Punish: The Birth of the Prison*. New York: Vintage. Print.

French, Warren. 1980. *Amiri Baraka*. Boston: Twayne Publishers. Print.

García, Angelica. 2005. *Teatro Pánico. Alejandro Jodorowsky en México*. Television program. Mexico City: CENIDIAP in collaboration with Canal 23 and CENART.TV.

Ginsberg, Allen. 1982. *Planet News 1961–1967*. San Francisco: City Lights Books. Print.

Giovanni, Nikki. 2004. "Interview by Julian Bond." University of Virginia. https://blackleadership.virginia.edu/transcript/giovanni-nikki.

Goldman, Shifra M., and Thomas Ybarro-Frausto. 1991. "The Political and Social Contexts of Chicano Art." In *Chicano Art: Resistance and Affirmation*, ed. Richard Griswold del Castillo, Teresa McKenna, and Yvonne Yarbro-Bejarano, 83–108. Los Angeles: Wight Art Gallery, University of California. Print.

Guralnick, Pete. 1986. *Sweet Soul Music: Rhythm and Blues and the Southern Dream of Freedom*. New York: Harper and Row. Print.

Hall, Stuart. 1990. "Cultural Identity and Diaspora." In *Identity: Community, Culture, and Difference*, ed. Jonathan Rutherford, 222–237. London: Lawrence and Wishart. Print.

Jackson, Carlos Francisco. 2009. *Chicana and Chicano art: ProtestArte*. Tucson: University of Arizona Press. Print.

Jappe, Elisabeth. 1993. *Performance – Ritual – Prozeß. Handbuch der Aktionskunst in Europa*. München/New York: Prestel Verlag. Print.

Jodorowsky, Alejandro. 1965a. "Hacía el 'efimero' pánico o ¡sacar el teatro del teatro!." In *Teatro pánico*, ed. Alejandro Jodorowsky, 12–13. México: Era. Print.

———. 1965b. *Teatro pánico*. Mexico City: Era. Print.

Jones, LeRoi. 1969. "Black Art." In *Black Magic: Sabotage Target Study Black Art: Collected Poetry 1961–1967*, ed. LeRoi Jones, 116–117. New York: The Bobbs-Merrill Company. Print.

Kaprow, Allan. 1995. "Excerpts form 'Assemblages, Environments & Happenings.'" In *Happenings and Other Acts*, ed. Mariellen R. Sandford, 197–205. London: Routledge. Print.

———. 1993. "Happenings in the New York Scene." In *Essays on the Blurring of Art and Life: Allan Kaprow*, ed. Jeff Kelley, 15–26. Berkley: U of California P, 1993. Print.

———. 1966. "18 Happenings in 6 Parts/The Script." In *Happenings: An Illustrated Anthology*, ed. Michael Kirby, 53–66. New York: Dutton. Print.

Kirby, Michael. 1965. *Happenings: An Illustrated Anthology*. New York: Dutton. Print.

Kusama, Yayoi. 2011. *Infinity Net. The Autobiography of Yayoi Kusama*. Chicago: The University of Chicago Press. Print.

Lenz, Günter H. 1986. "The Politics of Black Music and the Tradition of Poetry: Amiri Baraka and John Coltrane." *Jazzforschung/Jazz research* 18: 193–231. Print.

Madhubuti, Haki. 1984. "Sonia Sanchez." In *Black Women Writers, 1950-1980: A Critical Evaluation*, ed. Mari Evans, 419–432. New York: Doubleday. Print.

Martin, Bradford D. 2004. *The Theater Is in the Street: Politics and Public Performance in 1960s America*. Cambridge: University of Massachusetts Press. Print.

McLuhan, Marshall. 1967. *The Medium is the Massage: An Inventory of Effects*. London: Penguin Press. Print.

———. 1962. *The Gutenberg Galaxy: The Making of Typographic Man*. London: Routledge. Print.

Medina, Cuauhtémoc. 2006. "Recovering Panic." In *La era de la discrepancia: Arte y cultura visual en México/The Age of Discrepancies: Art and Visual Culture in Mexico; 1968–1997*, ed. Olivier Debroise. Mexico City: UNAM/Turner. Print.

Moore, Alan W. 2011. *Protest & Counterculture in New York City*. New York: Autonomomedia. Print.

Neal, Larry. 1968. "The Black Arts Movement." *Drama Review* 12: 29–39. Print.

Newman, Simon P. 1996. "Wearing Their Hearts on Their Sleeves: Reading the Tattoos of Early American Seafarers." In *American Bodies: Cultural Histories of the Physique*, ed. Tim Armstrong, 18–31. Sheffield: Sheffield Academic Press. Print.

Quinn, Kate. 2014. *Black Power in the Caribbean*. Miami: University Press of Florida. Print.

Raussert, Wilfried. 2003a. "Reinterpreting the Body: Gender, Utopia, and the Innovations of the Judson Dance Theater and the Living Theatre." In *New Beginnings in American Drama and Theatre*, ed. Christiane Schlote and Peter Zenziger, 434–435. Trier: WVT. Print.

———. 2003b. *Avantgarden in den USA. Zwischen Mainstream und Erneuerung*. Frankfurt a. M./New York: Campus. Print.

Reagon, Bernice Johnson. 1980. *Voices of the Civil Rights Movement, Black American Freedom Songs*. Washington: Smithsonian. Print.

Rojas, Rafael. 2016. *Fighting over Fidel: The New York Intellectuals and the Cuban Revolution*, translated by Carl Good. Princeton: Princeton University Press. Print.

Rosenthal, Cindy. 2011. "The Living Theatre's Arrested Development in Brazil: An Intersection of Activist Performances." In *Avantgarde Performance and Material Exchange: Vectors of the Radical*, ed. Mike Sell, 60–76. New York: Palgrave. Print.

Roszak, Theodore. 1995. *The Making of a Counterculture: Reflections on the Technocratic Society and Its Youthful Opposition*. Berkeley: University of California Press. Print.

Rothman, Angela. 2016. "Revolutionary Theatricality: Dramatized American Protest 1967–1968." *University of Oregon Libraries*, Scholars' Bank, 1–27. https://scholarsbank.uoregon.edu/xmlui/handle/1794/22258.

Rutherford, Jonathan, ed. 1990. "Cultural Identity and Diaspora." In *Identity: Community, Culture, and Difference*, ed. Jonathan Rutherford, 222–237. London: Lawrence and Wishart. Print.

Sansone, Livio. 2003. *Blackness without Ethnicity: Constructing Race in Brazil*. New York: Palgrave Macmillan. Print.

Schechner, Richard. 1994. *Performance Theory*. London/New York: Routledge. Print.

Sell, Mike. 2008. *Avant-garde Performance & the Limits of Criticism Approaching the Living Theatre, Fluxus, and the Black Arts Movement*. Ann Arbor: The University of Michigan Press. Print.

Shames, Stephen, and Bobby Seale. 2016. *Power to the People: The World of the Black Panthers*. London: New Abrams and Chronicle Books. Print.

Spencer, Catherine. 2015. "Performing Pop: Marta Minujín and the 'Argentine Image-Makers.'" *Tate Papers* 24. https://www.tate.org.uk/research/publications/tate-papers/24/performing-pop-marta-minujin-and-the-argentine-image-makers.

Steinitz, Matti. 2019. "'Calling Out Around the World.' How Soul Music Transnationalized the African-American Freedom Struggle in the Black Power Era 1965–1975." In *Sonic Politics. Mu-*

sic and Social Movements, ed. Olaf Kaltmeier and Wilfried Raussert, 88–106. London/New York: Routledge. Print.

Story, Isabel. 2018. "Debating the Revolution: The Evolving Role of the Visual Arts in Cuba." *Journal of Languages, Texts, and Society* 2: 1–24. Print.

Suvin, Darko. 1995. "Reflections on Happenings." In *Happenings and Other Acts*, ed. Mariellen R. Sandford, 285–309. London: Routledge. Print.

Varnedoe, Kirk. 1984. "Abstract Expressionism." In *Primitivism in the 20th Century Art: Affinity of the Tribal and the Modern*, ed. William Rubin, 615–659. Vol. II. New York: The Museum of Modern Art. Print.

Winant, Howard. 2012. "Foreword – A New Hemispheric Blackness." In *Comparative Perspectives on Afro-Latin America*, ed. Kwame Dixon and John Burdick, ix–xiv. Gainesville: University of Florida Press. Print.

Yúdice, George. 2003. *The Expediency of Culture: Uses of Culture in the Global Era*. Durham: Duke University Press. Print.

Zolov, Eric. 1999. *Refried Elvis: The Rise of the Mexican Counterculture*. Berkeley, CA: University of California Press. Print.

Chapter IV

Off the Grid: Art Practices and Public Space
in the Contemporary Period

Grid patterns continue to define urban structures in the Americas. They are also part of contemporary art practices that perform a re-modeling of public spaces. Seen in relation to each other, urban and art grid patterns highlight interAmerican entanglements that emerge from the visual and material transformation of public space and public sphere. Imagining and constructing a networked public and employing boundary-crossing performative practices in and off the grid characterize art's important contribution to the process of shaping the social in the Americas in the contemporary period.

The grid is considered the foundational architectural and urban structure to colonize and organize space in the Americas for purposes of spatial community-building and expansion. As Richard Sennett puts it, "It seemed that only the most arbitrary imposition could tame American vastness: an endless, unbounded grid." The grid "seemed to render space meaningless" (1991, 57). Yet, the grid contains tremendous power to shape the social in spatial terms. Functioning both horizontally and vertically, it supports the expansion of territory as well as the extension of architecture. To a large extent the grid has shaped the spatial conquest of the Americas and dictated urban structures of hierarchy, division, and marginalization. In the new media age, the grid adopts a new virtual extension.

As Zeynep Tufekci explains,

Now it appears that everything political is personal, since movement politics is experienced in environments that combine multiple contexts from the personal to the political, all homogenized because multiple audiences who might otherwise be separated by time and space are all on the same Facebook page. (2017, 272)

Internet networks build new powerful grid structures linking multiple locations over long distance, controlling and channeling the flow of information, but also revealing gaps and fissures in their structures that open venues for acts of divergence, dissidence, and counterhegemonic discourse. At the same time, governments have noticed the challenge posed by digital technology practices. In response they have developed counter measures, tightening grid structures by blocks and censorship.

While in the nineteenth century the flows and mobilities within the grid happened mostly through railroads, telegraphs, and newspapers, in the twentieth century telephone, radio, cinema, and television took dominance. In the early twenty-first century, digital technology, new media, and networking with the help of computers, smartphones, and the internet shape the flows and censorship of information. The new media have underscored that the public sphere is not uniform, and public space is ever more multilayered (Tufekci 2017, 5–6). Hence, the coffeehouses and salons that Jürgen Habermas (1989) once imagined as the site in which the public sphere emerged in rationalist discussion are now but a small piece in the puzzle of real and virtual social networking. The public has turned plural and consists of many "counterpublics" opposing hegemonic discourse (cf. Fraser 1990).

In recent years, the Reclaim-the Streets-Movement, comprising among others guerilla gardening, flashmobs, and biker manifestations, has spread throughout cities in the U.S. and Mexico and has advanced a new consciousness for mobile, mass democratic and pluricentric use of public streets and squares (Gretzki 2015, 235–245). Like the Reclaim-the-Streets-Movement, contemporary street art overall aims to reclaim public space for individual as well as communal use. A central idea, especially within collective street art projects, is to mobilize people to interact and participate in the recreation of urban spaces. Contemporary street art manifests both individual and collaborative artistic invasions of public space. Artistically, it valorizes the image, going beyond the tagging practices of the pure graffiti writers; it mediates between muralist, graffiti, and commercial art practices. Concerning commercial aspects, these artists frequently adopt and deconstruct brand names and tags in what is called "urban hacking" or "urban intervention." This practice wavers between subversion and collaboration with the markets that turn urban structures into venues of commerce and trade.

Within and beyond the new digital world, art practices in the contemporary period have become a driving force for social and cultural creativity. They are intensely intertwined with the cultural industry, unfold within and against hegemonic politics, and infuse everyday life culture with a mix of aesthetics and politics. They shape the urban in its cultural, social, and economic dimensions. Today's street art appears in museums and galleries, and creates new livable environments in socially conflictive urban spaces, yet, it also continues to voice dissidence and resistance. Art practices work within and against the grain when it comes to aesthetically recreating the social. It is safe to say that art practices in their aesthetic, performative, and critical guise have penetrated all spectra of social life in the twenty-first century. Consequently, they also take a leading role in redefining public space and its possibilities for capitalist subjectivity as well as communal coexistence (Illouz 2019).

Particularly with the beginning of the postmodern period, the struggle about and for public space has taken on multilayered dimensions. It revolves around visual enrichment and visual pollution that penetrate urban spaces throughout the Americas Street arts in particular reveal a visual entanglement of the South and the North in the Americas. The expansion of street continues despite municipal struggles to reduce and control its presence. Some governments have launched politics against visual pollution in megacities like São Paulo or Mexico City. While directed at lowering visual stress, these politics also operate to reduce the effects of the visual hybridization of the public sphere (Canclini 1990; Thies and Corona Berkin 2020). Yet, art practices in public space keep pushing further visual hybridization and provide interesting Pan-American tapestries of dialogic street arts that expose the transversal flows of theme, technique, ideology, and design between the North and the South. From the street to public places, the struggle for inclusion and participation keeps entering all domains of social interaction. Not surprisingly then, the world-wide web has become the perhaps most heated battleground in which actors compete in shaping, controlling and constructing new public spheres. New media channels not only encourage a rethinking of public space in small communal networks, blogging groups, or WhatsApp communities; they also provide new avenues for hacking government systems, manipulating election campaigns, and entering state defense systems. Artistic practices make use of these new forms of empowerment and also influence them by frequently using virtual formats to help shape the social.

Overall, we are witnessing a mobilization of artistic practices in various dimensions of public space. From the postmodern into the contemporary period, art practices are increasing in number and density in which artists choose sites of mobility to express their artistic mission. Art practices are thus responding to a heightened mobility and (denial of mobility) in contemporary times of globalization. Street crossings, highly frequented public parks, bus stations, metro stations, and airports, so called "non-places" (cf. Auge 1995), are turning into sites of artistic practice. At the same time, artists are giving these sites a sense of place by raising awareness of past and present entanglements of American histories and cultures in their public installations and performances. Embracing site-specificity and simultaneously adopting a nomadic new media stance, art practices are increasingly linking the local with the global and the South with the North. More convincingly than any social theory, it seems, contemporary art practices in public space are visualizing a profound interconnectedness that links people, ideas, cultural industries, and economies. They are nourishing networks with the purpose of spreading cultural creativity, extending market circuits, and infusing political networks that can be hegemonic and counter-hegemonic; they seek to share identity politics across multiple channels and create hybrid as well as participatory paradigms by borrowing from a rich spectrum of established and new public art practices.

By occupying and/or invading public space, art practices demand a renegotiation of the public sphere. In *On the Political*, Chantal Mouffe argues for a "vibrant 'agonistic' public sphere of contestation where different hegemonic political projects can be confronted" (2005, 3). This public sphere makes unlikely the resolution of conflicts via rational agreement, but it "nevertheless recognizes the legitimacy" of opposition (52). The art practices involved in the Zapatista movement, the Battle of Seattle, the Occupy movements, and the current Black Lives Matter movement, particularly strong in the U.S. and Canada, have addressed in their participatory and network outlook questions of justice, governance, citizenship, human rights, and cultural differences. As artistic and intellectual claims from within these movements make clear, the above issues are pushed forward to be debated and negotiated in different local, but also transnational and transcultural, contexts in an open and agonistic public discourse – in a world that needs to be understood as a multi-centered and multiply entangled world.

The current artistic and activist movements that challenge limits and monitoring of public space act against the background of multiple global challenges, menaces, and hazards. One way to conceive of this new interconnectedness is to acknowledge the ongoing devastation of the world. One of the leading proponents of a new cosmopolitan politics, David Held, speaks of "overlapping communities of fate" (2010, 168), denoting that environmental developments such as global warming, natural disasters, and diminishing resources render all people as a world community equally convicted and responsible. In a similar vein, Ulrich Beck uses the term "world risk society" (1999) to address ecological and technological questions of risk shared by all of us, which necessitate political experimentation to form a new type of global morality. Thinkers like Seyla Benhabib have put forth new ideas of a dialogic democracy in a "globalized world of uncertainty, hybridity, fluidity, and contestation" (2002, 186). While all artistic practices claiming public space as a democratic platform differ in radicalness and site-specificity, they unfold their agendas and actions largely within an understanding of dialogic democratic politics.

A recent example of dissident art practice would be the imbrication of art and protest in Oaxaca, Mexico. Street art and graffiti collectives emerged there in 2006 in a riot of visual slogans and statements accompanied by political demonstrations against the State Governor Ulises Ruiz Ortiz and his corrupt administration's violations of civic society. A mix of artists, demonstrators, and spontaneous participants joined to turn the city walls into a colorful canvas of artistic and social protest. Through a new stencil-style collective expression, this movement created new alternative imaginaries. The collective art of stenciling also led to workshops and projects lead among others by artists like Demián Flores that directly engaged with the social critique and political protest in Oaxaca. The coalition of artists and political groups lead to a close collaboration between the APPO (Popular Assembly of the Peoples of Oaxaca) and ASARO (Assembly of Revolutionary Artists of Oaxaca), resulting in the further proliferation of street stencils as a medium for local social struggle (Carillo and Barriendos 2015, 171, 181).

Out of these close ties between politics and street arts emerged the group *La Curtiduría*, which exists today as a cultural center that promotes and defends community life by means of visual and graphic arts (Carrillo and Barriendos 2015, 185). The visual occupation in the streets of Oaxaca meant that the artists created images of important figures of political life in Mexico such as the faces of Benito Juárez, first president of Mexico from Oaxaca and of indigenous origin; revolutionary leader Emiliano Zapata, using the battle cry "The land belongs to those who work it"; and Zapatista rebel Subcommandante Marcos. Mixed in with these depictions were also images of crickets wearing gas masks, young people throwing Molotov cocktails, young women in traditional dresses, and nature depictions such as cornfields (188). The visual art in the streets brought land politics right into the middle of the city, spotlighting issues of indigenous rights, land rights, and access and use of natural resources. The graffiti and street art collectives active in Oaxaca

stand for the political use of art and new public forms of cultural resistance. The activism in Oaxaca at the intersection of public protest
and art has created imaginaries of resistance and community that
have spread throughout the Americas, nourishing communal activism north and south of Mexico.

From Zapatista to the Battle of Seattle and
Occupy Wall Street: interAmerican connectedness

Radical art practice in the twenty-first century shows a strong interAmerican imaginary at its core. The Zapatista movement from
Chiapas in Mexico has influenced in many ways these art and activist practices that connect multiple public spaces on a local and global level. The Zapatista movement was one of the first social movements to claim presence on the internet, propagating networks of
"*convivencia*," solidarity, and communication, bringing together
radical activists from the North and the South. The Zapatista movement managed to bring the Third World Network from the Global
South into dialogue with radical thinkers from Northern labor, ecol-
ogy, and solidarity movements.

Hence, Fernando Coronil observed that "carried along by winds
of history that fan old flames and rouse new struggles, Latin America has become a diverse fabric of collective utopian dreams," linking these to the negotiation of temporalities. "The dialogue between
past and future informing current struggle," he writes, has "challenged place-bound, parochial conceptions of universality and has
generated global exchanges about reimagined worlds [that] now
unite South and North" (2011, 263–264). However, Coronil warns
that these "new imaginings may be co-opted or crushed" (264), giv-
en the unequal power structures within which these phenomena
have occurred. This new North-South coalition fueled the protest in
Seattle, calling both the People's Global Assembly and the World
Social Forum to join for the struggle against neoliberal capitalist
exploitation (McKee 2017, 50–51). The Zapatista movement contained important cultural and artistic elements that have helped fuel

the imagination of protest movements in the South and North. They emphasized the importance of the local in global times, projecting cultural elements like masks and dialogues with ancestral spirits to give their political protest a culturally anchored site. In addition, they used the internet to push their surreal politics of revolution and embraced artistically carnivalesque and socially provocative practices of political action around the globe, fueling also the imagination of the Critical Art Ensemble (CAE). Artists like Ricardo Dominguez and the CAE build on artistic rebels like Henry David Thoreau in challenging the semiotic codes of global politics and free trade in manifestoes such as *Electronic Civil Disobedience*. Net art became a tool for interfering with the digital networks of corporate and governmental institutions, as websites and internet servers were hacked. The artistic quality of Zapatista expressed through their surreal poetics opened venues for rethinking art, the public, and practices of social protest.

At first glance, Chiapas and Manhattan are worlds apart. The Zapatista movement and the Occupy movement seem equally distant. Both managed to capture worldwide attention, though. The imaginaries created by the Zapatista movement, with its mix of surrealist poetics and politics, have shaped grassroots visions of community-building and resistance against corruption and oppressive structures around the world. Many rich conjunctions of public art and the politics of democracy emerged in the period from the late 1980s, with the fall of the social welfare state, to the late 1990s. The Zapatista movement inspired major movements in the North against the neoliberal politics of exploitation. A watershed event occurred right at the turn to the new millennium in 1999. The Battle of Seattle highlighted the friction underneath contemporary capitalism at the level of trade policy and global economy (53).

And the Battle of Seattle also showed interAmerican imaginaries at work in the attempts to rethink the public sphere and the functions of radical art. From the Zapatista Revolution to the Battle of Seattle and the "Carnival Against Capital" in Quebec City during April 2001, imaginaries from the Global South fed the protest movements in the Northern hemisphere of the Americas. One can see this with the puppetry and street theater that were brought to Seattle by a group that would prove crucial to the Seattle project. A network of anarchist artists extending along the West coast from the United States to Canada, the group Art and Revolution were instrumental in weaving together various direct action-oriented environmental groups and various autonomous groups, thus launching the Direct Action Network (McKee 2017, 56). Artists took the lead in reporting for the media networks via Indymedia and strategizing actions. Puppetry took center stage as a specific form of street theater that embraced what is known as anti-closure in the art world. It rejected the solemnity and elitism of contemporary art and its related art historical self-references so often associated with postmodern artistic expression. Instead, puppet theatre fostered dialogue with the audience, encouraged direct participation, and celebrated the joy of communal artistic endeavor (56). Seattle became a showcase for art's multifaceted power to claim public spaces at the intersection of political, environmental, and artistic engagement. As McKee succinctly puts it, "Seattle opened a new horizon of aesthetics and politics" (58). A mix of carnivalesque puppet theatre, banners and costumes, Indymedia's self-organized public sphere, the action logics of internet shutdown, and the Yes Men's cyber inventions created an artistically based movement against neoliberal governance, Wall Street, The World Bank, and similar institutions.

The Battle for Seattle made clear that public space and the public sphere had taken on new complexity, fragmentation, and diversity as art created, claimed, and multiplied new forms of public spaces at the dawn of the new millennium.

Cultural creativity and the transformation of public spaces

With the turn to the twenty-first century, we witness the rise of the artivist (a synthesis of artist and activist). Artivism as a concept emerged from a 1997 gathering of Chicano artists from East Los Angeles and Zapatistas in Chiapas, Mexico, and it has hence become an umbrella term in the Americas for socially engaged artistic expression that bridges music, literature, and arts with community work (Raussert 2019, Interview with Quetzal Flores). With Cynthia Nikitin (2015), I share the conviction that "cultural creativity may well be the driving force of community revitalization in the twenty-first century. It promises more adaptive ways of seeing, understanding, experiencing, and transforming where we live, how we work, and what we dream."[1]

In the contemporary period, there is an increasing presence of art practices that reshape the social by reformulating, designing, and infiltrating public spaces as spaces of social encounter, aesthetic contemplation, and social and political interaction. Urban planning feeds on interAmerican dialogues. Ideas for new urban planning follow transversal flows, and what characterizes most of them is the important role that social and cultural creativity play in rethinking urban space. In Latin American and U.S. American cities these creative forms engage new communal forms within and against the commodification of public spaces. Spanning projects in Argentina, Brazil, Chile, Colombia, Peru, and Venezuela, the urban network and exhibition *Building Optimism: Public Space in South America* investigates ways that emerging architects and designers can trigger social change through designing public space. Drawing on visual arts such as photography, video, drawings, and models, the exhibition creatively immerses visitors in an understanding of how public spaces become social spaces – sites that respond to the unique circumstances and pressures of their communities (Exhibit 2016). Similarly, in 2013 the Detroit Economic Growth Corporation won a grant from ArtPlace America to display art in vacant storefronts and underperforming public spaces on a stretch of Livernois Avenue, between Seven and Eight Mile Roads in Detroit. The Revolve Detroit program engaged art and entrepreneurship to creatively transform the look of Detroit's historic neighborhoods. In collaboration

---

1   https://www.pps.org/article/creative-communities-and-arts-based-place-making.

with community and local groups the program brought forth the Livernois Community Storefront project, which functions as an urban site to connect and engage the local community on a regular basis. With its theater performances, poetry slams, design festivals, and art studios, it has helped business and culture thrive along this historic Avenue of Fashion, turning it into a place where entrepreneurship and artivism meet and dialogue.[2]

Finally, in the contemporary period, art practices also develop a strong sense of reflexivity about the public space itself. Artists turn to the grid as the fundamental matrix for urban structure and development and employ that grid in performative practices and artistic design as a tool for rethinking the subject's relationship to public space and public history. The grid as a skeleton of public space in the Americas becomes a laboratory for revisiting the utopian and dystopian dimensions of the Americas in their particularities and entanglements. As Darko Suvin reminds us, "Utopias are not flawless … Instead true utopias inspire transformation by envisioning how norms and individual relations are organized on a more perfect principle" (1988, 55). Numerous artists, among them Coco Fusco, Guillermo Gómez-Peña, and Kendrick Lamar revisit the grid, a material and metaphorical structure that represents utopia's original spatial design in the Americas, challenging and revising it through artistic practice and performance. By means of material and virtual installations, and literary, musical, and bodily performances, artists and artivists use the grid to recreate the social in the Americas against the backdrop of conflictive and productive interconnectedness.

When the world seemed to become one open public space

In November 1989, the Berlin wall came down. For a night and a day, the streets of Berlin became a seemingly boundless urban space. People climbed over the wall, danced on top of it, tore down parts of it; graffiti sprayers attached messages of freedom and

---

2   http://www.dcdc-udm.org/projects/catalysts/lightuplivernois/.

brotherhood, street artists broke the greyness of stones with colorful imagery. For many the world temporarily had turned into one open public space. For some in the West, utopia was fulfilled; for others in the East, another utopia had crashed into demise. Some declared the beginnings of a new free world, and others predicted the end of history. All lasted for only a little while, as the expanding neoliberal global markets created new divides, new conflicts, new inequality, and new walls. The attack on the Twin Towers on September 11, 2001 marked a violent climax in the struggles over power constellations in public space, here taking place in a new dimension. Public space was no longer contested in primarily horizontal terms. A new vertical dimension illustrated that public space in the new millennium had become a more complex, multiplied, multilayered, and multidirectional imaginary. In addition, the new expanding virtual spaces created new terrain for further differentiation. Art today reflects and responds to the new divisions and creates new imaginaries of public space in dispute, challenge, dialogue, and development.

Art and public space have collided and fused in changing relations in the new millenium. Art very much pursues site-specific events that have global implications. Art also asserts its presence in sites of conflict and crisis. One can see this in the Occupy movement, established itself in Manhattan's Wall Street, a symbolical and material center for global divisions between rich and poor, and a suitable location for protest and performance. Selecting the U.S.-Mexican border as a site for exhibits and performances, artists and artivists like Silvia Gruner, Guillermo Gómez-Peña, Quetzal Flores, and Martha Gonzalez have created new triads of site as cause, site as performance, and site as transcendence. During the 2006 protests against the corrupt governor in Oaxaca, Mexico, artists occupied the streets and spread their art and messages in the face of the menacing police and military presence. It is safe to say that art continues to claim its public role and occupies public spaces, whether it is commissioned or trespassing. The site-specific concepts of art and performance can be transmitted via today's media to translocal and global audiences.

Smartphones, blogs, internet videos, etc. transport local events into wide reaching networks of information. They also provide the basis for simultaneous forms of broadcasting and participation. New media illustrate that art has occupied the virtual space as an important public space for spreading aesthetics and political ideas on a global scale. Interactive forms of creating, sharing, and protesting challenge earlier democratic models. Virtual space is a site for aesthetic, economic, and political combat. While it helps to push neoliberal economics by speeding up the process of trade without borders, it also opens up spaces for grassroots social movements and related artistic efforts to impact local politics through the participatory appeal of global networks. Access to virtual space certainly mirrors power divisions between the Global North and the Global South, but at the same time it facilitates stronger links, more rapid exchanges, and mutual participatory projects between the two. This links various public spaces in the net and turns the public sphere into a multilayered, multi-sited complex beyond local or national control. Public space has become fluid, multiply combated, and difficult to control by single actors (cf. Bauman 2000).

Everyday life and art's ubiquitous presence in the streets

Public space has become the largest art gallery in the twenty-first century, exposing public art's dependencies on, and entanglements and exchanges with, commerce, the art market, local and global politics, urban development, and community-building. The omnipresence of street art in cities around the world shows the cutting-edge role of "American" public art in recent global developments. With their long trajectory of art and sign systems in streets and public places, the Americas are a propelling force behind a newly aestheticized and politicized urbanity. Collaboration and participation are the prominent markers of public art's current development, and street art has created a trans-American tapestry of aesthetic and political conquest of public spaces by street art cultures from Argentina to Canada. This process began in the 1970s but reached a new intensity and level of expansion in the twenty-first century. As walking various cities in the Americas reveals, art in the streets has experienced a renaissance. At the intersection of artistic expression and political commentary, graffiti, spray paint, posters, and murals infuse contemporary urban life with new visual semiotics. The city's public spaces are increasingly shaped by symbolic appropriation by grassroots movements, activists, and artists (Youkhana and Förster 2015, 7).

In urban centers in the Americas, street art, graffiti, and murals function as a medium for communication, resistance, and commercialization. They act from below and above, flourishing in newly established festivals as well as in subaltern spaces. The renaissance of street art shows the strong degree of interconnectedness of cultural production and social consciousness throughout the Americas (Raussert 2017). As a cultural practice that cherishes open air and public exposure, street art continues to shape urban communal developments and the aesthetic formation of a pluralistically conceived public sphere.

With respect to community-building, collaboration between street artists has gained new prominence, and community practice crosses local and transnational boundaries. Street art enjoys a major presence on a global scale with local issues at the center of attention (cf. Hunter 2012, 117). Just like the fast–paced developments of creation and destruction in contemporary cities exposed to natural and social impact, street art keeps changing and renewing itself on an almost daily basis. Contemporary graffiti artists such as Guadalajara's Daniel Neufeld are among those who design new directions, look for collaboration, and carry the spirit of street art as aesthetic and political statement into the twenty-first century (Neufeld and Haasser, 2010). One can get a good look at public art practices in the Americas by focusing on four of the grand metropolises in the Americas: Mexico City, New York City, Buenos Aires, and São Paulo. Contemporary street art in Mexico refers back to pre-Columbian roots; at the same time, it is full of local and global references. Artists like Dhear, Seher One, and Saner incorporate elements of regional Mexican wildlife, surrealism, and Japanese comic traditions, imbuing their art with a hallucinatory quality that is commonly associated with a psychedelic sense of place.

The muralist movement, started among others by Diego Rivera, José Clemente Orozco, and David Siqueiros in the 1920s, marks contemporary muralism's modern beginnings (cf. chapter II). These murals, commissioned and promoted by the Mexican government for their nationalistic, political, and social messages, can still be seen both inside and outside public buildings in Mexico City (Schacter 2013, 98). Contemporary street art in Mexico City eclectically builds on predecessors such as pre-Columbian art, the modernist Mexican mural movement, and open air murals of the 1950s done by John Gorman. While street artists in Mexico have a long history of collaborating with governmental institutions and academia, the tragic student massacre at Tlatelolco in 1968 ushered in a different wave of protest graffiti, posters, and murals. Graffiti in Mexican cities like Mexico City and Guadalajara experienced a punk wave in the 1970s. It became widespread with the arrival of hip hop culture on Mexican soil. In contemporary times, artists like Dhear, Neuzz, Sego, Seher One, and Saner shape the direction of the New School of Mexican Muralism.

These artists are representative of the contemporary diversity in Mexican street art. They share a compassion for phantasmagoric visual worlds. Dhear's murals depicts a permanent transformation of characters and animals. Sego brings street art adaptations of Oaxacan wildlife from the coastal area to the metropolis. Seher One integrates Japanese comic characters and global surrealism. Saner innovates pursues innovation and experiment via references to Nahual shamanic figures. Neuzz transforms characters and animals from indigenous folklore and Mexican popular culture with a mix of spray paint in urban street art expressions. Contemporary collaborative projects like *Intersticios Urbanos* by Said Dokins and Laura Garcia foster cooperation with other leading street artists from Argentina, Columbia, and Chile, thus sharing, expanding, and changing techniques and motifs, and developing new conceptualizations of what the public is.

New York City has exerted a major influence on independent public art, especially in the 1970s. In the twenty-first century, it remains a center for street artists, as well as creators of illicit art. While street art and graffiti flourish in cities from Toronto to San Francisco, it is New York that remains one of the world's most energetic and pioneering sites in the development of new styles and directions. From the early pioneers of spray can art such as Blade, Cost and Revs, Dondi, and Reas to contemporary practitioners like Espo, Katsu, and Swoon, New York continues as a hotbed of artistic innovation. The city had a head-start with respect to art in the streets in the 1970s. The graffiti movement's center was the subway and thus could spread rapidly throughout the city. Through the work of artists like Jean Michel Basquiat and Keith Haring, contemporary street art gained the art world's recognition. *Subway Art*, a film and book project released by Henry Chalfant and Martha Cooper in 1984, introduced New York graffiti to the world and helped make it a global movement. Revolting against the New York elite's efforts to keep the trains and the city clean, graffiti in the late 1980s returned to the streets. Writers like Joz and Easy artistically occupied public space. Artistic partnerships like Cost and Revs brought art in the street back to the art world's interest in downtown New York City. Particularly after the attacks of September 11 in 2001, the popular appeal of art in New York streets rekindled – with newly politically charged messages – and triggered of another global boom (Schacter 2013, 15–17).

The street art in Buenos Aires is closely associated with economic and political crisis. Stencils exploded as a fast and effective form of protest against the military junta in Argentina between 1976 and 1983. They experienced a second boom in the city streets during the economic crash of 2001. By that time the city of Buenos Aires was already rich in graffiti, on houses, walls, and most of all, public trains (Schacter 2013, 128–129). There is a strong nucleus of street artists in Buenos Aires. The city's native hip hop graffiti artists like The DOMA collective, Chu Gualicho, and NERF use various media such as stencils, paint, blow-up cartoon figures, large scale, and the Southern American medium of latex paint. A striking mobile presence can be seen in the hand-painted buses in Buenos Aires. There is a strong collective ethos in the street art scene that is also welcoming to visiting artists. It is not surprising, then, that artists from Peru like Entes and Pésimo, the Chilean group, AISLA, and the Paraguayan artist Oz have collaborated in street art projects. As Schacter has it, "Buenos Aires remains a hothouse for Latin American street art's ceaseless inventions" (129). While local issues are addressed, there continues to grow a transcultural consciousness of opposing inequality, injustice and exclusion in the context of the above artistic collaborations.

In São Paulo, Brazil, *Pichação* originated in the 1950s. It has become to Latin American graffiti what wildstyle means to graffiti in the U.S. and Canada. In street artist circles in the Americas, *Pichação* still marks a subcultural frontier between North and South (Schacter 2013, 113). Using abseiling and free-climbing techniques, the artists formed an activist protest movement that projected political messages and names of crews in the form of a cryptic alphabet on tall public buildings. They also exerted a major influence on hip hop graffiti writers such as Os, Vitché, and Zezao (to name but a few) who took center stage within the street art of Brazil in the 1980s. With the current political and economic crisis in Brazil, the net between political activism and art in the public has become bigger and tighter. This includes protest against long established patriarchal structures. Female artists like Jana Joana, Nína, Anarkia, and Fefe Talavera have gained prominence in the street art scenes of São Paulo and Rio de Janeiro. Artists in São Paulo hold on to subversive acts by going out with young graffiti crews to spread spray paint letters and latex based murals. Zezao literally works underground and transforms São Paulo's subterranean tunnels into galleries. Os Gemeos, a graffiti artist duo, developed mix styles of *Pichação*, national folklore, local symbols, and New York City-style graffiti that are instantly recognizable; their huge characters look down from tall buildings in São Paulo.

This style has also gone global, promoting Brazilian art in the streets worldwide. For instance, *The Giant in Boston*, a mural Os Gemeos installed in Boston in 2012, portrays a bizarre urban character wearing bright, colorful and mismatched clothing, his face wrapped in a scarf that reveals only his squinting eyes. This half-masked face created public debate and controversy when Christian communities felt threatened by what they saw as a stylized promotion of Muslim Arab culture. The mural was painted on an air intake structure on the Greenway in downtown Boston's Dewey Square and received plenty of controversial attention, as its cross-cultural expression provoked both admiration and rejection. The controversy illustrates that public art functions as matrix for renegotiating public space and contemplating the question of whose public space it is.[3]

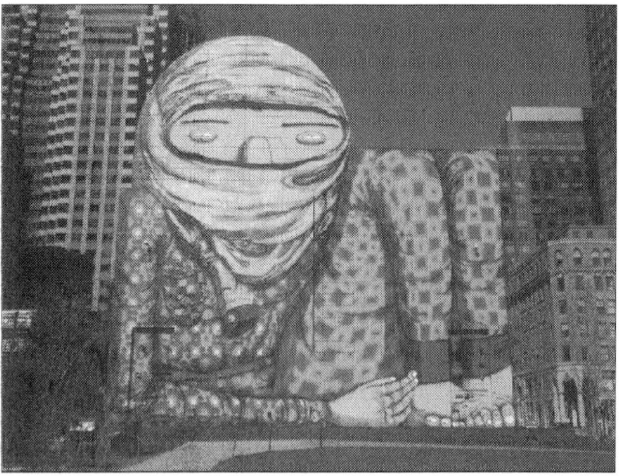

Figure 1: *The Giant in Boston* (©Wilfried Raussert, Boston 2013).

---

3   https://www.reuters.com/article/entertainment-us-usa-boston-mural/
    colorful-brazilian-mural-stirs-controversy-in-boston-idUSBRE8771NH
    20120809.

Collective and cooperative approaches to artistic expression as well as social critique characterize much of the contemporary graffiti and street art scene. In cities like New York, Rio de Janeiro, Mexico City, Oaxaca, and Santiago de Chile, huge communicative networks on a local and global scale support the artistic activity of street artists and graffiti writers. In addition, digital, communal, and body practices like performances legitimate street art culture. The network has increased recently due to a growing scholarly and intellectual interest in street art and its aesthetic and political significance. No longer respected simply by local communities, street art is now diffused through curators, exhibits, and museums, as well as scholarly books that have mushroomed in the market recently. Festival culture has embraced street art with events in New York, Guadalajara, and Rio de Janeiro.

Brazil may be the most prolific example that street art has also caught the attention of multinational companies seeking to promote their products with the flair of youth culture and alternative culture. This has led to collaborations in Rio de Janeiro between such companies as Adidas, Converse, Nike, and Pullman and the Urban art group in Rio's "Urban Art Core" event, a festival of graffiti culture and entrepreneurial spirit with open air exhibits in the courtyard of the Modern Art Museum (Ventura 2015, 135). Another public is addressed here. This includes lovers of art, tourists, and entrepreneurs. Nevertheless, the graffiti and street art culture that emerged from the *favelas* continues to make influential appeals for individual and communal recognition and resistance. In 1997, graffiti workshops and performances emerged in Rio de Janeiro, precisely in the urban periphery and low-income zone. The initial context was the Brazilian rap and drug scene led largely by the rapper drug dealer Marcio Amaro. Artists like Fabio Ema held workshops out of which artist collectives such as *Artistas Urbanos* [Urban Artists] and *Nacao* [Nation] launched their communal projects (131).

Fabio Ema is the best example for showing that, in Brazil, street art and graffiti have become vital assets to education and identity politics, from workshops for children in the *favelas* to events in public schools, prisons, and the poorest quarters of Rio de Janeiro. The case of Brazil demonstrates that the street is actually reaching into the institutions, and that street art and graffiti are important forms of self-expression before they enter larger social and political realms. One example is the work of Pamela Castro, a well-known painter and activist from within the *favelas*, who founded the organization *Rede Nami*. Her work combines the personal with the collective and wants to uplift the situation of women in Rio's *favelas*, to protect them from verbal and physical violence, to enlighten them about their rights as citizens, and to help them access services and resources (Ventura 2015, 131–132). Her visual art work that began in the Urban Art Workshop publicly supports women's rights to abortion, self-protection, and equal citizenship. In Brazil, we witness a conflictive yet vital coexistence of institutionalized, marketed, and resistant street art cultures; the street goes far indeed. Yet, it is important to remember that growing social and economic inequality means that some streets are not open for all.

From Basquiat, a world famous street artist welcomed into the temples of high art, to the *grafiteros* from Oaxaca who have reached out to galleries and museums, urban movements have a tendency to reduce their immediate political visibility and live on in the field of cultural production. This has been frequently criticized as a retreat from the street and a form of selling out to the art market. While it is true that they are hundreds of people more walking the streets than visiting museums, one can read the collaborations with art institutions also as an attempt to change the fields of cultural production and diffusion. Street art's recent entry into the museums has led to a change of context but not of texture; street art continues to have a vibrating presence in the streets. We can view this as an extension of the street into the museum in which it, luckily, cannot be confined. The question remains, however, as to how much more social visibility street art and graffiti art may gain in the context of galleries and museums.

Having received recognition from governments, companies, and museums, street art represents one of the most powerful forms of cultural creativity in contemporary times. Against all odds of segregation, ghettoization, and exclusion that we witness in urban developments across the Americas, street artists work hard to make public spaces fluid: streets, plazas, and (temporary) open spaces become venues for dance classes, football games, races, and ceremonies; in the logic of street art's transformative power, sidewalks become front row seats for people watching, promenading, and participating in conversations and spontaneous get-togethers. Importantly, cultural creativity in the streets aims to create democratic, equitable spaces open to everyone – in which most, if not all, can participate.

In *Arte y Color Para Rescatar México* [Art and Color to Save Mexico], Laura Uribe illustrates new networks between the economy, urban politics, and street artists (2017, 125–129). This project demonstrates that contemporary art is more than ever part of networks and participation culture. Eight cities and 700,000 people, as Uribe tells us, benefitted from the project *"Comex Por un México Bien Hecho"* [Comex For A Well Done Mexico]. In times of crisis due to narcotrafficking, transmigration, and growing social divides, this projects marks a new local and national effort to improve urban living conditions. The Mexican paint company Comex seeks to restore places in risk areas and give them back to the community. A national initiative that includes artists from other countries (primarily Latin American), it uses paint and visual signature as the most elemental tool in the recovery of declining urban spaces, filling them with colorful art. The goal is to create a new social ambience that is familiar and helps to empower new communal structures. The project took off in mid-2016 and has been implemented in cities such as Zacatecas, Puebla, Mexico City, Guadalajara, and Nuevo Léon.

Participatory structures are essential for making art part of the community and the community part of art. Hence the inhabitants of each community contribute actively to the artistic restorative work done in the streets. Around 700,000 people have been exposed to these transformative activities in at-risk urban spaces. The artistic work is embedded in a larger structure of social cultural work. The creation of murals also includes additional workshop initiatives on civil coexistence and risk awareness. The collaboration between universities (e.g. Tecnológico de Monterrey), federal state, and municipal governments shows that art once again plays a central role for community-building across economic, political, and cultural divides. In Chiapas 21, national and international artists collaborated in the painting of the *Ciudad Mural Tuxtla* [City Mural Tuxtla]. More than sixty volunteers and forty people who joined the artists to help paint underscored the participatory nature of this urban rescue initiative. Among the volunteers were many children and adolescents. By December 2017, Comex had invested 33,000 liters of paint in around 90,000 square meters of wall space Mexico, with the collaboration of more than 600 artists. As a result of this initiative, inhabitants of those urban zones previously considered risky – Iztapalapa in Mexico City, Casitas in Tuxtlá, Guiterrez – have reclaimed spaces that are now recreational and, most significantly, have become useful and appealing for people living in them.

As the above examples have shown, different centers combine to form an expanding interAmerican and transAmerican map of street art, highlighting the flows from South to North, North to South. In dialogue with distinct local urban cultures, transcultural collaborations between artivists and artists from different regions and nations increasingly permit us to think the Americas as a visually entangled space nourished by crosscultural influences.

Rethinking public space: art practices at sites of mobility and sites of tourist attraction

As a response to and reflection of mobility in times of accelerated globalization, art practices have entered and transformed airports, train stations, metro stations and bus stations as sites of mobility that connect local and global aspects of culture. These sites are intersections for flows of people, ideas, and goods in everyday life. Art seeks these sites as potential platforms for mobilizing ideas of community, social connectedness, and inclusion. Seizing the opportunity for outreach in these highly frequented locations, art practices recreate the social within everyday mobility. Performances and installations frequently fuse historical consciousness, communal vision, aestheticization of everyday culture. Public music performances like Quetzal's "Tragafuegos" at a bus station in Los Angeles express new forms of community-building, taking into account the elements of cultural change, exchange, and diasporic experience. As the Youtube video *Here and Now: Quetzal "Tragafuegos"* shows, the lyrics, music, and performance in the event turn the bus stop into a vibrant contact zone for different people on their travels.[4] The music event self-reflexively performs the effervescence of communal bonding. Art practice here enters the social space as a surprising act of slowing down mobility. The performance of the band members includes participatory elements that invite passersby to enter a transitory circle of music-making. Most important, the performance establishes sound and rhythm as a community-building force in the usually anonymous public space of rapid transit, transforming a "non-place" (Auge 1995) into a social contact zone with potential for inclusion, participation, and dialogue.

Art practice in public space has become a common educational tool to spread culture and history on the fly, so-to-speak. A cooperation between the Atlantic History Center, Georgia State University, and airport art at Atlanta Hartfield International Airport has produced changing collaborative exhibitions that comprise a multitude of artistic genres and expressions, creating a postmodern synthesis of museum, archive, and art gallery in Concourse E of the Atlanta Hartfield International Airport. In the fall of 2011, the Atlanta History Center, in cooperation with Heritage Preservation students from Georgia State University, launched the exhibition "Atlanta History," which presented major steps in the city's development in ten thematic sections. The purpose behind the exhibition is to show the cultural heritage and historical significance of the city and its region. As the general showcase of the Atlanta History exhibition announces, "The subjects are as diverse as the people of Atlanta and

---

4   https://www.youtube.com/watch?v=c4YqrJuDmTE.

the events that have shaped the city" (Showcase, Atlanta, 21. Nov. 2012). While the exhibits emphasize local color and locality, they unfold a global interconnectedness by including international artists who have chosen Atlanta as a temporary or permanent home.

Why stop and think more about the conceptualization of these exhibits in such highly frequented public sites of mobility? The presence of art fills these "non-places" with social meaning. This peculiar mix of museum, art gallery, and transit zone lets us experience locally and globally entangled histories while we are on the move. The encounter between traveler and conceptual art and history project triggers individual and collective journeys of cultural memory and aesthetic vision. Many of the artistic and historic pieces from the 2013 showcases highlight the strong presence of African American culture in the South and underscore African American cultural, political, and economic achievement in Atlanta and the rest of Georgia. They highlight Atlanta's pivotal role not only for black cultural and artistic expression but underscore the city's important history of black entrepreneurship, struggle, and political agency. And they refer to the rich musical traditions such as the blues that have emerged from the American South and changed popular music throughout the world.

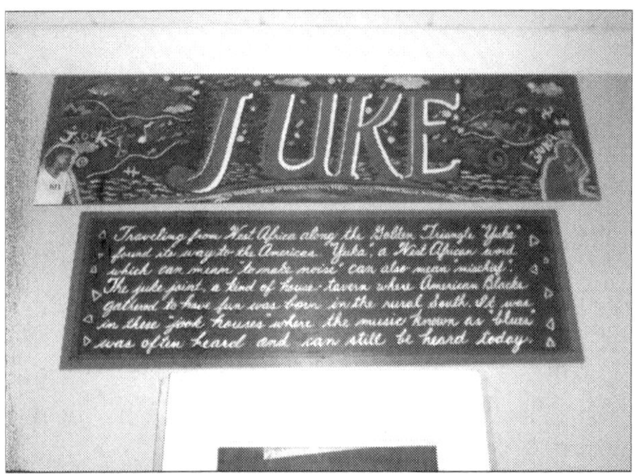

Figure 2: "Juke tabloid," Atlanta Airport, 2013 (© Wilfried Raussert).

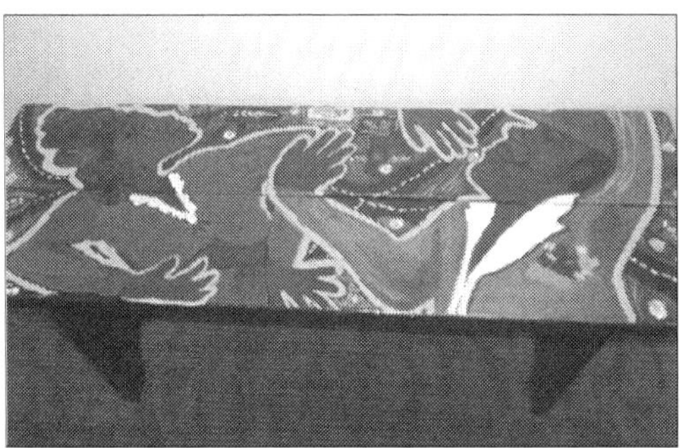

Figure 3: "Juke joint bench," Atlanta Airport, 2013 (© Wilfried Raussert).

Likewise, they function as a gateway to the larger American South, its global embeddedness, and its still peculiar position on the U.S. cultural and political spectrum. Many artifacts greet the arriving international traveler even before she reaches customs and immigration. By depicting landscape, nature, city, history, and cultural production, the exhibits conceptualize a holistic approach to the city, state, and larger region of the American South. Art practices in the airport represent an educational tool as well as a platform for promoting tourism and economic investment.

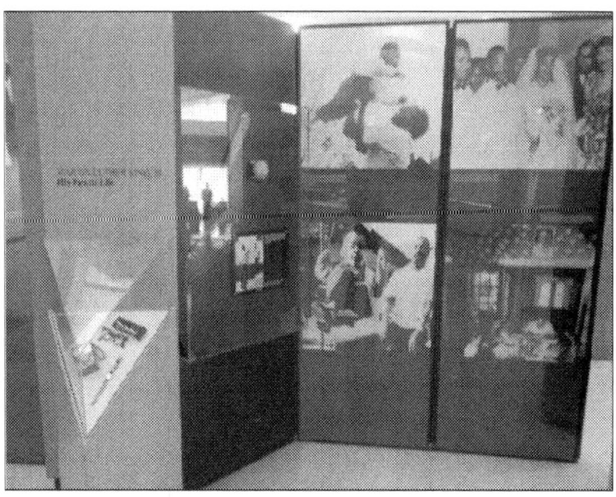

Figure 4: "Martin Luther King showcase," Atlanta Airport, 2014
(© Wilfried Raussert).

Airports are nodal points of global movement and mobility studies, as Peter Adey reminds us, and, thus "[they] are indicative of the increasingly mobile world in which we live, and must owe its momentum to the popular fluid and mobile thought of philosophers such as Gilles Deleuze, Feliz Guattari, Ian Chambers and Paul Virillio" (2002, 501). Adey concludes that "this new paradigm [of living] has moved beyond static idealizations of society towards theories that are marked by terms such as nomadism, displacement, speed and movement" (501). The showcases of the city and region's history redirect the traveler to the past. The various exhibitions and installations record the region's cultural production of past and present and install artistic visions of migration and mobility in the Americas and beyond, encouraging the traveler's reflection on these topics. By engaging with these art projects, he or she moves in and out of entangled temporalities. These temporalities emerge from the triad of history's obsession with the past, art's enthusiasm for vision and abstraction, and the traveler's interrupted and redirected motion in time and space as spectator.

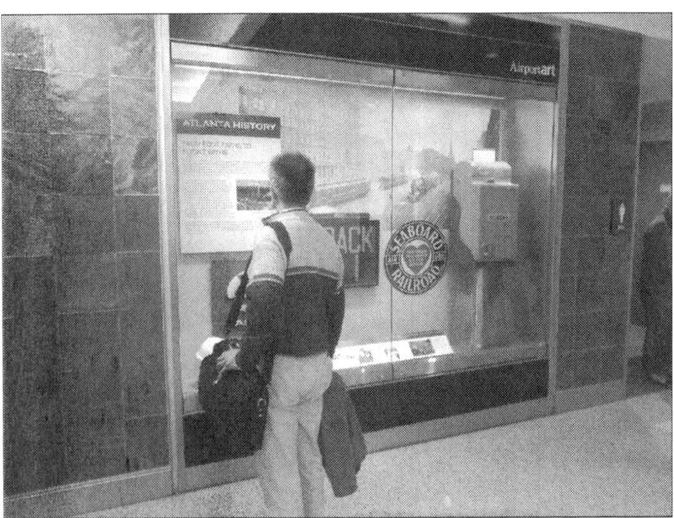

Figure 5: "Traveler and Atlanta history showcase," Atlanta Airport, 2014 (© Wilfried Raussert).

The exhibitions of photographs, paintings, and installations function as a changing historical archive and visualized aesthetic reflection of culture in process. Exploring the nexus between global mobility and locality, the exhibits visually transfer the city with its local and global connections into the heart of the airport. A sense of the social as the site of home, work, and production collides with a notion of the social as mobile. The art practices expose and renegotiate the power of cultural and social creativity even in sites of transit. Potentially, a new vision of the social emerges in this temporary contact zone, as subject and culture are equally thrown into a state of mobilization.

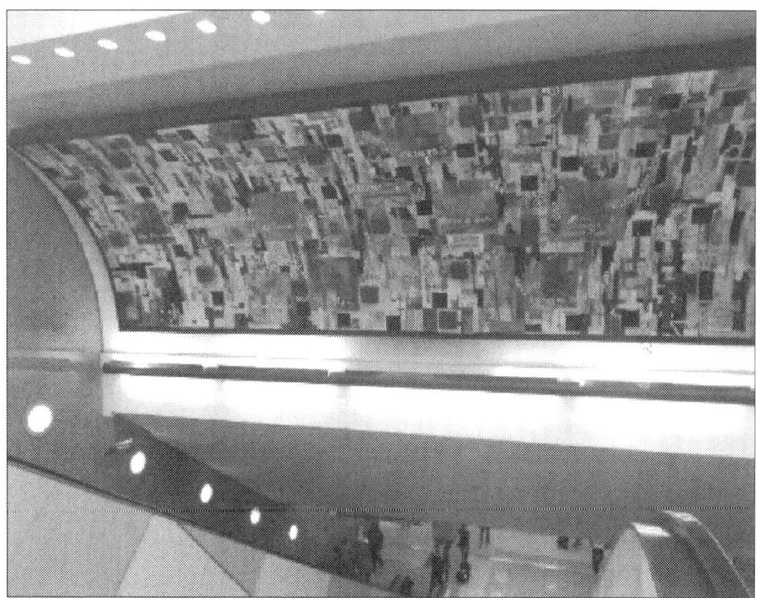

Figure 6: "Saints," Atlanta Airport, 2013 (© Wilfried Raussert).

Installed between the ground floor and the E-platform in 1996, the *Saints* mural by Brad Radcliff nicely illustrates these forms of mobilization. In patchwork style, the mural expresses horizontal and vertical movements. The mural explores the theme of migration by incorporating old photos, stencil, symbols of power, paint, and text about various aspects of African American culture. The traveler herself views the mural in an upward or downward movement on the stairway, thus physically and aesthetically moving through time and space. The airport becomes a site in which bodies and aesthetics are put in motion in a steady process of connection and disconnection. While the airport as public space is extremely controlled and monitored, through art it gains new potential for envisioning relations between self, other, and place.

As John Urry suggests in a blueprint for the study of mobility, "the turn [to mobility studies] connects the analyses of different forms of travel, transport, and communication with the multiple ways in which economic and social life is performed and organized through time and various spaces" (2007, 6). Defining the mobility turn as "post-disciplinary," Urry not only refers to the transdisciplinary potential of a focus on mobility studies but also highlights "how all social entities, from a single household to large scale corporations, presuppose many different forms of actual and potential movement" (6). The exhibition awaits the airport traveler in his transition from one place to another and piques his curiosity for a place behind the site of transit. By bringing the city's culture and history into the airport, the Atlanta History and Airport Art Project transforms the site from a "non-place" (Auge 1995; Bender 2001, 78) into a place of cultural, historical, and social importance. Seen through the cultural production of the exhibit, the airport takes on the important function of mediator between local and the global, the local history and the global traveler. While the traveler moves toward a future destination, the history showcases not only interrupt the sojourner's progressive move; they nudge him to project himself back in time. They invite him to reconsider public space as a sphere beyond consumption, and the transit zone as a site of heritage, culture, and education.

Reclaiming tourist spots as cultural and historical markers: New York, Havana, Tijuana

A central feature of contemporary performance art is to reclaim public spaces that have become popular tourist spots. While these public places present performances geared especially toward the tourist gaze, artists and activists transform them by a new dissident element of critique and protest. Edgar Heap of Birds works with and about ancestral lands in the U.S. and Canada; he included popular tourist sites like New York in his decolonial remapping of the U.S. in the 1990s. In this multi-sited performance, he presented the U.S. as an occupied territory. Installing site-markers in various public spaces in different U.S. American cities and states, he highlighted the precolonial and colonial divisions of space. With site-markers like "New York Today Your Host Is Shinnecock" he renamed and reclaimed dispossessed ancestral lands (McKee 2017, 47). Tourist pleasure turns into a history lesson, and public space once again becomes a matter of renegotiation. In common with most of Edgar Heap of Birds' public work, "the enameled signs are sited at interfaces of difference" (Fisher n.d., n. pag.).

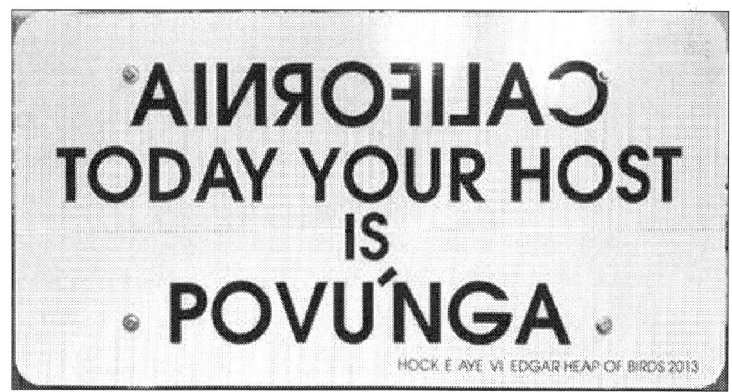

Figure 7: "Today Your Host Is" (© Edgar Heap of Birds, 2013).

These are places of real or symbolic exchange or conflict between alternative usages and meanings of public space, and between Native American and non-Native American historical interpretation.

Critical research and archival works are at the basis of the artist's attentiveness to the sites' temporal and spatial aspects. Public space and any particular locality can only be reinterpreted through the stories and experiences that have created it. As Fisher puts it, "the subversive charge of Heap of Birds' interventions in official history lies both in its usurpation of the power to name and construct meaning and its treatment of the archive as living, not dead space" (n. pag.). Heap of Birds' provocative site-markers take the viewer out of her comfort zone and unravel the long and often forgotten histories of place. In addition, they give public space a dynamic dimension shaped by historical and contemporary cultural encounters and occupations.

Between comfort zone and resistance, religion, popular art, and musical performance mark street life in Cuba's capital Havana. Cuba's revolutionary image, tropical environment, and conflictive embeddedness in global history are just a few reasons why Cuba has become as a hotspot of global tourism. In response to political and economic instability in Cuba, the encounter between art and public space gained new momentum in the late 1980s – the beginning of the Cuban crisis – when politically and socially engaged performance events "exploded in public space" (Fusco 2015, 10). These performances presented critical views on the state of the nation in provocative and unexpected ways.

The arrival of the digital age ushered in a second wave on the island. Political activism and dissident performance art found its outlet on the local and global web. Public and performance art in the context of Cuban tourist culture continues to draw upon a rich spectrum of vernacular performance traditions that abound in Cuban popular culture, in street carnivals, and syncretic religious events and processions. Public space is crucial for giving heightened visibility to these performances of social life and change. For instance, artists like María Magdalena Campos-Pons, Manuel Mendive, Leandro Solo, and Tania Bruguera integrate elements of *santería*, the most widely practiced Afro-Cuban syncretic religion on the island, into their street performances. The performance art seen in the streets in Cuba shows that public space is a battleground for recognition and power, but also a site of belonging and living community. Los Carpinteros' conga line and the gyrating hand-painted dancers of Manuel Mendive's processions brought musical and religious spectacle to the streets in the 1990s. These types of showcased performances used local popular performance traditions and the tropicalized images of Cuba to foster tourism and support the local economy. Artists from the Cuban art-student collectives launched projects to embellish public spaces and reclaim them for public communal living. At the same time, they enhanced aesthetic aspects of art and performance, bringing Cuban art into the global art market (Fusco 2015, 34–35). Steeped in island traditions, popular culture and spirituality fuel and camouflage public performance culture. Hence, tourist events repeatedly turn into frames for performances of social critique and protest. As Coco Fusco emphasizes, "the other principal argument about the notable presence of performance relates to Cuban art pedagogy and its openness to avant-garde practices" (44). A spirit of new critical performance art that emerged in the 1980s and 1990s in Cuba continues to be present in the twenty-first century. Despite continuous censorship, performance artists including rappers, DJs, and visual artists have pushed dissident subcultures into visibility, and these subcultures have a distinctively performative character. For instance, artists and activists use cell phones (legalized in Cuba in 2008) to document their protest performances, including skirmishes with the police related to them. Through this recent online presence, Cuban artivists claim public space on the island as artistic and countercultural territory, and manage to connect their projects with other movements in the Americas and around the globe.

A hot spot for American tourists, Tijuana holds a double position as attractive cultural other and, due to its border location, heterotopic menace to political and social control (Foucault 2002). The latter has particularly intrigued artists and activists to rethink public space in performances, installations, and street art. Challenging borders as major dividing lines between public spaces, the San Diego/Tijuana-based "Border Arts Workshop/Taller de Arte Fronterizo (BAW/TAF)" has become a driving force in questioning national territory, closed public space, and geopolitical imaginaries of North America since the late twentieth century. The group was founded in 1984 by a binational set of artists, activists, intellectuals, journalists, and scholars. Among the founding members were Isaac Artenstein, David Avalos, Sara-Jo Berman, Guillermo Gómez-Peña, Víctor Ochoa, Michael Schnorr, and Jude Ederhart. Many of the BAW/TAF artists were affiliated with San Diego's *Centro Cultural de la Raza*, a Chican@ arts center founded in 1970. Considering "the border" a central theme of their activities, they selected border cities like Tijuana and the very border itself as sites for their performances.

Performing in the heart of Mexican and American border tourism, the group's projects were often carried out with the objective to redefine public space and public sphere in binational dialogues. From the beginning, the group's artistic activities and performances imagined communities beyond the boundary separating the neighboring nations in North America. They addressed social, cultural, political, and economic conflicts emerging from immigration and border politics, forms of exclusion and divisions frequently tearing families and communities apart. Their aim was to create communal visions that could overcome the most conflictive boundary in North America (Prieto 2018, n. pag.). Silvia Gruner's *The Middle of the Road/La mitad del camino* (1992) – made possible by Insite, an organization that commissioned cultural and art projects in the Tijuana-San Diego Region – represented one of the most spectacular ephemeral art installations along the U.S.-Mexican Wall. The piece was created in collaboration with the local community (Oles 2014, 386). Originally from Mexico City, Gruner was drawn to working directly on the border fence. She selected a stretch of fence running along the residential neighborhood of Colonia Libertad in Tijuana. The installation integrated more than a hundred replicas of the Aztec goddess Tlazolteotl in a birthing position on metal stools, which Gruner mounted directly onto the border fence. Gruner used this image of fertility to counter the division and closure of public space.

Near the turn of the twenty-first century, collaborations by the Mexican American artist Guillermo Gómez-Peña and Cuban American artist Coco Fusco used public-space performances to expand the traditional definition of the border, dramatizing a fluid border between colonizing and colonized cultures in the Americas.

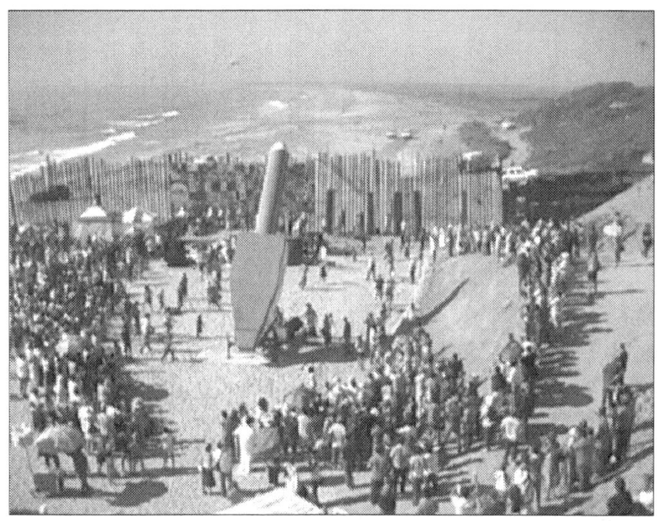

Figure 8: One flew over the void (© Javier Tellez Bala Perdid).

In 2005 Javier Tellez's flying human cannonball across the border in Tijuana territory certainly marked a performative climax in re-thinking mobility in monitored public spaces.

Site-specificity and nomadic extension across the Americas

Contemporary art and performance in public spaces tends to be site-specific and nomadic at the same time. While "the global village utopia" formed the backdrop of many public space performances and artistic conceptions in the 1960s and 1970s, the contemporary scene intensifies existing local-global networks, stressing the importance of site-specificity in combination with larger outreach. Site-specific describes the work of contemporary Mexican artist Rafael Lozano-Hemmer, who fuses art, technology, and public spaces with a direct appeal to the participation of the people. He challenges utopian ideals based on technology and progress, asking whether technology equals progress. Technology serves art to achieve a high degree of accessibility. With technological performance art works "Vectorial Elevation, Relational Architecture" (2000) and "Voz Alta, Relational Architecture" (2008) – the latter commissioned as a memorial for the 1968 student massacre at Tlatelolco –, Lozano-Hemmer invited large numbers of people to participate in his events, which were constructed as "open text[s]" (Flores 2013, 11).

"Voz Alta" returned to the site of the state's crime against the students. The work was conceived as a performance of collective memory shared in public. In the piece, participants spoke freely into a megaphone placed on the *Plaza de las Tres Culturas*, the site of the massacre and a public space symbolically layered with references to multiple historical epochs. The voices of the participants amplified by the megaphone called forth sequences of flashes. A 10 kW searchlight translated the voices in light rays that changed their brightness according to the rising or falling volume of the human voice. As the rays hit the top of the building of the former Ministry of Foreign Affairs, now hosting the cultural center of Tlatelolco, the beams were relayed by three additional searchlights pointed to other public sites like the Zócalo Square and the Monument to the Revolution. The lights silently spread the voices over the roofs of the Mexican metropolis, while 96.1 FM Radio UNAM transmitted the voices in live performance. As Lozano-Hemmer's archive recalls, "the three lights on the building played back recordings of survivors, interviews with intellectuals and politicians, music from 1968, and radio art pieces commissioned by Radio UNAM"[5] when participants were gone and the light on the plaza was off.

The public event mixed archival material with contemporary performance of memory and vision. There was no censorship on the participants' contributions and thousands of people joined the artist

---

5   http://www.lozano-hemmer.com/voz_alta.php.

to pay homage to the victims of 1968. Former student protest entered into dialogue with contemporary protest against governmental corruption and violence related to drug trafficking and sexual abuse. The event was participatory and included statements from witnesses and survivors, street poetry, shout-outs, ad hoc art performances, and calls for protest, but also visions for the future like marriage proposals. The performative in the political (Butler 1997) and the performative in the private joined hands in a spectacle of illuminating memory and sonic protest. The relational architectural design of the performance event made it possible that the light beams, admittedly dependent on weather conditions, could traverse the whole metropolis and turn the act of remembering into a translocal public event. The site-specific character of the event provided a basis for memory work and knowledge production about the tragic event from October 3rd 1968. Likewise, it created a platform for personal, communal, anti-government, anti-hierarchy, and anti-corruption messages to be shared on the radio and as part of the light show.

While this event showed that technology could shrink the metropolis into a focus on local history, Lozano-Hemmer's interactive installation *Vectorial Elevation: Relational Architecture 4*, staged eight years earlier on Mexico's arguably most emblematic public space, the Zócalo, created a global network of participants who artistically welcomed the new millenium. The light show included eighteen searchlights distributed around the perimeter of the plaza. These lights projected beams from 7,000 watt xenon lamps into the evening sky, and Mexico City provided the urban scene in which lights could be observed from a radius of fifteen kilometers. While the megaphone could be heard only at the site, the light show on the Zócalo could be seen around the globe through an interactive internet site. Although a space-time fusion (Harvey 1989) creating a complete simultaneity could not be achieved, a sequence of globally created designs projected into the sky. Web users all over the world would access an online interface both to create and watch designs through three-dimensional simulation. Their creations were stored in a queue and sequentially projected "in real time and space" (Flores 2013, 7). Each design lasted for six seconds before being re-placed by the next light image. The interactive concept emphasized creativity, process, motion, and participation. It denied structures of center, hierarchy, and power. Neither the installation's mastermind Lozano-Hemmer, nor any of the web users, could control the sequence in which the designs appeared.

The project comprised more than 700,000 internet participants from eighty-nine countries, marking a milestone in public art history. How many millions of people witnessed the light shows during the two-week project in Mexico City can only be guessed. The public spaces envisioned were virtual and real. Neither the overall concept nor the individual designs could lay a claim for utopia. Rather, the installation manifested a desire for global self-expression. For Lozano-Hemmer technology serves as a medium of participatory culture and a horizontal approach to knowledge production and memory work. It is no longer loaded with a clear-cut vision of progression. He designs and temporarily occupies public spaces, making them spaces of motion and interconnection, without fixed design but with shifting sites of agency. The meaning of the memory work or artistic expression emerges in dialogue with the spectators as participants. Each spectator and each action adds new levels of meaning. His art is participatory but far from utopic. The participation denies control. Neither the individual nor the collective has a definitive say in the visual, sonic, and semiotic messages produced. Lozano-Hemmer keeps challenging the reign of the individual artist and "the utopic ideals of collectivism" (Flores 2013, 11).

Hemmer-Lozano's work is just one important example of the high level of creativity in Latin America in regards to designing political spectacle, which also shines through in examples of earlier public art events. *Ay South America* and *Poem Rains*, two examples from Chile, represent memory work and new visions for the artistic use of air space. As with Lozano-Hemmer's projects, site-specificity and nomadic diffusion characterize these performances in different contexts of recent Chilean history. In Chile, the return to democracy in 1990 also meant the beginning of neo-liberal policies to steer the country's economy and promote its image abroad. Street art as a form of social protest has a long trajectory in Chile, from the early workshops of *Siqueiros* in the 1940s, through the performances protesting the Pinochet dictatorship, to contemporary art collectives that push new communal ideas and concepts of socioeconomic justice in times of democratically framed neoliberal economics and politics.

The current artist collectives' invasion of the public sphere is certainly less daring and dangerous than it would have been in times of state repression, but it is no less imaginative and radical in its occupancy of public space. The Casagrande collective builds upon earlier radical artistic and political projects like *Ay Sudamérica* [Ay South America]. Signifying on the bombing of poems over Santiago de Chile in 1981 – an artistic air strike protesting the Pinochet dictatorship's violence and repression, referring specifically to the regime's bombing of the Government Palace to remove the government of the *Unidad Popular* – Casagrande launched a similar initiative in the twenty-first century with *Poem Rains*. In cities around the globe such as Santiago de Chile, Guernica, London, and Berlin, among others, poems were dropped from the sky. All these cities had been bombed at some point in their history. The *Poem Rains* events commemorated these historical attacks, creating awareness and staging bonding and solidarity in an extended public space (Lagos Preller 2015, 141–144).

In the U.S., the Occupy Movement also drew on revisions of public space along horizontal and vertical lines. The desire to reinvent collectivism resulted in The Illuminator, a mobile and high-powered public projection during the Occupy Movement's activities in Manhattan. Most of the movement's events received worldwide media coverage. Thus, events could count on a surplus of media diffusion from outside the movement. The multi-levelled event signaled its illuminating function in its title. For some critics it remains the most impactful public art project of the Occupy movement. Combining presence in the streets with a technologically created presence in the air, it connected various public spaces and enhanced artistic models of participatory culture. On November 17th 2011, the Occupy Movement announced its two month anniversary in the Zuccotti Park. The Illuminator was the greatest gift of the movement's alliance of art and protest.

Perhaps with Walt Whitman's vision of America as multitude in mind, hundreds of marchers crossed Brooklyn Bridge with hopes for a just world. They shouted slogans, poems, and other short texts on the ground in dialogue with the tremendous light projection on the Verizon building in Manhattan. The projection contained multiple signatures, slogans, and texts representative of the Occupy mission. This multi-sited presence made the aesthetic and political signs visible to the police who were in the air and on the ground. For the marchers, the projection created the sense that their messages literally traveled through space and gained high visibility in the city. The event was site specific with Brooklyn Bridge and the Verizon building as markers of local New York identity. And the event was nomadic as the Occupy movement as a whole "in its mobility and replicability as a meme, translating freely between images, objects, and worlds across time and space through media networks" (McKee 2017, 103) reached out globally.

The images projected onto the Version appeared to have an empowering effect on the marchers, bringing them together in an intense moment of shared political desire. The transmitted images on the web helped create local and global circles of supporters diffusing political objectives even further. Out of the Occupy Wall Street Movement emerged the Illuminator Art Collective, which has continued its support of grassroots movements, environmental groups, and big political organizations like Greenpeace in their struggles against capitalist and environmentalist exploitation. The collective has staged hundreds of interventions in public spaces – both geographical and virtual – as acts of incitement and invitation. According to their mission, they transform the street from a site of transit to a democratic space of engagement, conflict, and dialogue.[6]

---

6   http://www.blunderbussmag.com/author/theilluminator/.

When looking at recent collaborations between artists in protest movements from Seattle to Occupy, in which Judith Butler also appeared as a public speaker in Zuccotti Park, it becomes evident that the theoretical framework of Judith Butler and Athena Athanasiou's concept of "dispossession" offers a new understanding of "the human" and the "social" in circumstances of oppression and/or marginalization (Butler and Athanasiou, 2013). The concept also sheds light on agency and artivism in the public, especially through their understanding of spaces of appearance as general constructs that enable "the human" to *perform* his/her dispossession, and thereby resist it. This agency need not be bound to a specific medium, but materializes dispossession *through* the bodily performance.

The Illuminator performance as a collaborative multimedia projection and the marching individual chanting slogans across Brooklyn Bridge illustrate the multi-media facets of performing "dispossession" in public in the recent Occupy movement. Butler and Athanasiou (2013, 84) unfold a normative understanding of political or economic dispossession that marginalizes different people worldwide by depriving them of citizenship, property, or land. It is Athanasiou who develops that "dispossession persists beyond the colony and the postcolony":

> In the context of neoliberal forms of capital – combined with tightened migration policies and the abjection of stateless people, *sans papiers*, 'illegal' immigrants – bodies (that is, human capital) are becoming increasingly disposable, dispossessed by capital and its exploitative excess, uncountable and unaccounted for. (29)

The mix of political and artistic protest from the Occupy and Zapatista movements continues to thrive in contemporary action-networks struggling with the misery of global migration in contemporary times. As Tufekci reminds us, "the longevity and durability of these networks means that know-how, especially infrastructural know-how, can be shared across time and place" (2017, 86). A site-specific movement, Occupy erected a library in Zuccotti Park, as did many other Occupy encampments around the globe. Through new media networks shared knowledge and practices traveled fast.

Grid, cage, and public space in contemporary urban spectacle cultures

Contemporary urban culture celebrates festivals, spectacles, and the re-aestheticization of public space. Leftist and neo-Marxist intellectuals have criticized the spectacularization of urban spaces (Debord 1995; Zukin 1995). The general critical direction asserts that the culture of spectacles commodifies all forms of social, cultural, and political life. Yet, critics like Daniel Goldstein and Kevin Fox Gotham arrive at a more complex vision of spectacle culture. Aside from clearly present commodity interests, they locate a potential for resistance, rebellion and subversion in urban spectacles in contemporary times. Goldstein claims that "spectacles, like other public events, are systems for not only the performance but also the creation or transformation of social order" (2004, 16). With a nod to the New Orleans Mardi Gras, Gotham maintains that public spectacles have the potential to create "a radical critique especially with respect to class and race inequalities" (2005, 235).

Gotham sees contemporary urban cultures increasingly expressing themselves through festival-related spectacle, from sports events to film and book festivals, from carnival and Christopher Street parades to street art festivals. Undoubtedly, spectacle cultures are deeply embedded in commodity culture and market circuits, but they are also important loopholes through which the social status quo can be challenged. Two examples from performance culture shall serve as a point of departure for exploring how public space can simultaneously be envisioned as a site of colonial and neocolonial oppression and a site of visionary knowledge production. Both instances show that art practices in public remain crucial for rethinking and redistributing public space. In Guillermo Gómez-Peña's and Coco Fusco's "The Couple in the Cage" performance tour and in Kendrick Lamar's 2016 chain-gang Grammy performance, public space is envisioned as a grid-patterned cage, confining and porous at the same time.

These performances illustrate the increasing complexity when it comes to defining public space and the public sphere. As well-established performance artists, Gómez-Peña and Fusco started their "Couple in the Cage" tour in 1992, five hundred years after Christopher Columbus's arrival in the Americas. For two years they travelled through various Western metropolises in the Americas and Europe, presenting themselves as undiscovered Amerindians from an island in the Gulf of Mexico that had somehow been overlooked for five centuries. Their tour had a mobile and global presence, as they claimed various urban sites such as the British Museum in London for public performance. At the same time, they challenged and questioned the very concept of openness in public spaces. Employing the cage as locus of an interactive performance they addressed the audience directly and reacted to spectators' comments and wishes. Hence, public space and cage became relational sites. While performing in public, the couple never left the cage. Combining dressing and naming practices, they performed "natives" from "Guatinau," an imagined homeland, and called themselves tongue-in-cheek "Guatinauis." A small donation box in front of the cage signaled that for a small fee, the female Guatinaui would perform a "traditional" dance (to rap music), and the male Guatinaui would tell "authentic" Amerindian stories (in a made-up language). In addition, they would both pose for photos with visitors. As a caged couple, Gómez-Peña and Fusco brought imagined colonies to the urban centers. In the style of postmodern parody, they staged the colonial encounter as a zoo-like experience, leaving their audiences in a state of perplexity, amusement, and disgust.

For many spectators the scenery indeed appeared "real" and "authentic." The performances created a complex spatio-temporal link between coloniality and late modernity, between the cage as symbol of human enslavement and the public space as potential site of participation, interaction, and dialogue. Their tour playfully revealed that "knowledge [can] not only be accumulated in Europe and the US and, from there, spread all over the world. Knowledge is produced, accumulated, and critically used everywhere" (Mignolo 2005, 115). Even more importantly, their performance revealed that knowledge production is in the hands of those who control production as well as diffusion. As internationally established performance artists, Gómez-Peña and Fusco could gain access to highly visible public sites and channel the knowledge they wanted to share according to their means. They imaginatively posed their production of knowledge against Western versions of colonial histories and imaginaries of indigenous cultures, thus challenging and mobilizing modes and sites of knowledge production.

As Stuart Hall emphasizes,

> Europe brought its own cultural categories, languages, images and ideas to the New World in order to describe and represent it. It tried to fit the New World into existing conceptual frameworks, classifying it according to its own norms, and absorbing it into western traditions of representation. (1996, 204)

Sources that the colonial discourse drew on were the writings of Classical philosophers like Plato and Aristotle, religious sources that created knowledge by reinterpreting "geography in terms of the Bible" (Hall 1996, 207), and mythology, which "transformed the outer world into an enchanted garden, alive with misshapen peoples and oddities" (207). Yet, the most fertile source of information were traveler's tales –"a discourse where description faded imperceptibly into legend" (207). The combination of these sources created an image of the New World that the settlers internalized before they set foot in the New World. "Europeans had outsailed, outshot, and outwitted peoples who had no wish to be 'explored,' no need to be 'discovered,' and no desire to be 'exploited.' The Europeans stood vis-a-vis the Others, impositions of dominant power" (204). In the case of "The Couple in the Cage," it is, subversively, the reinvented indigenous from the New World who is the traveler occupying public spaces in the West and presenting "knowledge" through the masks of costume, body paint, made-up language, and interactive parody – thus pushing the boundaries of knowledge production and diffusion.

As a couple in the cage, Gómez-Peña and Fusco turned the public sites of their performances into unexpected educational sites, shaking the very foundations of established knowledge production through interaction, participatory culture, and the simulacrum of public space as a cage. As Sara Mills reminds us, "discourses do not exist in a vacuum but are in constant conflict with other discourses and other social practices which inform them over questions of truth and authority" (1997, 17).

Their events revealed public sites to be performative and fluid, yet, also porous and enclosed, oscillating between spaces of free interaction and social/economic entrapment. Public spaces in Gómez-Peña and Fusco's performances remain ambiguous, dangerous, and far from utopian, as they are sites of control, surveillance, manipulation, and consumption, in addition to being sites of free dialogue and individual expression. Yet, they remain the chosen loci of enunciation to challenge colonial and neocolonial forms of knowledge production, and to perform the political.

A second example is Kendrick Lamar's artistic return to the grid as performance space. His Grammy award performance from 2016 is a quintessential example of sonic dissent that emerges from the very center of stardom within the pop music world. Minutes after Lamar received his fifth Grammy of the night for Best Rap Album in February 2016, he delivered a spectacle-like performance to raise historical consciousness and voice his rage against racial injustice. Performing a medley that included songs like "Alright" and "The Blacker the Berry," he approached the microphone chained to other black men in a makeshift prison block. Next to the musicians of the chain gang there were musicians performing from within a prison cage. The performance ended with the debut of an emphatic new verse about modern slavery, in memory of Trayvon Martin: "On February 26th I lost my life, too." A new call for solidarity and brotherhood was performed, televised, and spread through the new media instantaneously. His performance at the Grammy awards combined artistic craftsmanship, spectacle, and political action, with a gigantic fire behind the stage visually emphasizing his musical demand for awareness and justice (cf. Makarechi 2016).[7] With the appearance of a stage on fire, musicians also broke loose from their chains.

Lamar's provocative performance created a collage of historical time in which he related the balls and chains of slavery with the current prison situation in the United States, and with racism on a global scale. He created a powerful image of a threatening historical continuum that enslaves anew and prolongs colonial slavery into neocolonial practices of racist jurisdiction and police practice. For marginalized groups the political message included a "social imperative to perform" (Yúdice 2003, 40). Lamar's reclaiming the stage as a public space of protest is part of what Daphne Brooks calls a "new wave of black pop protest music" that "captures and grapples with racial catastrophe in the twenty-first century: the prison-industrial complex, globalised wealth inequality and the violent expenditure of women and children" (2016, n. pag.). Lamar's vanguard performance style also has found its way into video art. For instance, the choreography for the *Alright* video stages Lamar with a group of young African American males riding in a car carried by white police officers.

The video juggles with spatial metaphors. Lamar moves above the city with a bird's-eye view of the world below. The spatially superior position is accompanied by rap dance movements underscoring the cherished physical freedom that contrasts sharply with the lyrics, which express critique, sadness, anger, and resistance. While floating above the city, Lamar transcends the ground scenes of white armed policemen pushing a young African American onto the pavement. His bold city flight eventually attracts the attention of a police officer, who pretends to fire a bullet at him through a finger gun. Lamar enacts his empowerment through the performative of urban

---

7   http://www.vanityfair.com/hollywood/2016/02/kendrick-lamar-2016-grammys-performance.

song and dance. "If we are always named by others" – a condition that Butler and Athanasiou highlight – "then the name signifies a certain dispossession from the start. If we seek to name ourselves, it is still within a language that we never made" (2013, 137). Performativity, however, provides a solution, according to Athanasiou: "Naming implies a performative which is necessarily interwoven in the fabric of appropriation that authorizes it, while at the same time it remains somehow capable of exposing and exceeding its prescribed limits" (138). Performativity's potential to challenge "ways in which the wrongs of oppression and dispossession are not audible within hegemonic discourses" (132) is doubly heightened when the performative emerges from within the very temples of cultural industry and its massive impact on the public sphere, as Lamar's performance and video underscore (Raussert 2021).

The examples from Lamar, Goméz-Pena, and Cusco illustrate that contemporary artists engage with public space with a high level of self-reflexivity. Their performances bear a meta-level of meaning and show how deeply engaged vanguard as well as pop artists are in the process of rethinking the social via public performance. Self-reflectively they address the role of the artist in the public and engage with art's ubiquitous presence in contemporary society. The trope of the public space gets reinterpreted via the cage metaphor which is based on a multi-dimensional grid patterns-reminiscent of the urban planning grid patterns and the architectural design of skyscrapers that promises endless expansion. At the same time, the grid encloses and confines. The artists use the cage with awareness that they are also caught in it. In addition, they are aware that they are part of the networks of economy, market, audience-response, and the concept-producing industry. The cage makes permanent surveillance part of the performative act. The dispossessed performer and the disoriented spectator enter into a playful dialogue that blurs the boundaries between fiction and fact. No matter how mobile the tour through Western metropolises may appear, the performers, like the audience, remained entangled by projections, imaginaries, and structures framed by a porous yet limiting cage.

To conclude, let me link public space, cage, and the "Entangled Americas" project's hypothetical spatial reference point – the Americas as space of entanglement – through the grid. The grid holds a central historical role in urban planning. While predecessors can be found in ancient Rome as well as in the urban structures developed by Aztec and Incan cultures, the grid becomes a powerful tool to modernize American spaces from coloniality to contemporary times. Together with the temporal concept utopia, the spatial concept of the grid marks the very beginning of settlement in the colonies in the New World. Both the English term "America" and the Spanish "América" have historically functioned as signifiers of utopia and independence. As Quijano and Wallerstein have pointed out, the differences lie within utopian conceptualizations: "North America's 'utopia of social equality and liberty' and Latin America's indigenous "utopia of reciprocity, solidarity, and direct democracy" (Quijano and Wallerstein 1992, 556–557).

The grid's presence as modern urban utopia ranges from South to North and East to West in the American hemisphere. As Kaltmeier puts it, the Latin American grid bears "a strategic role for the colonization of space" (2011, 5). The cage in the performances is modelled on the grid. The grid in the Americas has great significance in urban and architectural design, from the rectangular blocks that mark cities like Chicago and New York to their skyscrapers (Sennett 1991, 52). Both, in Latin America, where the grid had already a pre-Columbian history, and in North America, the grid became a tool for colonizing space and installing white hegemony (Kaltmeier 2011, 6–7). With reference to the U.S., Richard Sennett maintains that the grid serves as a force for expansion. While he refers to westward and imperialist expansion, I would add that it functions as a mobile and repeatable structure for horizontal and vertical expansion. We may think of urban planning and skyrocketing architectural designs. Public space in the Americas, then, needs to be broadly negotiated within an overarching grid pattern. Like the spectacle performance of Kendrick Lamar during the 2016 Grammy ceremony, in which musicians performed from within a cage symbolizing African American confinement in contemporary U.S. prisons, the spectacle performances by Gomёz-Pena and Cusco interpret the grid as a fundamental "American" structure – a "space of entanglement" that sets spatial limits to utopia but also provides open spaces between the metal, steel, and iron through which voices of the dispossessed can pass and through which new forms of participation, interaction, and community emerge. These new forms desire for new critical utopias by rethinking the social within and against the grid.

Concluding thoughts

The traveling of imaginaries through the new media creates even more profound connections between worlds that seem geographically, geopolitically, economically, religiously, and culturally very distant from each other. South and North take turns in providing important alternative imaginaries to spur and perform new conceptualizations of public space and futurist visions in the Americas, even in the twenty-first century. These new visions involve a rethinking of public space, access to public spaces, and the connectivity and conflictual relation of public spheres. Frequently, they are born out of disillusionment with existing structures. At the same time, they advocate a recognition of otherness, acceptance of territorial rights, and greater local and global awareness of the politics of dispossession that unfortunately continue to grow the divide between rich and poor on a global scale.

With shifting emphasis on poetics and politics and differing calls for sovereignty, art practices in the Americas can look back to a long history of rethinking public spaces and imaginatively constructing communities. From colonial times to neocolonial forms of dispossession, the imaginative and economic struggles over public spaces have shaped and been shaped by art practices that engage with the street, the plaza, and virtual space in the Americas. Art practices continue to thrive as a tool for reinventing the social and rethinking public space in our contemporary networked public.

While it may sound utopian, the often underestimated potential of cultural creativity may well be one of the most powerful tools for creating open and inviting public spaces and a dialogic, networked public of difference and exchange, in and off the grid.

Works cited

Adey, Peter. 2002. "Secure and Sorted Mobilities: Examples from the Airport." *Surveillance & Society*: 500–519. https://ojs.library. queensu.ca/index.php/surveillance-and-society/article/view/33 33.

Auge, Marc. 1995. *Non-Places: Introduction to an Anthropology of Supermodernity. Place.* New York: Verso. Print.

Bauman, Zygmunt. 2000. *Liquid Modernity.* Cambridge: Polity Press. Print.

Beck, Ulrich. 1999. *World Risk Society.* New York: Polity Press. Print.

Bender, Barbara. 2001. "Landscapes on-the-Move." *Journal of Social Archeology* 1.1: 75–89. Print.

Benhabib, Seyla. 2002. *The Claims of Culture: Equality and Diversity in the Global Era.* Princeton, NJ: Princeton University Press. Print.

Brooks, Daphne. 2016. "How BlackLivesMatter Started a Musical Revolution." *The Guardian.* https://www.theguardian.com/ profile/daphne-a-brooks.

Butler, Judith. 1997. *Excitable Speech: A Politics of the Performative.* London/New York: Routledge. Print.

Butler, Judith, and Athena Athanasiou. 2013. *Dispossession: The Performative in the Political.* New York: Polity Press. Print.

Canclini, García. 1990. *Culturas híbridas. Estrategias para entrar y salir de la modernidad.* México, D.F.: Grijalbo. Print.

Carrillo, Sofía, and Joaquín Barriendos. 2015. "STENCIL IXTLIL XÓCHITL: Demián Flores, La Curtiduría, and the Visual Guerilla in Oaxaca." In *Grafficity: Visual Practices and Contesta-*

tions in Urban Space, ed. Eva Youkhana and Larissa Förster, 171–192. Paderborn: Wilhelm Fink. Print.

Coronil, Fernando. 2011. "The Future in Question: History and Utopia in Latin America (1989-2010)." In *Business as Usual. The Roots of the Financial Global Meltdown*, ed. Craig Calhoun and Georgi Derluguian, 231–292. New York: New York University Press. Print.

Debord, Guy. 1995. *The Society of the Spectacle*. New York: Zone Books. Print.

Exhibit. 2016. "Discover Design for Urban Life in South America that Builds on Radical Optimism." Pittsburgh: The Heinz Architectural Center, Carnegie Museums. https://cmoa.org/exhibition /building-optimism.

Fisher, Jean. "Remembering the Future: Tradional and Modernity in the Work of Hock E Ayey VI Edgar Heap of Bird." n.d. http:// www.jeanfisher.com/remembering-the-future-tradition-and-modernity-in-the-work-of-hock-e-aye-vi-edgar-heap-of-birds/.

Flores, Tatiana. 2013. *Mexico's Revolutionary Avant-Gardes: From Estridentism to !30-30!*. New Haven/London: Yale University Press. Print.

Foucault, Michel. 2002. *Discipline and Punish. The Birth of the Prison*. New York: Vintage Books. Print.

Fraser, Nancy. 1990. *Rethinking the Public Sphere: A Contribution to the Critique of Actually Existing Democracy*. Milwaukee: University of Wisconsin. Print.

Fusco, Coco. 2015. *Dangerous Moves: Performance and Politicis in Cuba*. London: Tate Publishing. Print.

Goldstein, Daniel. 2004. *The Spectacular City: Violence and Performance in Urban Bolivia*. Durham: Duke University Press. Print.

Gotham, Kevin Fox. 2005. "Theorizing Urban Spectacles: Festivals, Tourism and the Transformation of Urban Space." *City* 9.2: 225–246. Print.

Gretzki, Allan. 2015. "Graffiti, Streetart und Culture Jamming zwischen urbanem Protest und Kommerzialisierung." In *Grafficity:*

Visual Practices and Contestations in Urban Space, ed. Eva Youkhana and Larissa Förster, 235–265. Paderborn: Wilhelm Fink. Print.

Habermas, Jürgen. 1989. *The Structural Transformation of the Public Sphere: An Inquiry into a Category of Bourgeois Society*. Cambridge: MIT Press. Print.

Hall, Stuart. 1996. "The West and the Rest: Discourse and Power." In *Modernity: An Introduction to Modern Societies*, ed. Stuart Hall, David Held, Don Hubert, and Kenneth Thompson, 184–227. Oxford: Blackwell. Print.

Harvey, David. 1989. *The Condition of Postmodernity: An Inquiry into the Origins of Cultural Change*. Blackwell. Print.

Held, David. 2010. *Cosmopolitanism: Ideals and Realities*. Cambridge: Polity Press. Print.

Hunter, Garry. 2012. *Street Art Around the World*. Canterbury: Arcturus 117. Print.

Illouz, Eva. 2019. "Capitalist Subjectivity and the Internet." Talk. Berlin: Alexander von Humboldt Institut für Internet und Gesellschaft.

Kaltmeier, Olaf. 2011. "Introduction." In *Selling EthniCity: Urban Cultural Politics in the Americas*, ed. Olaf Kaltmeier, 1–20. Farnham: Ashgate. Print.

Lagos Preller, Theobaldo. 2015. "Fall of Presence(s): The Art Projects ¡Ay, Sudamérica! and 'Poem Rain.'" In *Grafficity: Visual Practices and Contestations in Urban Space*, ed. Eva Youkhana and Larissa Förster, 141–169. Paderborn: Wilhelm Fink. Print.

Makarechi, Kia. 2016. "Watch Kendrick Lamar Escape Handcuffs in 2016 Grammys Performance." https://www.vanityfair.com/hollywood/2016/02/kendrick-lamar-2016-grammys-performance.

McKee, Yates. 2017. *Strike Art. Contemporary Art and the Post-Occupy Condition*. New York: Verso. Print.

Mignolo, Walter. 2005. *The Idea of Latin America*. Malden: Blackwell. Print.

Mills, Sara. *Discourse*. 1997. London/New York: Routledge. Print.

Mouffe, Chantal. 2005. *On the Political*. London/New York: Routledge. Print.

Neufeld, Daniel, and Jérémie Haasser. 2010. *Arte Urbano GDL*. Guadalajara: Consejo Estatal para la Cultura y las Artes. Print.

Nikitin, Cynthia. 2015. "Communities and Arts-Based Placemaking." In *Project for Public Spaces*. https://www.pps.org/article/creative-communities-and-arts-based-placemaking.

Oles, James. 2014. *Arte y architectura en México*. Mexico City: Taurus Historia. Print.

Prieto, Antonio. 2018. *Border Art as a Political Strategy*. http://isla.igc.org/Features/Border/mex6.html.

Quijano, Anibal, and Immanuel Wallerstein. 1992. "Americanity as a Concept, or the Americas in the Modern World System." *International Sociological Association* 1.134: 549–557. Print.

Raussert, Wilfried. 2021. *'What's Going On': How Music Shapes the Social*. Trier: WVT, New Orleans: UNO Press. Print.

———. 2019. "Interview with Quetzal Flores." Interview. Bielefeld: Center for InterAmerican Studies.

———. 2017. *Art Begins in the Streets. Art Lives in the Streets*. Bielefeld: kipu. Print.

Schacter, Rafael. 2013. *The World Atlas of Street Art and Graffiti*. London: Aurum Press Limited. Print.

Sennett, Richard. 1991. *The Conscience of the Eye: The Design and Social Life of Cities*. New York: Faber and Faber. Print.

Suvin, Darko. 1988. *Positions and Presuppositions in Science Fiction*. Kent: Kent State University Press. Print.

Thies, Sebastian, and Sarah Corona Berkin. 2020. "Visual Cultures." In *The Routledge Handbook to Culture and Media in the Americas*, ed. Wilfried Raussert, Giselle Anatol, Sarah Corona Berkin, José Carlos Lozano, and Sebastian Thies, entry 45. London/New York: Routledge. Print.

Tufekci, Zeynep. 2017. *Twitter and Tear Gas: The Power and Fragility of Networked Protest*. New Haven: Yale University Press. Print.

Uribe, Laura. 2017. "Arte y Color Para Rescatar México." In *Aire*, 125–129. Print.

Urry, John. 2007. *Mobilities*. Cambridge: Polity Press. Print.

Ventura, Tereza. 2015. "Graffiti Practices in Rio de Janeiro and Berlin. A Comparative Perspective." In *Grafficity: Visual Practices and Contestations in Urban Space*, ed. Eva Youkhana and Larissa Förster, 121–140. Paderborn: Wilhelm Fink. Print.

Youkhana, Eva, and Larissa Förster, 2015. "Introduction." In *Grafficity: Visual Practices and Contestations in Urban Space*, ed. Eva Youkhana and Larissa Förster, 7-17. Köln: Morphomata. Print.

Yúdice, George. 2003. *The Expediency of Culture: Uses of Culture in the Global Era*. Durham: Duke University Press. Print.

Zukin, Sharon. 1995. *The Cultures of Cities*. Oxford/Malden: Blackwell. Print.

Epilogue

From the early twentieth century to the contemporary period, artists in the Americas have appropriated public space and public sites to reinvent the social and social relations. While art and cultural practice, strangely enough, go frequently unnoticed and underrated in their function as creator of social meaning, at the end of this book it appears safe to say that artistic practice has established itself as an effective tool for redefining human relationships to public space and rethinking social diversity in public spheres. Public art has demonstrated its self-reflexive capacity to uncover conflicts and breaks in the spheres of the social, and its power to articulate them to a broader public. As shown in the three periods of artistic development and articulation examined in this book, public art has an extraordinary capacity to adjust itself to the "fluidity of the social" (Bauman 2000, 25). Not only this; beyond the confines of state censorship, the dictates of cultural industries, and the expansion of capitalist culture, it continues to serve as a vehicle for dissent and *reinvention* of that social in times of cultural, economic, and political crisis, by utilizing traditional as well as new media public spaces.

Critics like Bruno Latour have rearticulated the "crisis" of the social in the beginning of the twenty-first century. In the "cartographies of the social," Latour detects tension, conflict, and contradiction (2005, 34). For him, considering interrelations between political, economic, and cultural forces are key to rethinking the social in a relational way. To capture and analyze public space and public sphere in relation to the emergence of the social, this book has considered art practice in public space as essential to understanding the social as a process, something always in a state of becoming (Deleuze and Guattari 1987) and creatively transformable. Art practices, particularly when they occupy public space, are uniquely equipped to reflect the social in dialogue with multiple competing public spheres. In addition, they deserve recognition for reflecting crisis and creating models for social interaction among human actors and between them and nonhuman actors.

Artists and writers have proven tremendously creative in producing social, cultural, and political visions, particularly when working out of a profound desire to infuse public sites with creative imagination (cf. Galante 2008). While often simply discredited as public showmen, entertainers, and exhibitionists, artists, one should acknowledge, demonstrate courage and strength when they leave the comfort zones of regulated art worlds, galleries, theaters, and literary salons for the streets. Practicing art in public requires an immediate and direct confrontation with the world and the people inhabiting it. It also necessitates adjusting one's creative imagination to the needs of a group, community, or network. And it requires rethinking art practice in real life situations, because public spaces not only provide visibility and recognition, but also represent danger zones in which people, ideas, and imaginaries may clash.

Chantal Mouffe (2007) goes so far as to define public space as a battleground on which different hegemonic projects are confronted, without any possibility of final reconciliation. Mouffe would certainly also agree that critical artistic practices help subvert dominant ideologies in what she labels an "agonistic" model of public space, as these practices can visualize that which is repressed and eliminated by the consensus of contemporary post-political democracy. We can place the various art practices discussed within Mouffe's conception of public space and see that the experience of art practice going public has been controversial, conflictive, transgressive, and innovative in its attempts to work within and against the grid patterns of spatial control in the twentieth and twenty-first century.

For Mouffe, "public spaces are always plural and the agonistic confrontation takes place on a multiplicity of discursive surfaces" (2007, 3). She denies any underlying principle of unity. In her thinking, public spaces are "always striated and hegemonically structured" (3). This also holds true for those urban structures based upon foundational grid patterns. It also rings true for the extended and diversified public space of television in the 1950s and 1960s, as well as that of the new media in the digital age, with its algorhythmically-determined grid patterns of control and hierarchy. While there is no fixed or predetermined center that controls the diversity of spaces, "diverse forms of articulation always exist among them" (3).

As this book has shown, art practices represent one of the central forms of articulation in public space. They are profoundly dialogic, powerfully interactive, and relentlessly creative in rethinking not only ways of articulation but the constituency of public space itself. I also want to insist on a second point: They play a vital role in hegemonic struggles over forms of articulation and contribute to the conflictive dialogue about and among diverse public spaces. For a long time, art practice has been continuously reshaping discourses in and about public space in the Americas. Not confined to isolated spheres of imagination and creation, it is embedded in power relations and struggles of dominance. Artists act within institutional and cultural industry frames, they frequently transgress them to create space for new visions. While they are without a doubt tied to the larger cultural industry paradigms of capitalist culture and cultural politics in our age of globalization (García Canclini 1987, 1995; Yúdice 2003), they are also capable of departing from well-worn paths to challenge norms and standards of cultural production. As I wish to emphasize, it is chiefly in public space that art practice unfolds its full potential to shape everyday life culture and redirect the course of the social in any given place and time.

Cultural production and social vision in the Americas, as the three historical periods show, have strongly profited from art practices pushing into the realms of public space and public sphere. While there is no linear development of art practices in relation to public space, different degrees of radical intensity can be distinguished that mark artistic engagement with and in public space from the early twentieth to the twenty-first century. In its early modernist phase, art practice in public space predominantly occurred within the context of public institutions and their related architectural sites; in most instances, artistic projects on walls and in public buildings were also supported by institutional commission. While challenging spatial divisions and hierarchies in their art works, artists like the muralists worked principally within the grid patterns of public buildings and sites. When art and cultural practice took to the streets in Harlem and Jamaica in the early twentieth century, the parades and performances generally followed routes in accordance with the regulations of city officials.

The turbulent 1960s witnessed a massive artistic presence in the streets. Streets became a site of political expression and confrontation, and art practices provided models for social and political action. Breaking down the fourth wall of theatre conventions, taking performances into streets, parks, and plazas, artists took radical and daring steps to diversify the public sphere and to occupy public spaces where the social, in its cultural and political aspects, could be reinvented. Some performance artists continued within urban structures, but many of them sought to break out of the urban grid of control and surveillance, as in the music festivals of Woodstock and Ávandaro. Created in dialogue with Cuban revolutionary cultural practices, the Black Panther movement's artistic and cultural articulations served as a means to create alternative black-controlled grid patterns for communal urban living.

In the contemporary period we are witnessing performance artists approach new public sites and routes to create new visions of the social. In spatial terms, it is striking that many performances and events exhibit a site-specific yet nomadic character, as they respond to the challenges of intensified mobilization and globalization. While art practices shape the new media and open new channels for reaching multiple public spheres, their dissemination is at the same time channeled and censored by hegemonic struggles within the new media networks. As the act of selecting sites of conflict and confrontation like the U.S.-Mexican border for performance acts illustrates, many artists take on the struggle over articulation in public spaces by confronting the hegemon directly. Public art practice confronts politics in a very site-specific way, presenting new social visions through immediate and direct engagement with the social sphere, the art world, and the cultural industries. By tapping into the channels of the contemporary digital age, they manage to use newly emerging grid patterns also to work in ways that resist hegemonic surveillance and control.

Analyzing the development of art practice in public space in different historical epochs reveals that widely assumed power hierarchies between North and South in the Americas lose their validity when it comes to art practices that shape the use of public space and redefine articulations of the social in relation to public space. Artistic flows from the South and the North take turns throughout the twentieth and into the twenty-first century in creating complex interAmerican webs of artistically inspired visions of the social in public art.

Artists work within and against the grid structures monitoring and controlling public space. They are also active agents in creating and redefining them. The modernist period saw artists who foremost created art in public within the grid structures of urban architectural design. The postmodern period experienced an expansion of grid structures through media like television and witnessed regular attempts of artists to loosen grid structures or break through grid patterns. In the contemporary digital age, artists display a high degree of self-reflexivity about the relation between artistic practice in public space and steadily expanding grid structures that provide global dissemination yet create new ways of monitoring and controlling public space.

Contemporary populist movements from the North to the South attempt to negate diversity, reduce access to public space, and eliminate plural socialities. The social and political rhetoric of political leaders like Jair Bolsonaro in Brazil and Donald Trump in the U.S. promotes a version of public space that negates the advances of human rights, civil rights, and multicultural politics of earlier decades. Historians like David Frye have pointed out that we are living in an age in which the construction of walls to divide social and geopolitical spaces has reached a new high. These dividing lines shape the grid patterns of urban segmentation and fragmentation, they impact the accessibility of mobility and migration routes, and they enhance the divide between rich and poor throughout North and South America.

Against these developments, contemporary art practice has sought out public spaces that are sites of crisis and conflict in order to create new social visions in the midst of power struggles over the flows of goods, people, ideas, and media in the twenty-first century. As the public art practices in the current Black Lives Matter movement in the U.S. and Canada powerfully demonstrate (Raussert 2021, 58–63, 142–164), the hegemonic and counterhegemonic struggle over articulations within and about public spaces goes on. Cultural and art practice continue to aesthetically and socially shape the public spaces of contemporary American societies.

Works cited

Bauman, Zygmunt. 2000. *Liquid Modernity*. Cambridge: Polity Press. Print.

Deleuze, Gilles, and Félix Guattari. 1987. *A Thousand Plateaus: Capitalism and Schizophrenia*. Minneapolis: University of Minnesota Press. Print.

Frye, David. 2019. *Walls: A History of Civilization in Blood and Brick*. New York: Simon & Schuster. Print.

Galante, Raffaela. 2008. "La cultura sí importa." *Crítica* 952: 46–50. Print.

García Canclini, Nestor. 1995. *Consumidores y Ciudadanos. Conflictos multiculturales de la globalización*. México D.F., México: Grijalbo. Print.

———, ed. 1987. *Las políticas culturales en América Latina*. México: Grijalbo. Print.

Latour, Bruno. 2005. *Reassembling the Social: An Introduction to Actor-Network-Theory*. Oxford: Oxford University Press. Print.

Mouffe, Chantal. 2007. "Art as an Agonistic Intervention in Public Space." In *Art as a Public Issue: How Art and its Institutions*

Reinvent the Public Dimension, ed. Chantal Mouffe, 1–7. Rotterdam/Amsterdam: NAI Publishers. Print.

Raussert, Wilfried. 2021. *'What's Going on': How Music Shapes the Social*. Trier: WVT, New Orleans: UNO Press. Print.

Yúdice, George. 2003. *The Expediency of Culture: Uses of Culture in the Global Era*. Durham: Duke University Press. Print.

Inter-American Studies

Cultures – Societies – History

Estudios Interamericanos

Culturas – Sociedades – Historia

This interdisciplinary series examines national and transnational issues in the cultures, societies, and histories of the Americas. It creates a forum for a critical academic dialogue between North and South, promoting an inter-American paradigm that shifts the scholarly focus from methodological nationalism to the wider context of the Western Hemisphere.

Vol. 1
Raab, Josef, Sebastian Thies, and Daniela Noll-Opitz, eds. *Screening the Americas: Narration of Nation in Documentary Film / Proyectando las Américas: Narración de la nación en el cine documental.* 2011. 472 pp.

WVT Wissenschaftlicher Verlag Trier	ISBN 978-3-86821-331-7	€ 29,50
Bilingual Press / Editorial Bilingüe	ISBN 978-1-931010-83-2	$ 29.50

Vol. 2
Raussert, Wilfried, and Michelle Habell-Pallán, eds. *Cornbread and Cuchifritos: Ethnic Identity Politics, Transnationalization, and Transculturation in American Urban Popular Music.* 2011. 292 pp.

WVT Wissenschaftlicher Verlag Trier	ISBN 978-3-86821-265-5	€ 29,50
Bilingual Press / Editorial Bilingüe	ISBN 978- 1-931010-80-1	$ 29.50

Vol. 3
Butler, Martin, Jens Martin Gurr, and Olaf Kaltmeier, eds. *EthniCities: Metropolitan Cultures and Ethnic Identities in the Americas.* 2011. 268 pp.

WVT Wissenschaftlicher Verlag Trier	ISBN 978-3-86821-310-2	€ 29,50
Bilingual Press / Editorial Bilingüe	ISBN 978-1-931010-81-8	$ 29.50

Vol. 4
Gurr, Jens Martin, and Wilfried Raussert, eds. *Cityscapes in the Americas and Beyond: Representations of Urban Complexity in Literature and Film.* 2011. 300 pp.

WVT Wissenschaftlicher Verlag Trier	ISBN 978-3-86821-324-9	€ 29,50
Bilingual Press / Editorial Bilingüe	ISBN 978-1-931010-82-5	$ 29.50

Vol. 5

Kirschner, Luz Angélica, ed. *Expanding* Latinidad: *An Inter-American Perspective.* 2012. 292 pp.

WVT Wissenschaftlicher Verlag Trier	ISBN 978-3-86821-309-6	€ 29,50
Bilingual Press / Editorial Bilingüe	ISBN 978-1-931010-84-9	$ 29.50

Vol. 6

Raussert, Wilfried, and Graciela Martínez-Zalce, eds. *(Re)Discovering 'America': Road Movies and Other Travel Narratives in North America / (Re)Descubriendo 'América': Road movie y otras narrativas de viaje en América del Norte.* 2012. 252 pp.

WVT Wissenschaftlicher Verlag Trier	ISBN 978-3-86821-384-3	€ 29,50
Bilingual Press / Editorial Bilingüe	ISBN 978-1-931010-91-7	$ 29.50

Vol. 7

Kaltmeier, Olaf, ed. *Transnational Americas: Envisioning Inter-American Area Studies in Globalization Processes.* 2013. 278 pp.

WVT Wissenschaftlicher Verlag Trier	ISBN 978-3-86821-415-4	€ 29,50
Bilingual Press / Editorial Bilingüe	ISBN 978-1-931010-92-4	$ 29.50

Vol. 8

Raab, Josef, and Alexander Greiffenstern, eds. *Interculturalism in North America: Canada, the United States, Mexico, and Beyond.* 2013. 312 pp.

WVT Wissenschaftlicher Verlag Trier	ISBN 978-3-86821-460-4	€ 29,50
Bilingual Press / Editorial Bilingüe	ISBN 978-1-931010-99-3	$ 29.50

Vol. 9

Raab, Josef, ed. *New World Colors: Ethnicity, Belonging, and Difference in the Americas.* 2014. 418 pp.

WVT Wissenschaftlicher Verlag Trier	ISBN 978-3-86821-461-1	€ 29,50
Bilingual Press / Editorial Bilingüe	ISBN 978-1-939743-00-8	$ 39.50

Vol. 10

Roth, Julia. *Occidental Readings, Decolonial Practices: A Selection on Gender, Genre, and Coloniality in the Americas.* 2014. 284 pp.

WVT Wissenschaftlicher Verlag Trier	ISBN 978-3-86821-446-8	€ 26,50
Bilingual Press / Editorial Bilingüe	ISBN 978-1-939743-07-7	$ 32.50

Vol. 11

Thies, Sebastian, Gabriele Pisarz-Ramirez, and Luzelena Gutiérrez de Velasco, eds. *Of Fatherlands and Motherlands: Gender and Nation in the Americas / De Patrias y Matrias: Género y nación en las Américas.* 2015. 344 pp.

WVT Wissenschaftlicher Verlag Trier	ISBN 978-3-86821-528-1	€ 29,50
Bilingual Press / Editorial Bilingüe	ISBN 978-1-939743-08-4	$ 39.50

Vol. 12
Fuchs, Rebecca. *Caribbeanness as a Global Phenomenon: Junot Díaz, Edwidge Danticat, and Cristina García.* 2014. 298 pp.

WVT Wissenschaftlicher Verlag Trier	ISBN 978-3-86821-533-5	€ 26,50
Bilingual Press / Editorial Bilingüe	ISBN 978-1-939743-09-1	$ 32.50

Vol. 13
Andres, Julia. *¡Cuéntame algo! – Chicana Narrative Beyond the Borderlands.* 2015. 202 pp.

WVT Wissenschaftlicher Verlag Trier	ISBN 978-3-86821-569-4	€ 25,00
Bilingual Press / Editorial Bilingüe	ISBN 978-1-939743-11-4	$ 28.50

Vol. 14
Hertlein, Saskia. *Tales of Transformation: Emerging Adulthood, Migration, and Ethnicity in Contemporary American Literature.* 2014. 228 pp.

WVT Wissenschaftlicher Verlag Trier	ISBN 978-3-86821-570-0	€ 25,00
Bilingual Press / Editorial Bilingüe	ISBN 978-1-939743-10-7	$ 31.50

Vol. 15
Raab, Josef, and Saskia Hertlein, eds. *Spaces – Communities – Discourses: Charting Identity and Belonging in the Americas.* 2016. 382 pp.

WVT Wissenschaftlicher Verlag Trier	ISBN 978-3-86821-590-8	€ 29,50
Bilingual Press / Editorial Bilingüe	ISBN 978-1-939743-13-8	$ 39.50

Vol. 16
Mehring, Frank, ed. *The Mexico Diary: Winold Reiss between Vogue Mexico and Harlem Renaissance. An Illustrated Trilingual Edition with Commentary and Musical Interpretation* (includes color plates and audio CD). 2016. 244 pp.

WVT Wissenschaftlicher Verlag Trier	ISBN 978-3-86821-594-6	€ 29,50
Bilingual Press / Editorial Bilingüe	ISBN 978-1-939743-14-5	$ 39.50

Vol. 17
Raussert, Wilfried, Brian Rozema, Yolanda Campos, and Marius Littschwager, eds. *Key Tropes in Inter-American Studies: Perspectives from the* forum for inter-american research (fiar). 2015. 374 pp.

WVT Wissenschaftlicher Verlag Trier	ISBN 978-3-86821-627-1	€ 29,50
Bilingual Press / Editorial Bilingüe	ISBN 978-1-939743-16-9	$ 39.50

Vol. 19
Rehm, Lukas, Jochen Kemner, and Olaf Kaltmeier, eds. *Politics of Entanglement in the Americas: Connecting Transnational Flows and Local Perspectives.* 2017. 226 pp.

WVT Wissenschaftlicher Verlag Trier	ISBN 978-3-86821-675-2	€ 27,50
Bilingual Press / Editorial Bilingüe	ISBN 978-1-939743-17-6	$ 32.50

Vol. 20

Britt Arredondo, Christopher. *Imperial Idiocy: A Reflection on Forced Displacement in the Americas*. 2017. 194 pp.

WVT Wissenschaftlicher Verlag Trier	ISBN 978-3-86821-706-3	€ 26,50
Bilingual Press / Editorial Bilingüe	ISBN 978-1-939743-20-6	$ 30.00

Vol. 21

Schemien, Alexia. *Of Virgins, Curanderas, and Wrestler Saints: Un/Doing Religion in Contemporary Mexican American Literature*. 2018. 218 pp..

WVT Wissenschaftlicher Verlag Trier	ISBN 978-3-86821-724-7	€ 27,50
Bilingual Press / Editorial Bilingüe	ISBN 978-1-939743-22-0	$ 32.50

Vol. 22

Fulger, Maria Diana. *The Cuban Post-Socialist Exotic: Contemporary U.S. American Travel Narratives about Cuba*. 2020. 266 pp.

WVT Wissenschaftlicher Verlag Trier	ISBN 978-3-86821-769-8	€ 32,50
Bilingual Press / Editorial Bilingüe	ISBN 978-1-939743-27-5	$ 36.00

Vol. 24

Kaltmeier, Olaf, Mirko Petersen, Wilfried Raussert, and Julia Roth, eds. *Cherishing the Past, Envisioning the Future. Entangled Practises of Heritage and Utopia in the Americas*. 2021. 176 pp.

WVT Wissenschaftlicher Verlag Trier	ISBN 978-3-86821-804-6	€ 23,50
UNO University of New Orleans Press	ISBN 978-1-60801-206-0	$ 27.50

Vol. 26

Raussert, Wilfried. *'What's Going On': How Music Shapes the Social*. 2021. 224 pp.

WVT Wissenschaftlicher Verlag Trier	ISBN 978-3-86821-811-4	€ 28,50
UNO University of New Orleans Press	ISBN 978-1-60801-199-5	$ 34.00

Vol. 27

Frank-Job, Barbara. *Immigration as a Process: Temporality Concepts in Blogs of Latin American Immigrants to Québec*. 2021. 138 pp.

WVT Wissenschaftlicher Verlag Trier	ISBN 978-3-86821-820-6	€ 20,00
UNO University of New Orleans Press	ISBN 978-1-60801-215-2	$ 24.00

Vol. 28

Roth, Julia. *Can Feminism Trump Populism? Right-Wing Trends and Intersectional Contestations in the Americas*. 2021. 168 pp.

WVT Wissenschaftlicher Verlag Trier	ISBN 978-3-86821-821-3	€ 23,00
UNO University of New Orleans Press	ISBN 978-1-60801-205-3	$ 26.00

Vol. 30
Buitrago Valencia, Clara. *Missionaries: Migrants or Expatriates? Guatemalan Pentecostal Leaders in Los Angeles.* 2021. 236 pp.
WVT Wissenschaftlicher Verlag Trier   ISBN 978-3-86821-818-3   € 28,50
UNO University of New Orleans Press   ISBN 978-1-60801-210-7 $ 34.50

Vol. 31
Schwabe, Nicole. *De-Centering History Education: Creating Knowledge of Global Entanglements.* 2021. 92 pp.
WVT Wissenschaftlicher Verlag Trier   ISBN 978-3-86821-828-2   € 18,00
UNO University of New Orleans Press   ISBN 978-1-60801-214-5 $ 21.00

Vol. 32
Manke, Albert. *Coping with Discrimination and Exclusion. Experiences of Free Chinese Migrants in the Americas in a Transregional and Diachronic Perspective.* 2021. 162 pp.
WVT Wissenschaftlicher Verlag Trier   ISBN 978-3-86821-829-9   € 23,00
UNO University of New Orleans Press   ISBN 978-1-60801-207-7 $ 27.00

Vol. 33
Rohland, Eleonora. *Entangled Histories and the Environment? Socio-Environmental Transformations in the Caribbean, 1492-1800.* 2021. 92 pp.
WVT Wissenschaftlicher Verlag Trier   ISBN 978-3-86821-833-6   € 18,00
UNO University of New Orleans Press   ISBN 978-1-60801-208-4 $ 21.00

Vol. 34
Kaltmeier, Olaf. *National Parks from North to South. An Entangled History of Conservation and Colonization in Argentina.* 2021. 208 pp.
WVT Wissenschaftlicher Verlag Trier   ISBN 978-3-86821-834-3   € 27,50
UNO University of New Orleans Press   ISBN 978-1-60801-204-6 $ 32.50

Vol. 35
Raussert, Wilfried. *Off the Grid. Art Practices and Public Space.* 2021. 232 pp.
WVT Wissenschaftlicher Verlag Trier   ISBN 978-3-86821-835-0   € 29,50
UNO University of New Orleans Press   ISBN 978-1-60801-213-8 $ 34.50

Vol. 36
Ravasio, Paola. *This Train Is Not Bound to Glory. A Study of Literary Trainscapes.* 2021. 114 pp.
WVT Wissenschaftlicher Verlag Trier   ISBN 978-3-86821-836-7   € 18,00
UNO University of New Orleans Press   ISBN 978-1-60801-216-9 $ 21.00

Vol. 37
Schäfer, Heinrich Wilhelm. *Protestant 'Sects' and the Spirit of (Anti-)Imperialism. Religious Entanglements in the Americas.* 2021. 242 pp.
WVT Wissenschaftlicher Verlag Trier   ISBN 978-3-86821-855-9   € 29,50
UNO University of New Orleans Press   ISBN 978-1-60801-209-1 $ 34.50